IMMORTAL HOUNDS

3

Ryo Yasohachi

VERTICAL COMICS

Table of Contents

Characters

Escape Artists
A dark organization that hides Vectors from the police.

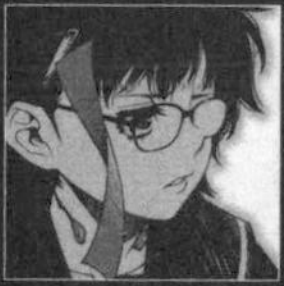

Rin Kazama
A girl who has infiltrated the MPD; essentially a hound. Called "Rin" by the MPD and "Fuurin" by the organization.

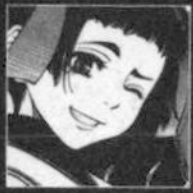

Kiriko
Helps Vectors escape alongside Rin. Competent but treated like a novice.

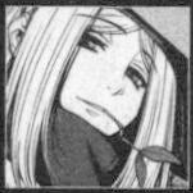

Karigane
An Escape Artist debuting in this volume.

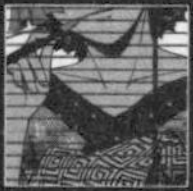

Mama
A mysterious woman who manages the Escape Artists' girl soldiers.

Tousai Precinct
A group of three led by Kenzaki comprises the Anti-Vector Unit.

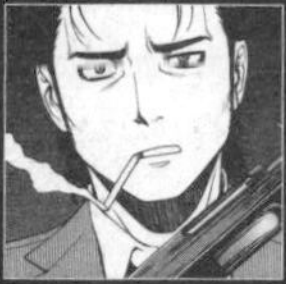

Shin'ichi Kenzaki
Chief. His sister, Ikumi, was killed by a Vector. An "immortal hound" who pursues culprits.

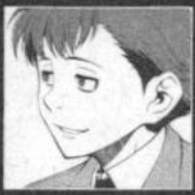

Masaki Wakabayashi
Kenzaki's subordinate. Easygoing but has a devious side.

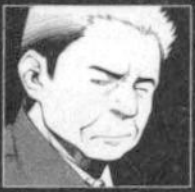

Kouzou Shigematsu
Kenzaki's subordinate despite being his elder. A great marksman. Nicknamed "Shige."

UNDO
Short for the United Nations Disease-control Office

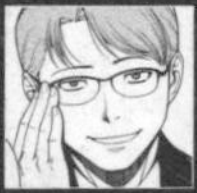

Kanai
Director. The UNDO has no right to carry out investigations or make arrests. Carries out executions of Vectors captured by the police.

Rescue

Remove

Vectors
A group of murderers who spread Resurrection Deficiency Syndrome (RDS). Those who love them become incapable of revival.

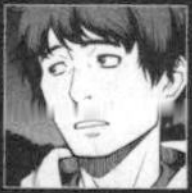

Teruyoshi Kouda
The Vector who killed Ikumi Kenzaki's sister. Currently active as an Escape Artist.

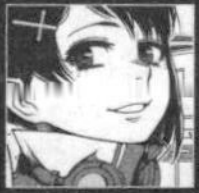

"Snow White"
A Vector who has killed 99 men. Is constantly on the move, quickly changing location.

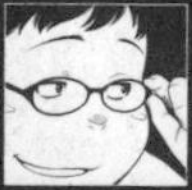

Tsutomu Takamiya
A Vector who has killed three women working night jobs. Called "Fatass" by Kenzaki.

Previous Volume Summary

In another world, "death" does not exist. The criminals known as Vectors were somehow transported from a world of mortality into this world. Kenzaki's unit is in pursuit of a Vector named Snow White. She is a mass murderer who works by infiltrating groups of nerds and charming them. Kenzaki has agreed to cooperate with UNDO in order to hunt down Snow White.

16 Love's Location

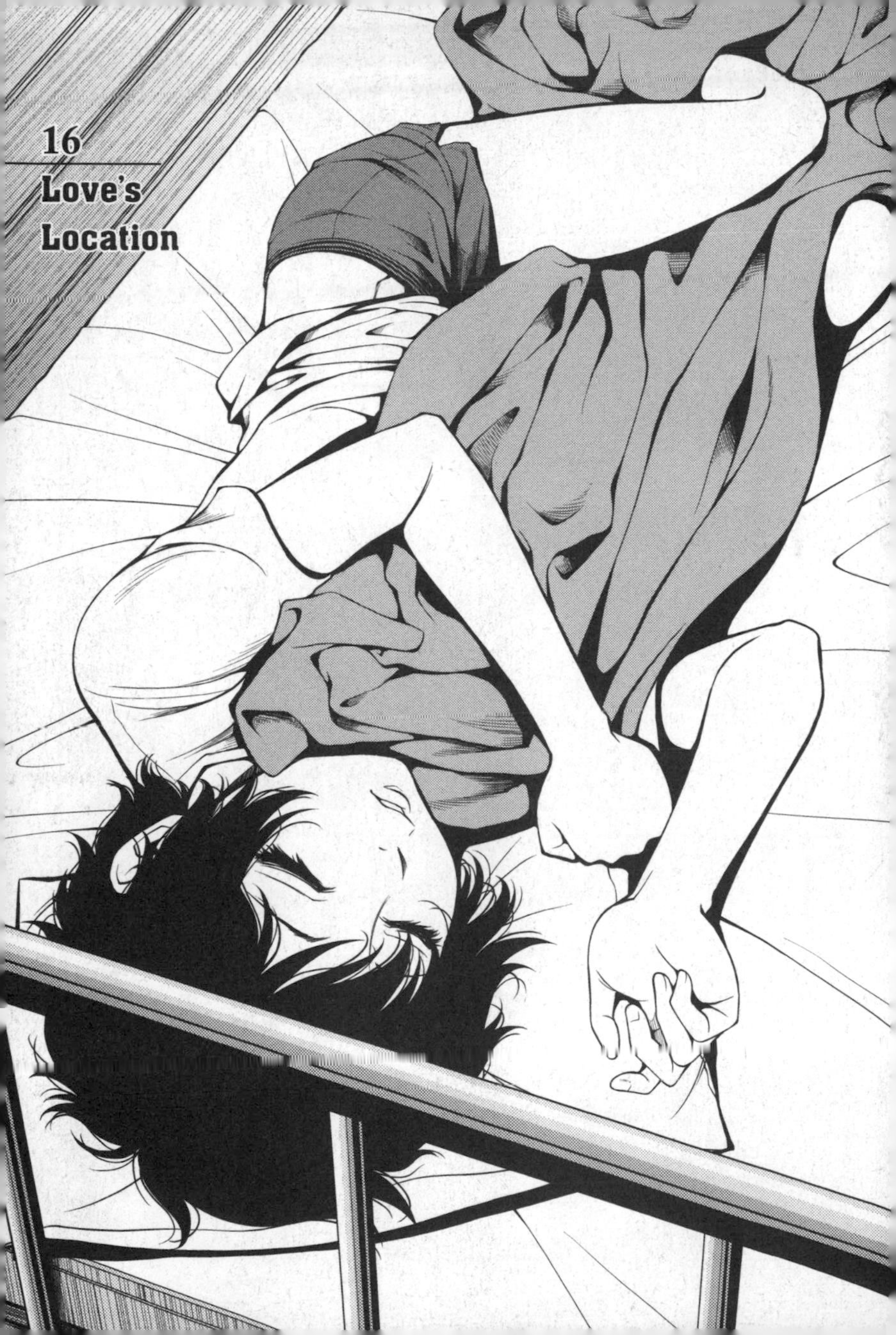

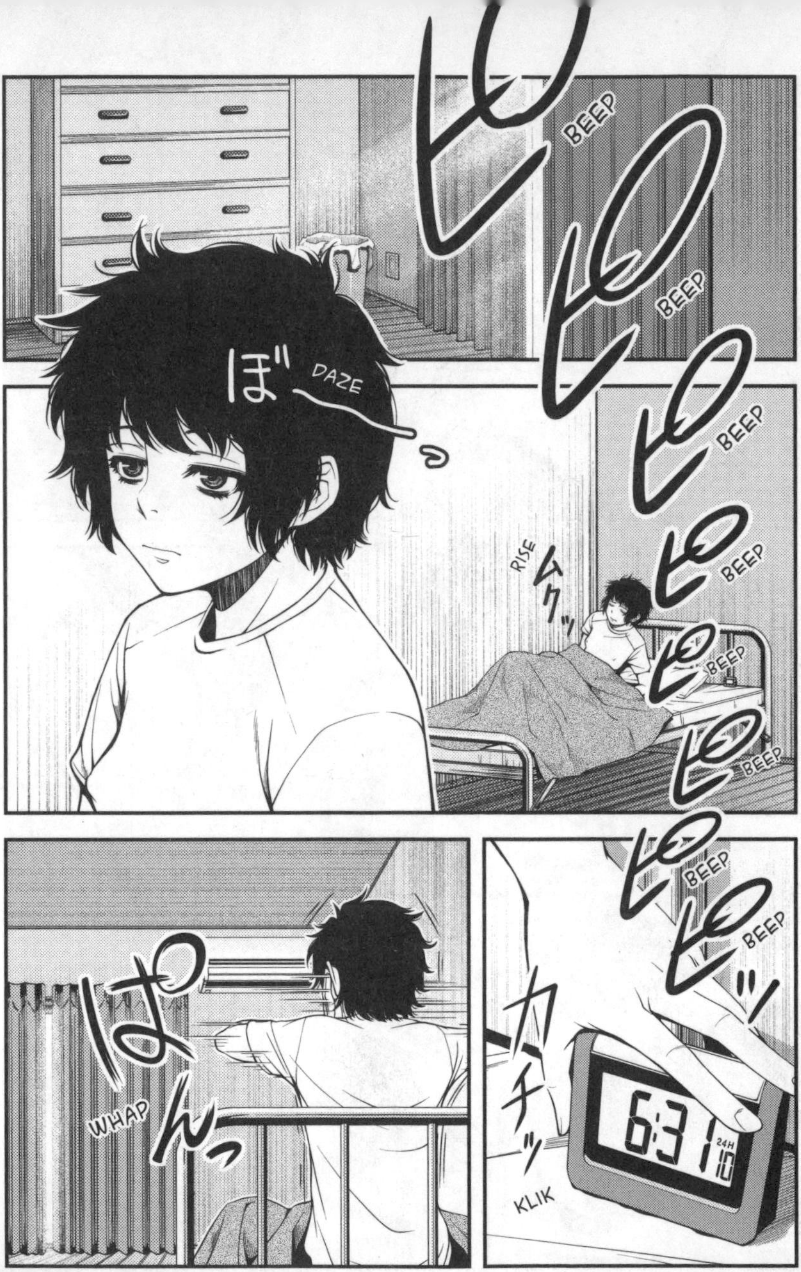
BEEP
BEEP
BEEP
BEEP
BEEP
BEEP
BEEP
BEEP
ぼ～っ
DAZE
ムクッ
RISE
カチッ
KLIK
ぱんっ
WHAP

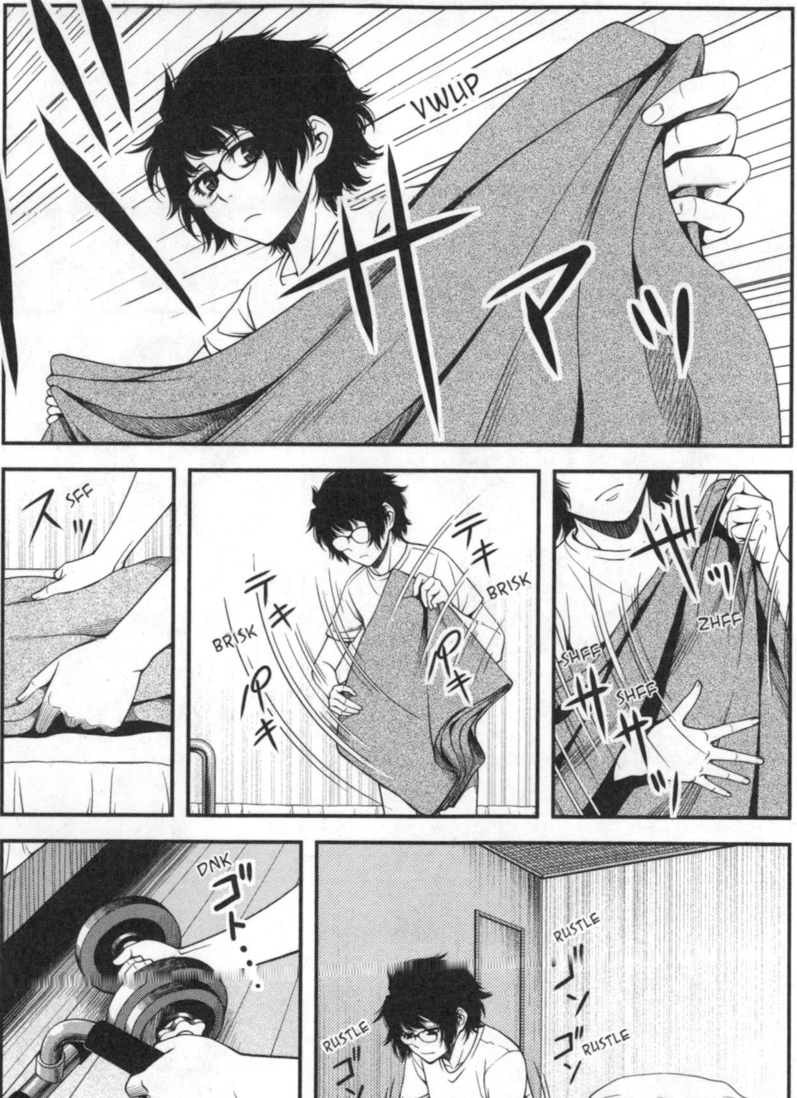
ザァッ
VWUP
ザッ
ZHFF
ザザ
SHFF
SHFF
テキパキ
BRISK
テキパキ
BRISK
スッ
SFF
ゴソ
RUSTLE
ゴソ
RUSTLE
ゴソ
RUSTLE
ゴト…
DNK

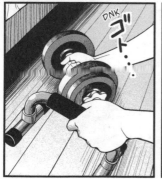

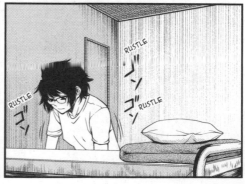

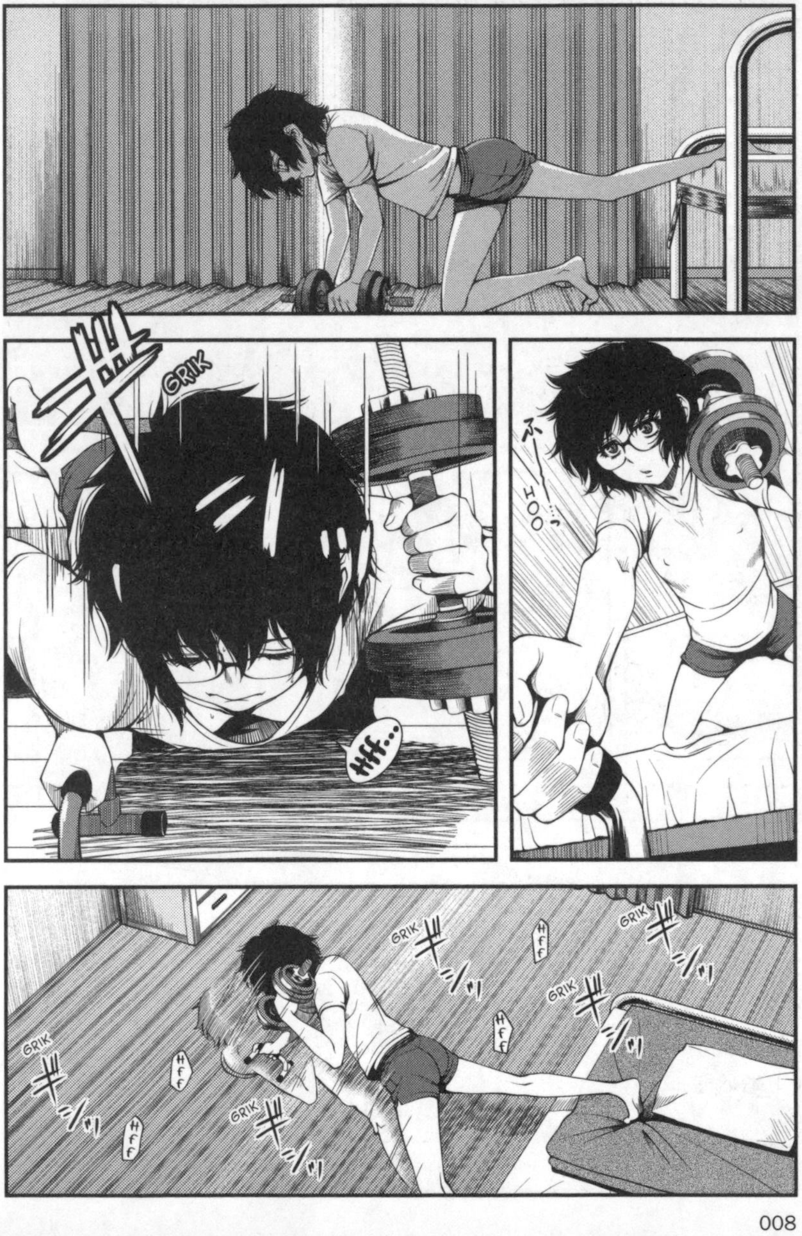
ふー……
HOO...
GRIK
Hff...
GRIK
Hff
GRIK
GRIK
Hff
GRIK
Hff
GRIK
Hff

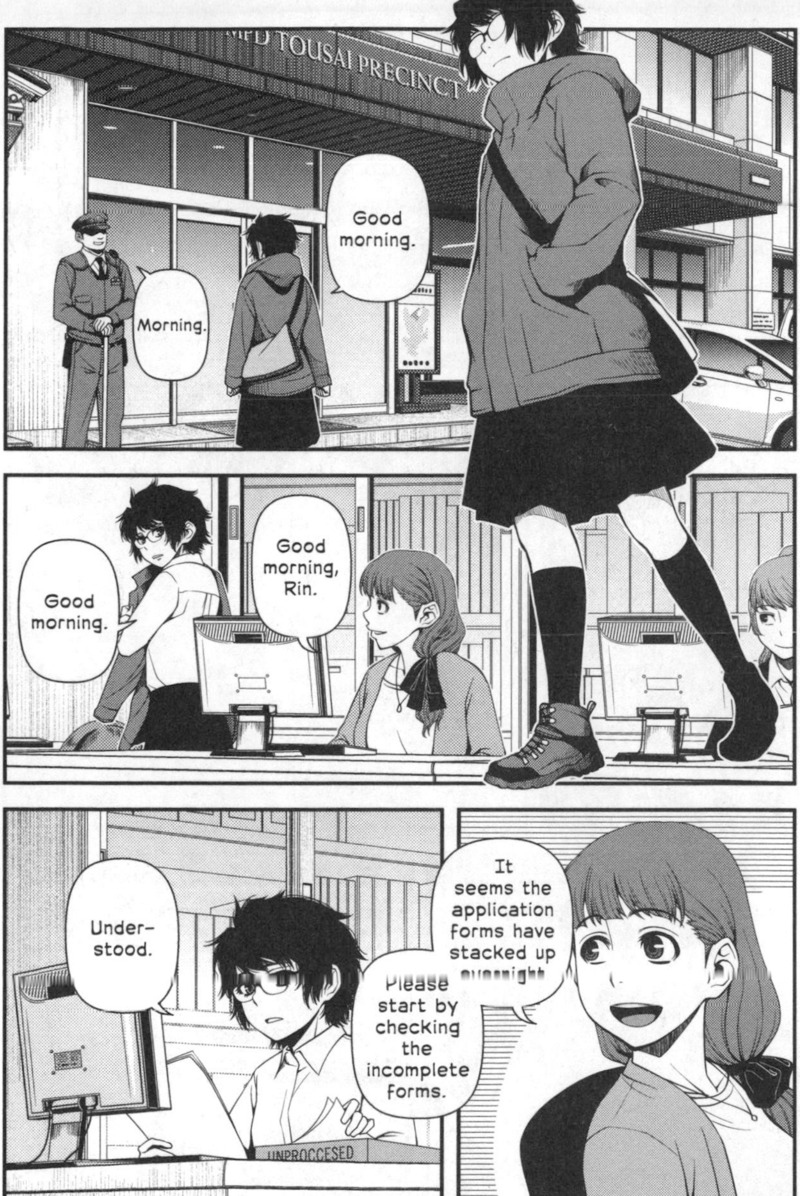
MPD TOUSAI PRECINCT
Good morning.
Morning.
Good morning, Rin.
Good morning.
It seems the application forms have stacked up
Please start by checking the incomplete forms.
Understood.
UNPROCCESED

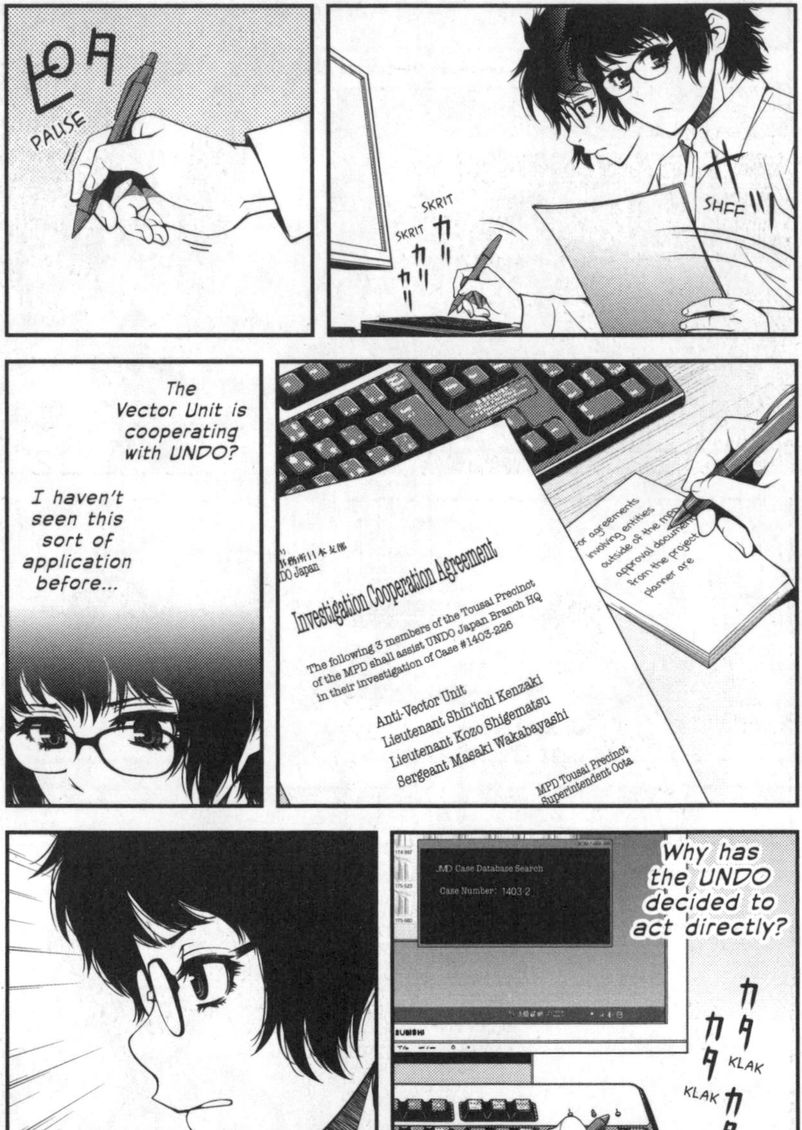
シャ
SHFF
カリ
SKRIT
カリカリ
SKRIT
ピタ
PAUSE
For agreements
involving entities
outside of the MP
approval documen
from the project
planner are
UNDO Japan
Investigation Cooperation Agreement
The following 3 members of the Tousai Precinct of the MPD shall assist UNDO Japan Branch HQ in their investigation of Case #1403-226
Anti-Vector Unit
Lieutenant Shin'ichi Kenzaki
Lieutenant Kozo Shigematsu
Sergeant Masaki Wakabayashi
MPD Tousai Precinct
Superintendent Oota
The Vector Unit is cooperating with UNDO?
I haven't seen this sort of application before...
Why has the UNDO decided to act directly?
JMD Case Database Search
Case Number: 1403-2
カタ
KLAK
カタ
KLAK
カタ
KLAK

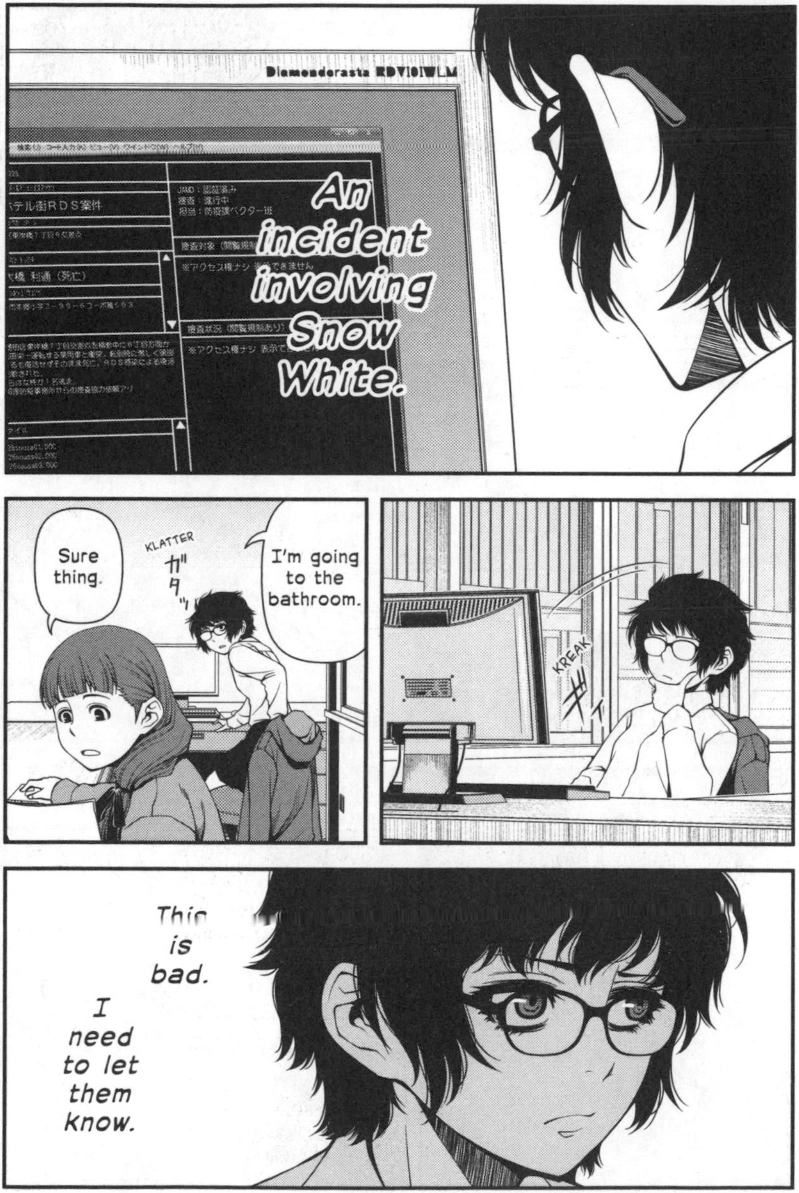
Diamondorasta RDV10IWLM
An incident involving Snow White.
KREAK
ギィ
I'm going to the bathroom.
Sure thing.
KLATTER
ガタッ
This is bad.
I need to let them know.

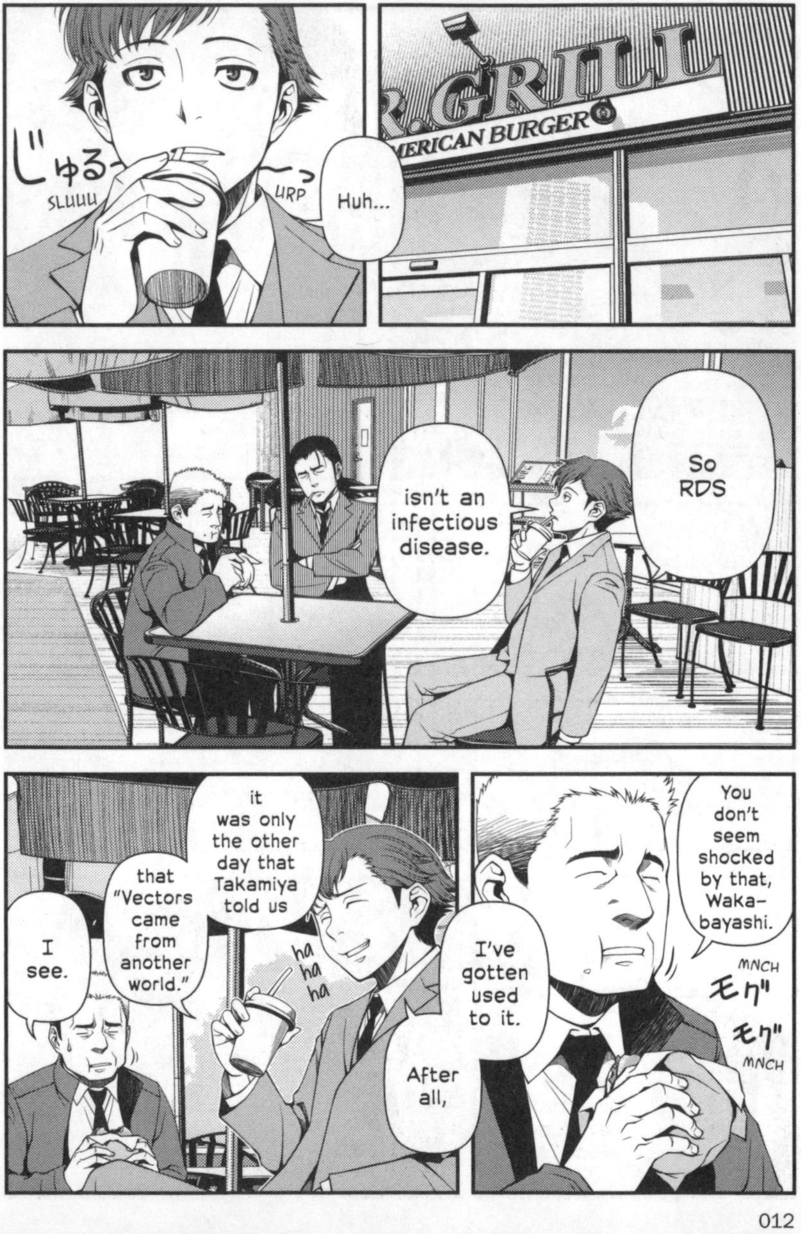
R.GRILL
MERICAN BURGER
Huh...
じゅるー
SLUUU
~っ
URP
So RDS
isn't an infectious disease.
You don't seem shocked by that, Waka-bayashi.
モグ
MNCH
モグ
MNCH
I've gotten used to it.
After all,
it was only the other day that Takamiya told us
that "Vectors came from another world."
ha ha ha
I see.

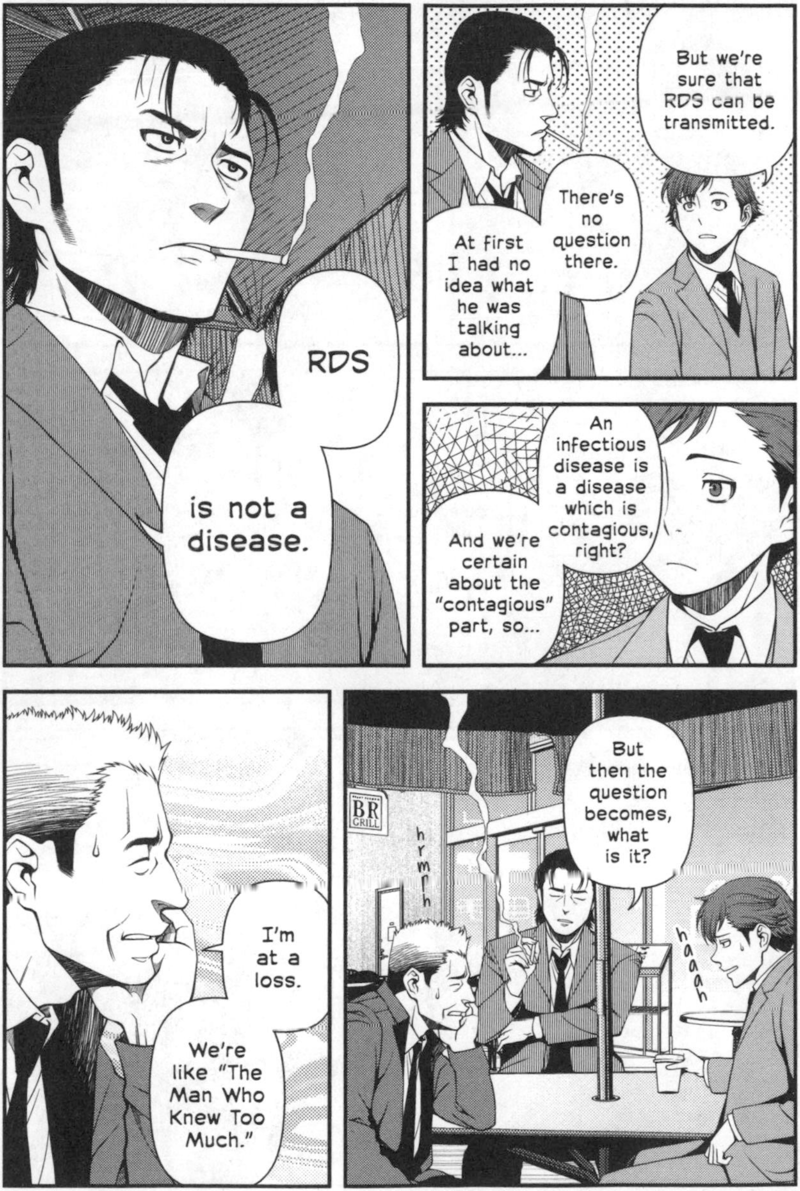
But we're sure that RDS can be transmitted.
There's no question there.
At first I had no idea what he was talking about...
An infectious disease is a disease which is contagious, right?
And we're certain about the "contagious" part, so...
RDS
is not a disease.
But then the question becomes, what is it?
BR GRILL
hrmph
haaah
I'm at a loss.
We're like "The Man Who Knew Too Much."

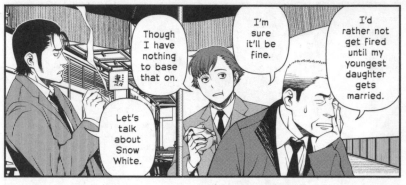

I'd rather not get fired until my youngest daughter gets married.
I'm sure it'll be fine.
Though I have nothing to base that on.
Let's talk about Snow White.
First, our course of action for the investiga-tion...
Sorry, can I leave it to you, Shige?
I'm clueless here.
Oh, right,
you're not internet-savvy.
There are thousands of online games,
and players number in the tens of thou-sands,
so it won't be possible to capture Snow White by searching with a fine-tooth comb.
But based on the pattern of victims, we can narrow it down somewhat.
The people we gathered last time were teammates on an FPS*, right?

*FPS = First Person Shooter

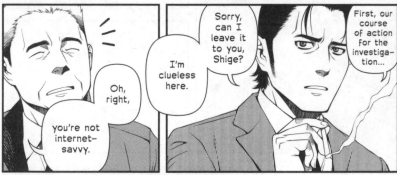

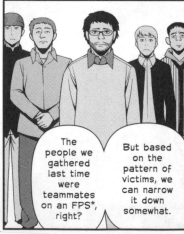

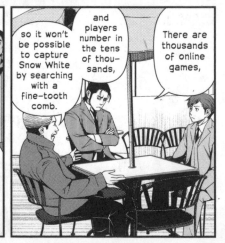

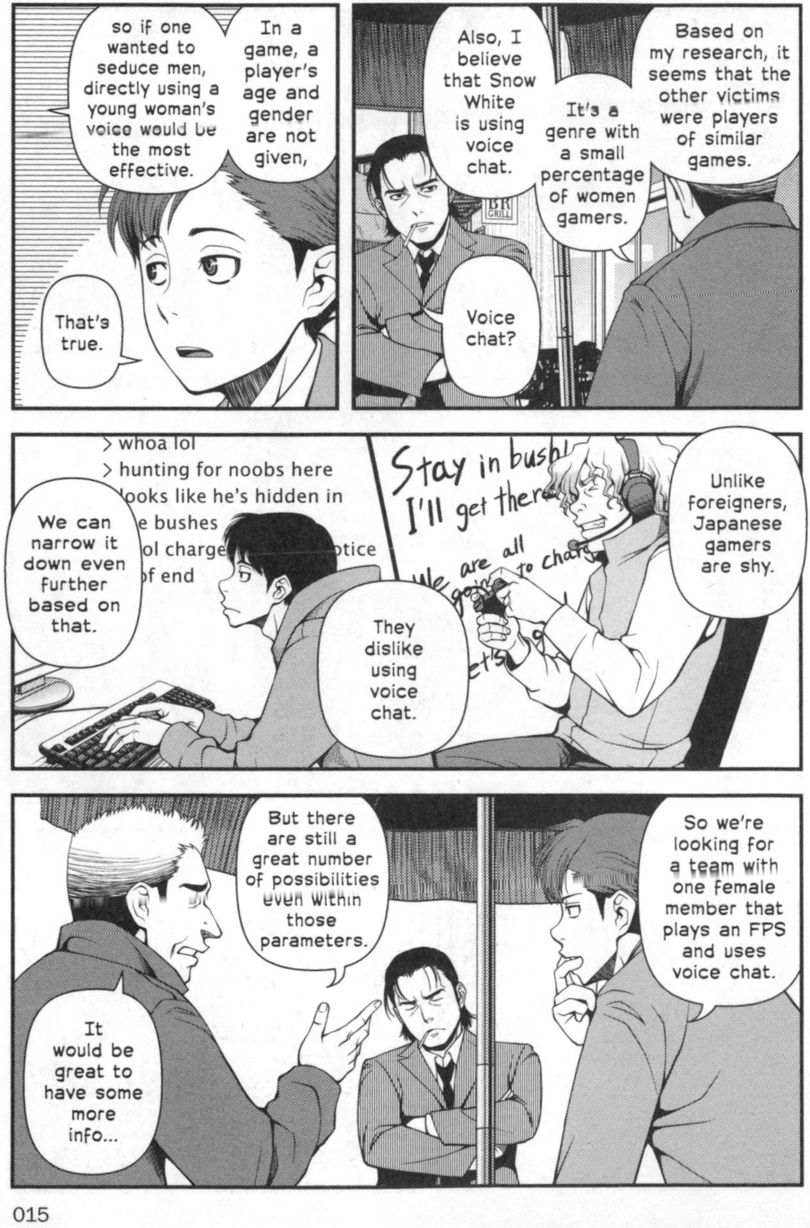
Based on my research, it seems that the other victims were players of similar games.
It's a genre with a small percentage of women gamers.
Also, I believe that Snow White is using voice chat.
Voice chat?
In a game, a player's age and gender are not given,
so if one wanted to seduce men, directly using a young woman's voice would be the most effective.
That's true.
Unlike foreigners, Japanese gamers are shy.
They dislike using voice chat.
> whoa lol
> hunting for noobs here
We can narrow it down even further based on that.
So we're looking for a team with one female member that plays an FPS and uses voice chat.
But there are still a great number of possibilities even within those parameters.
It would be great to have some more info...

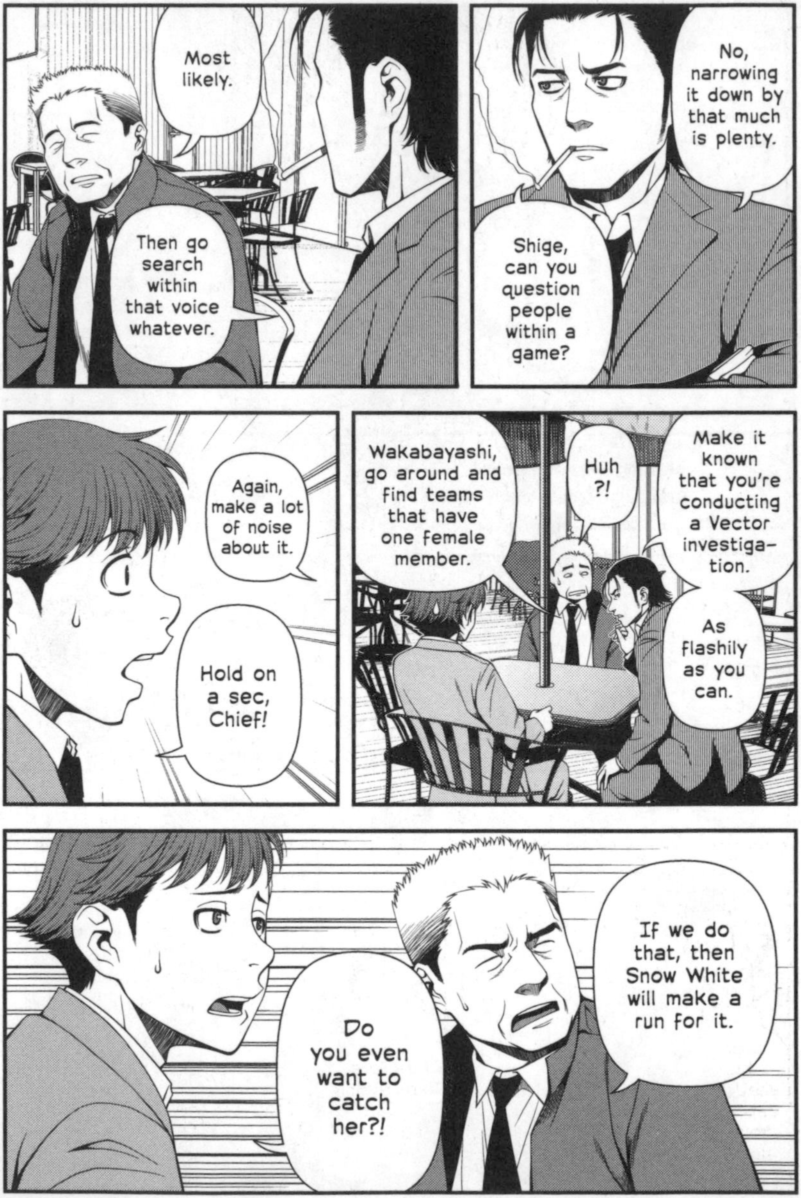

No, narrowing it down by that much is plenty.
Shige, can you question people within a game?
Most likely.
Then go search within that voice whatever.
Make it known that you're conducting a Vector investigation.
Huh ?!
Wakabayashi, go around and find teams that have one female member.
As flashily as you can.
Again, make a lot of noise about it.
Hold on a sec, Chief!
If we do that, then Snow White will make a run for it.
Do you even want to catch her?!

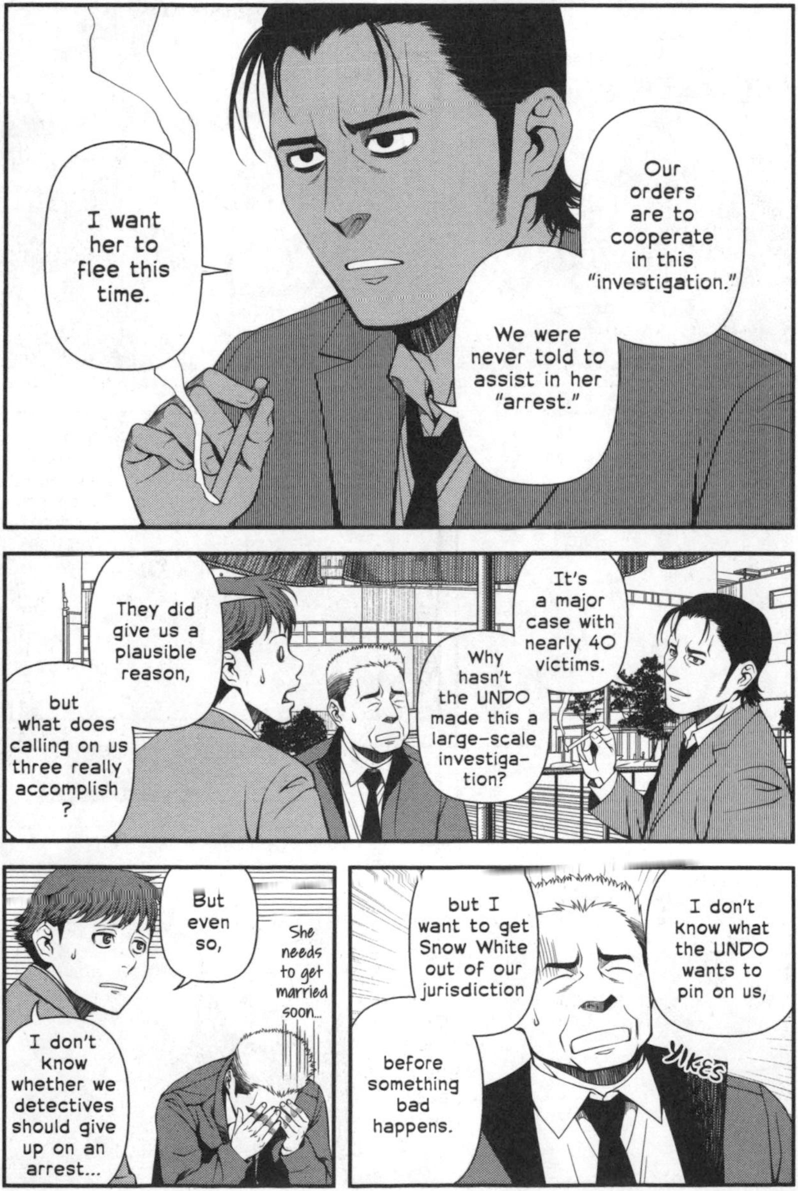
Our orders are to cooperate in this "investigation."
We were never told to assist in her "arrest."
I want her to flee this time.
It's a major case with nearly 40 victims.
Why hasn't the UNDO made this a large-scale investigation?
They did give us a plausible reason,
but what does calling on us three really accomplish?
I don't know what the UNDO wants to pin on us,
but I want to get Snow White out of our jurisdiction
before something bad happens.
YIKES
But even so,
I don't know whether we detectives should give up on an arrest...
She needs to get married soon...

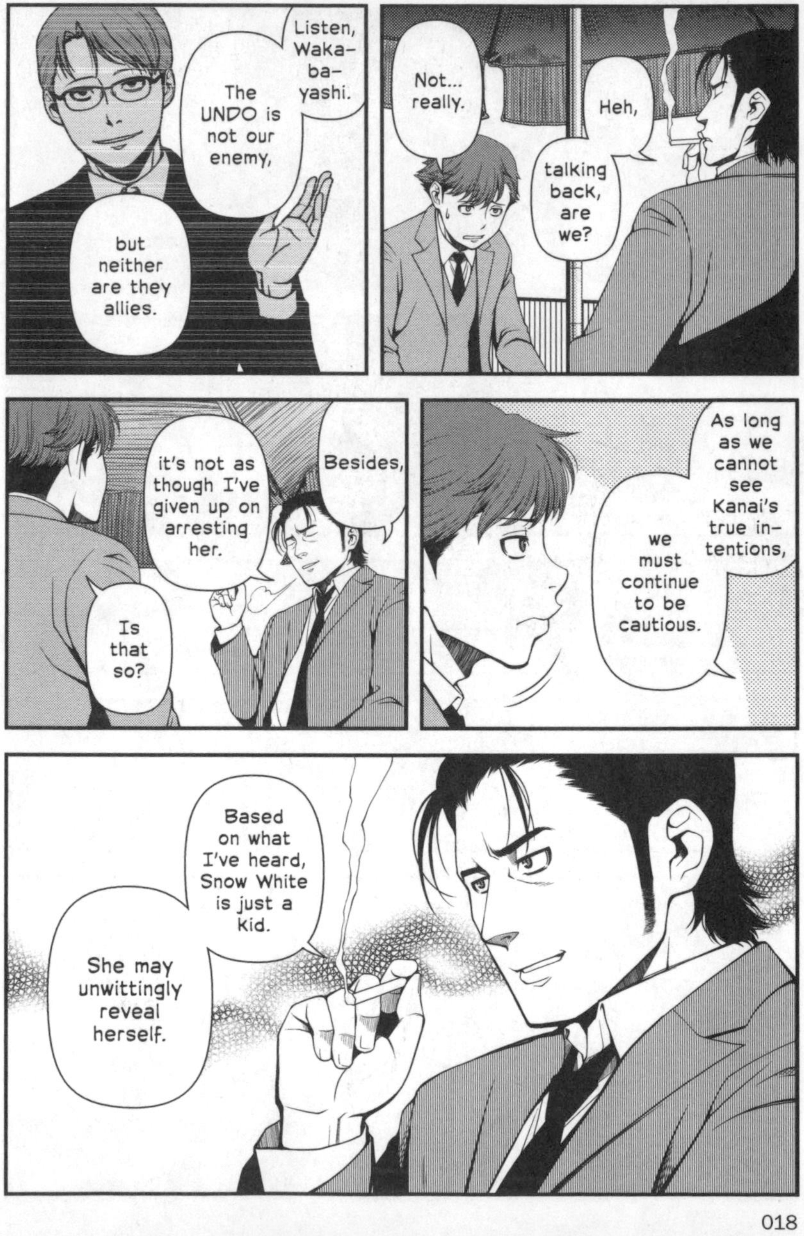
Heh,
talking back, are we?
Not... really.
Listen, Waka-ba-yashi.
The UNDO is not our enemy,
but neither are they allies.
As long as we cannot see Kanai's true in-tentions,
we must continue to be cautious.
Besides,
it's not as though I've given up on arresting her.
Is that so?
Based on what I've heard, Snow White is just a kid.
She may unwittingly reveal herself.

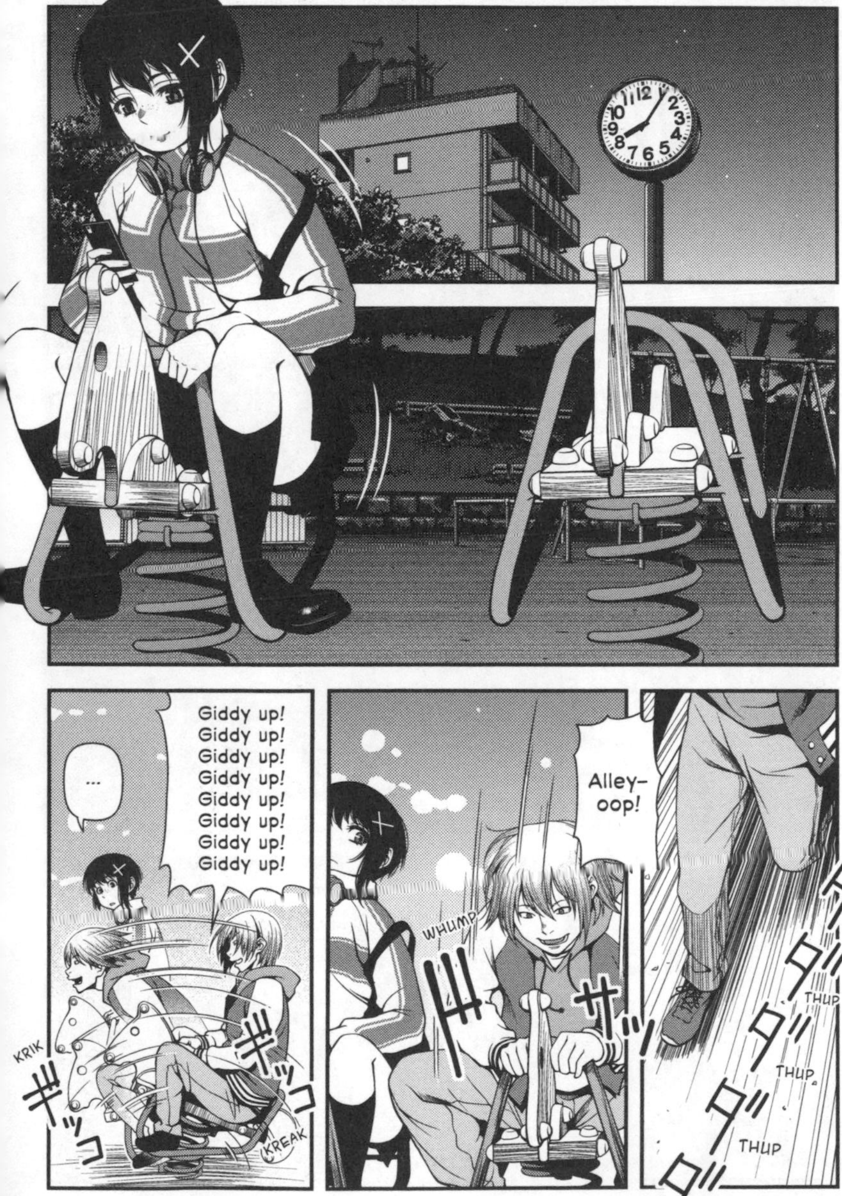
THUP
THUP
THUP
THUP
THUP
Alley-oop!
WHUMP
Giddy up! Giddy up! Giddy up! Giddy up! Giddy up! Giddy up! Giddy up! Giddy up!
...
KRIK
ギッコ
ギッコ
KREAK

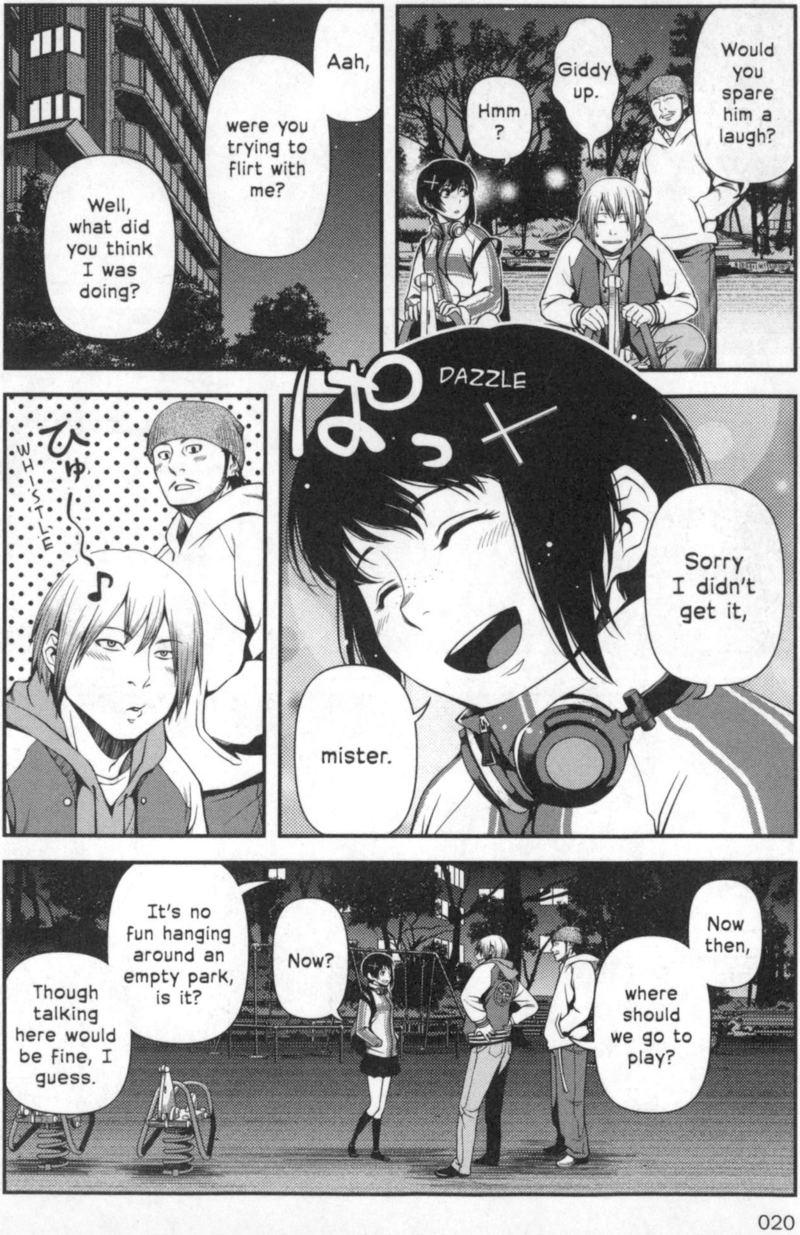
Would you spare him a laugh?
Giddy up.
Hmm?
Aah,
were you trying to flirt with me?
Well, what did you think I was doing?
ぱっ
DAZZLE
Sorry I didn't get it,
mister.
ひゅ～
WHISTLE
♪
Now then,
where should we go to play?
Now?
It's no fun hanging around an empty park, is it?
Though talking here would be fine, I guess.

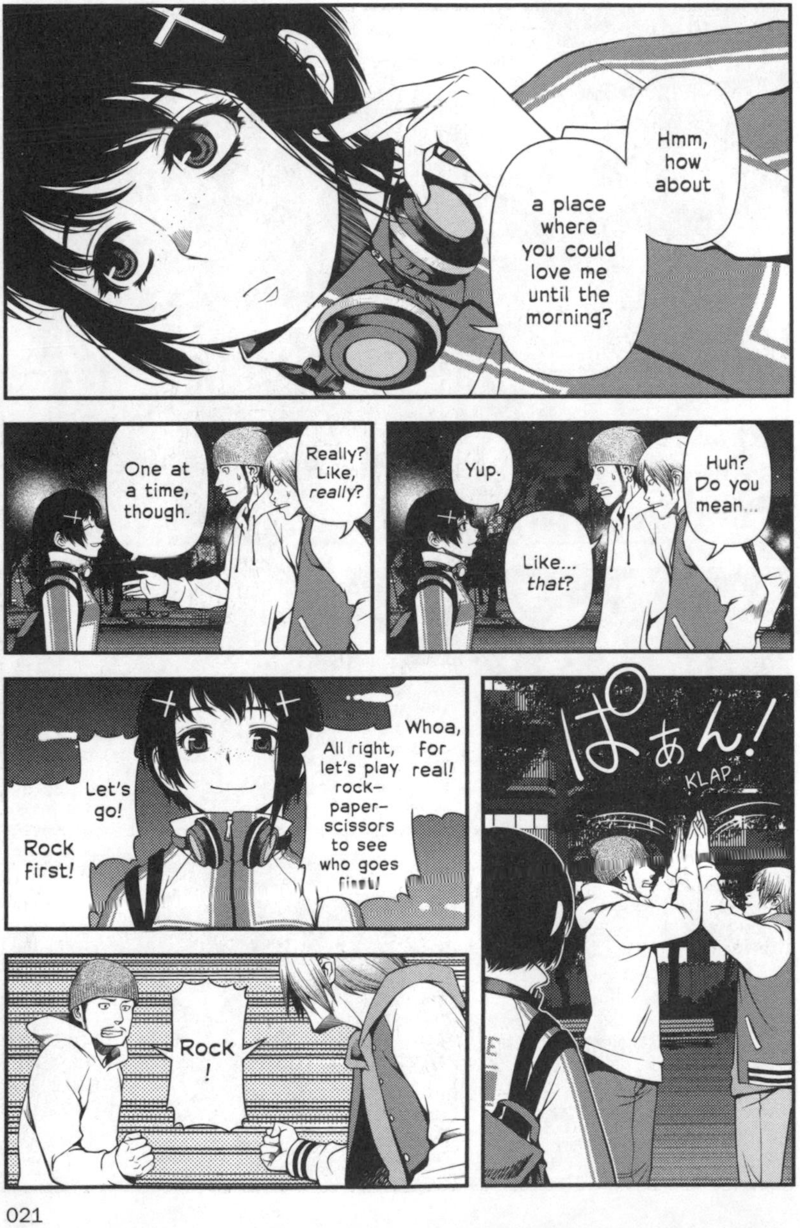
Hmm, how about
a place where you could love me until the morning?
Huh? Do you mean...
Like... *that*?
Yup.
Really? Like, *really*?
One at a time, though.
ぱぁん!
KLAP
Whoa, for real!
All right, let's play rock-paper-scissors to see who goes first!
Let's go!
Rock first!
Rock!

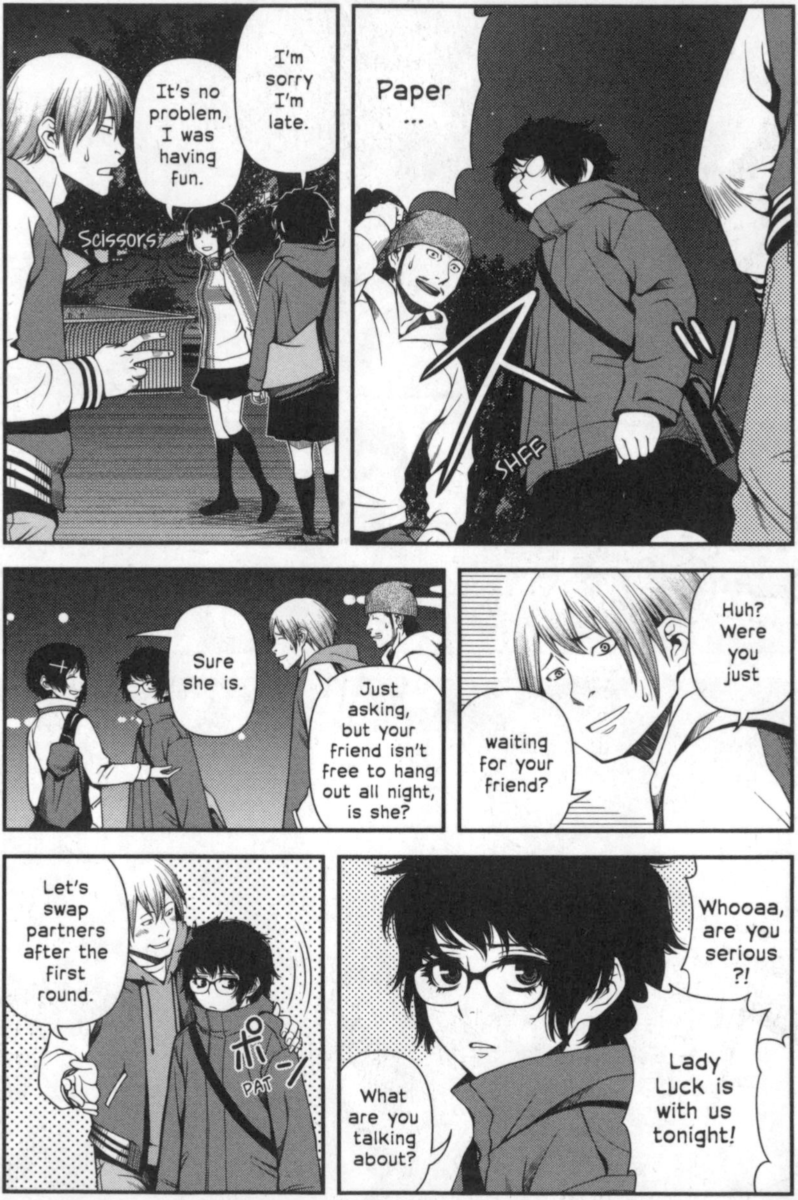
Paper ...
SHFF
I'm sorry I'm late.
It's no problem, I was having fun.
Scissors ...
Huh? Were you just
waiting for your friend?
Just asking, but your friend isn't free to hang out all night, is she?
Sure she is.
Whooaa, are you serious?!
Lady Luck is with us tonight!
What are you talking about?
PAT
Let's swap partners after the first round.

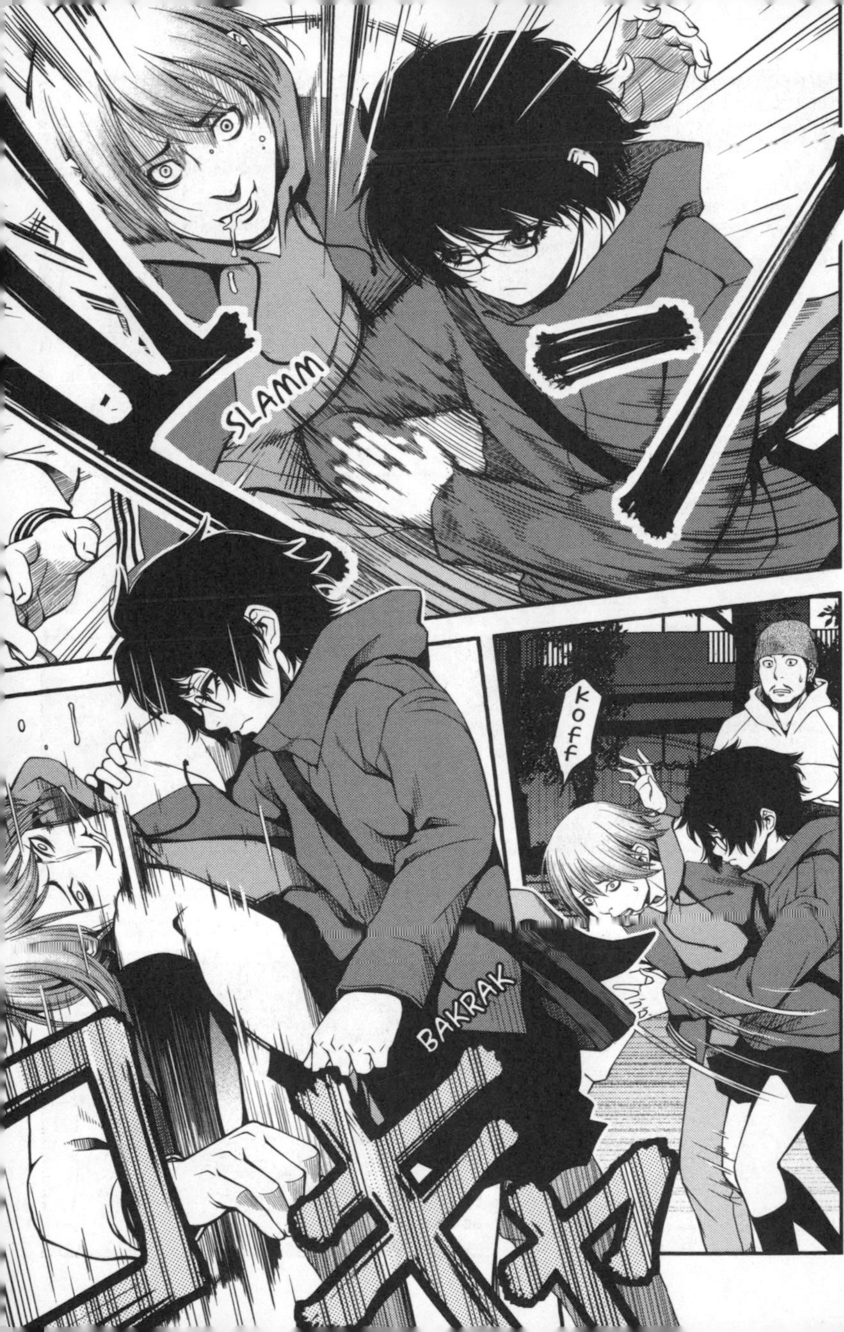
SLAMM
KOFF
BAKRAK

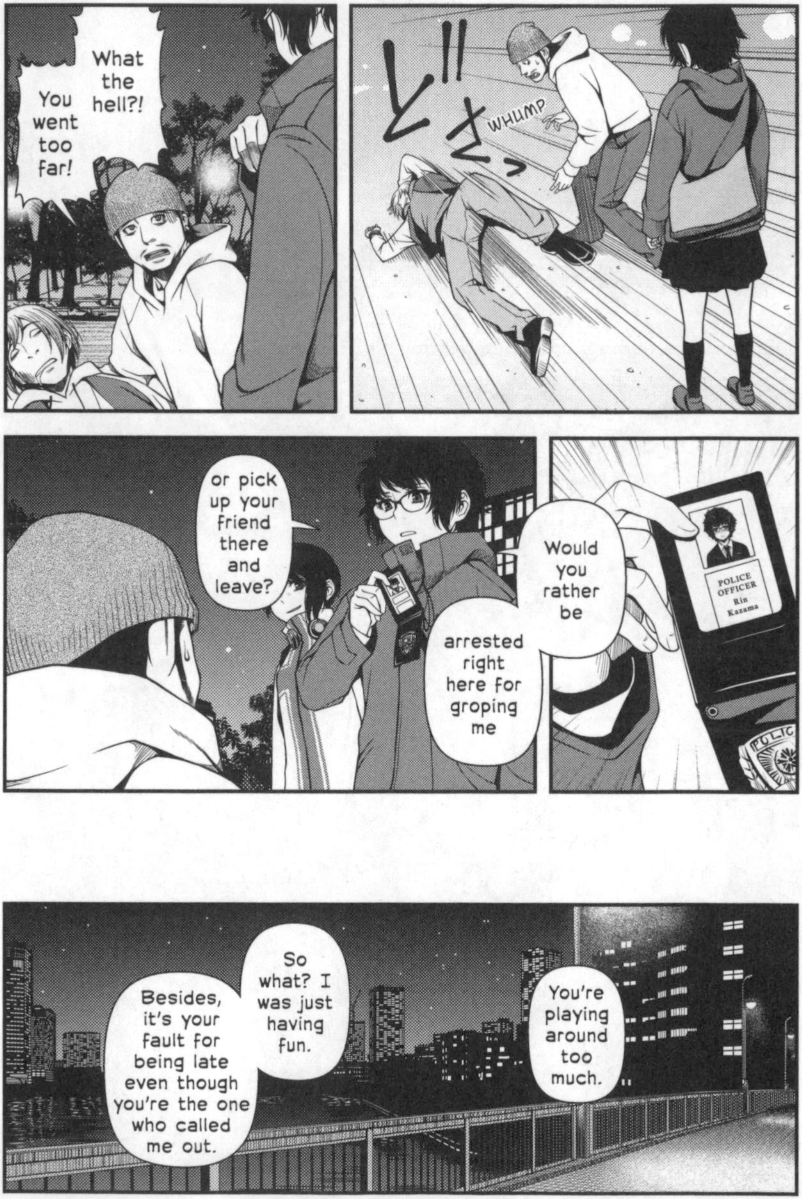
どさっ
WHUMP
What the hell?!
You went too far!
Would you rather be
arrested right here for groping me
POLICE OFFICER Rin Kazama
or pick up your friend there and leave?
You're playing around too much.
So what? I was just having fun.
Besides, it's your fault for being late even though you're the one who called me out.

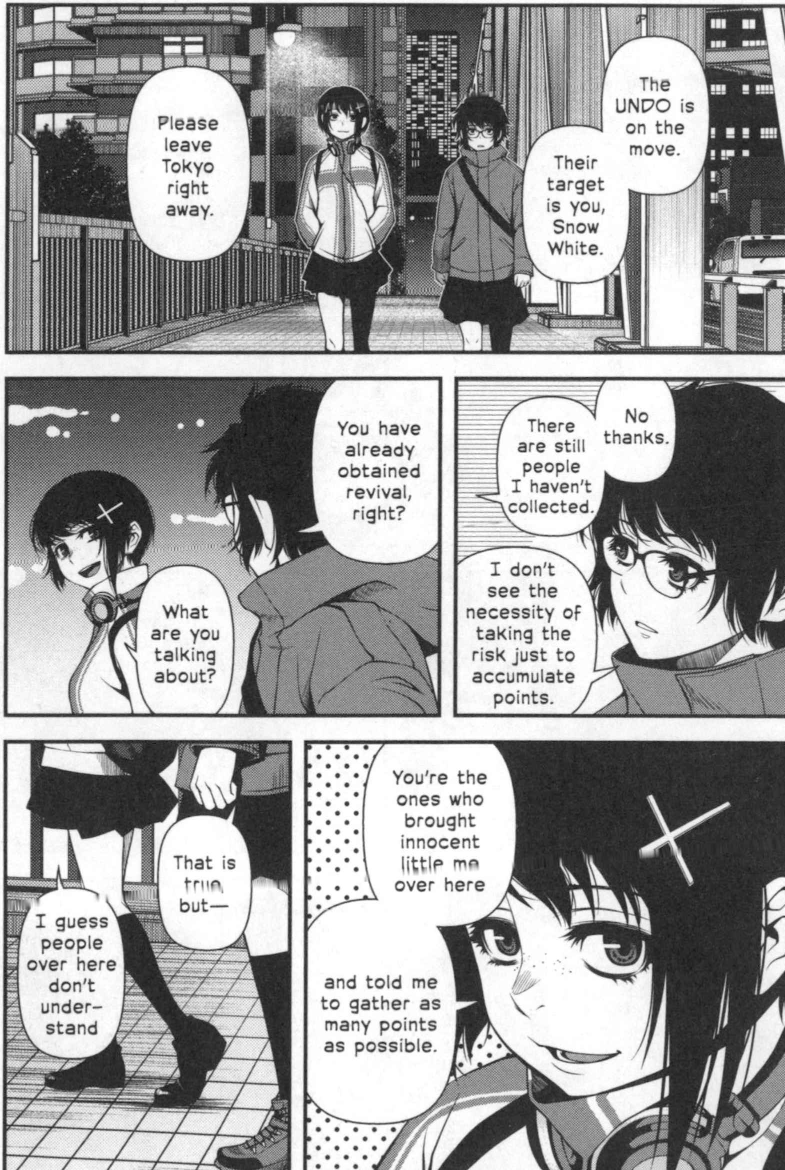
The UNDO is on the move.
Their target is you, Snow White.
Please leave Tokyo right away.
No thanks.
There are still people I haven't collected.
I don't see the necessity of taking the risk just to accumulate points.
You have already obtained revival, right?
What are you talking about?
You're the ones who brought innocent little me over here
and told me to gather as many points as possible.
That is true, but—
I guess people over here don't under-stand

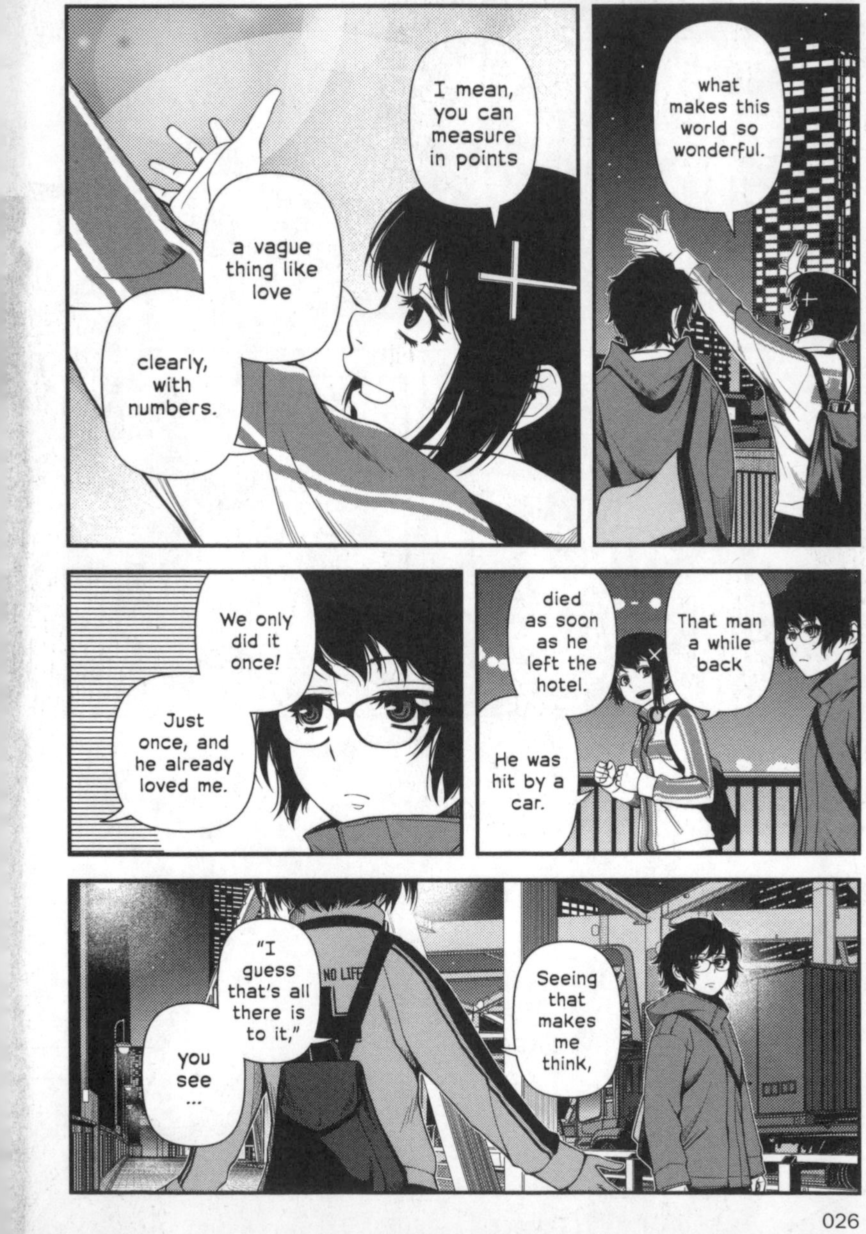
what makes this world so wonderful.
I mean, you can measure in points
a vague thing like love
clearly, with numbers.
That man a while back
died as soon as he left the hotel.
He was hit by a car.
We only did it once!
Just once, and he already loved me.
Seeing that makes me think,
"I guess that's all there is to it,"
you see ...

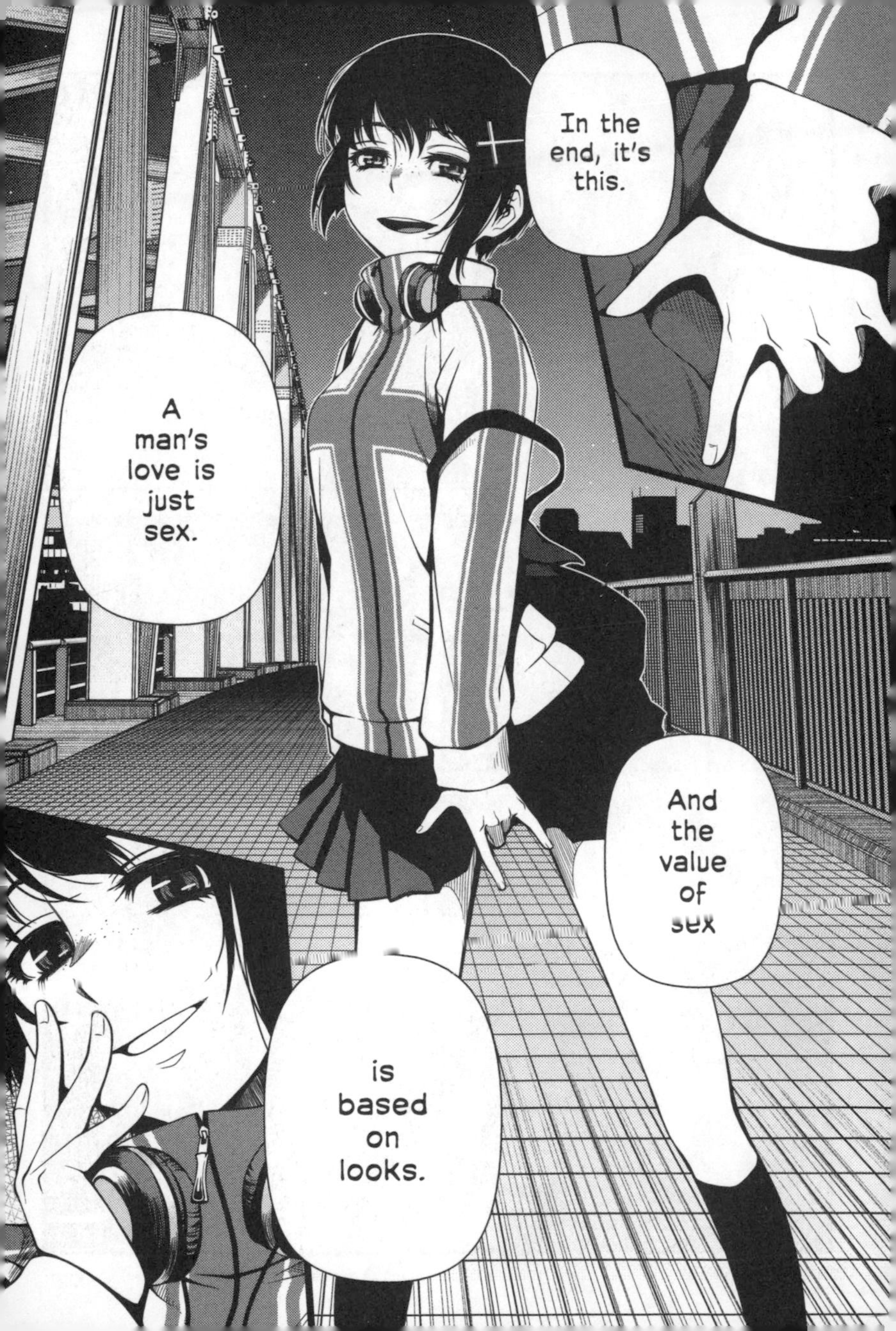
In the end, it's this.
A man's love is just sex.
And the value of sex
is based on looks.

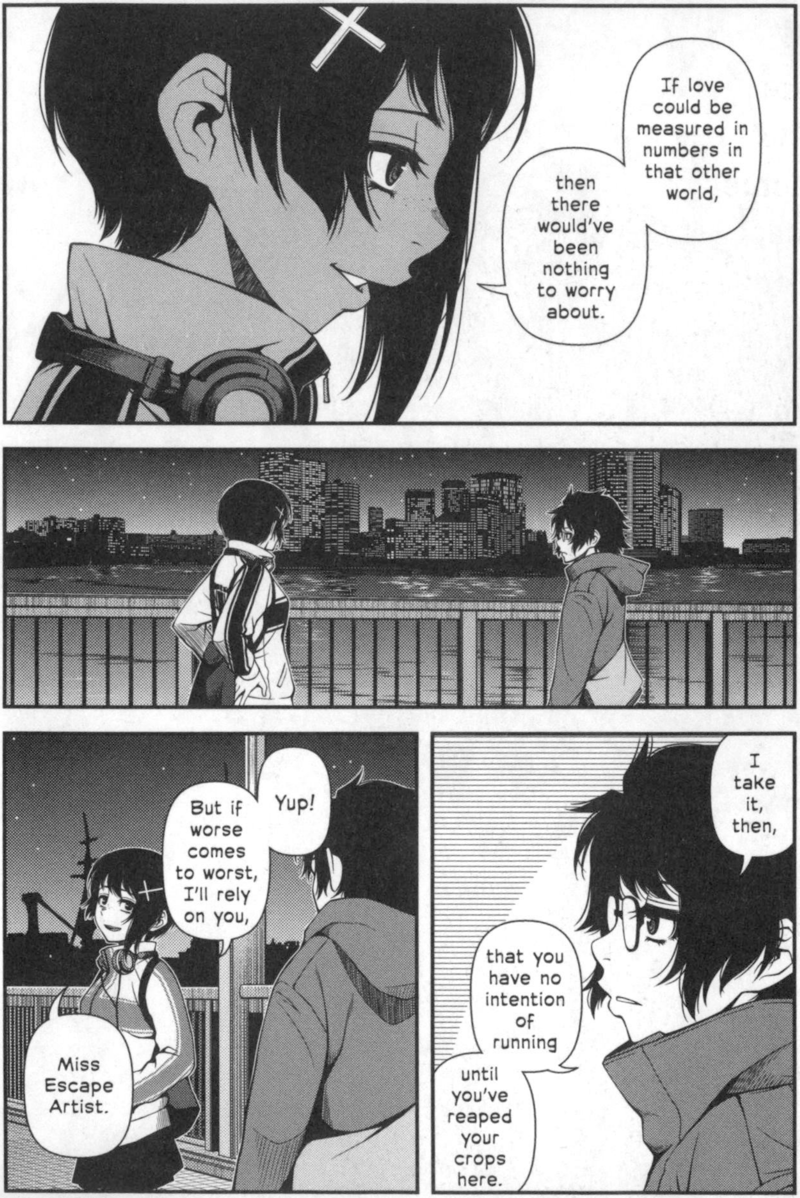
If love could be measured in numbers in that other world,
then there would've been nothing to worry about.
I take it, then,
that you have no intention of running
until you've reaped your crops here.
Yup!
But if worse comes to worst, I'll rely on you,
Miss Escape Artist.

17

Are You Home, Mr. Tobita?

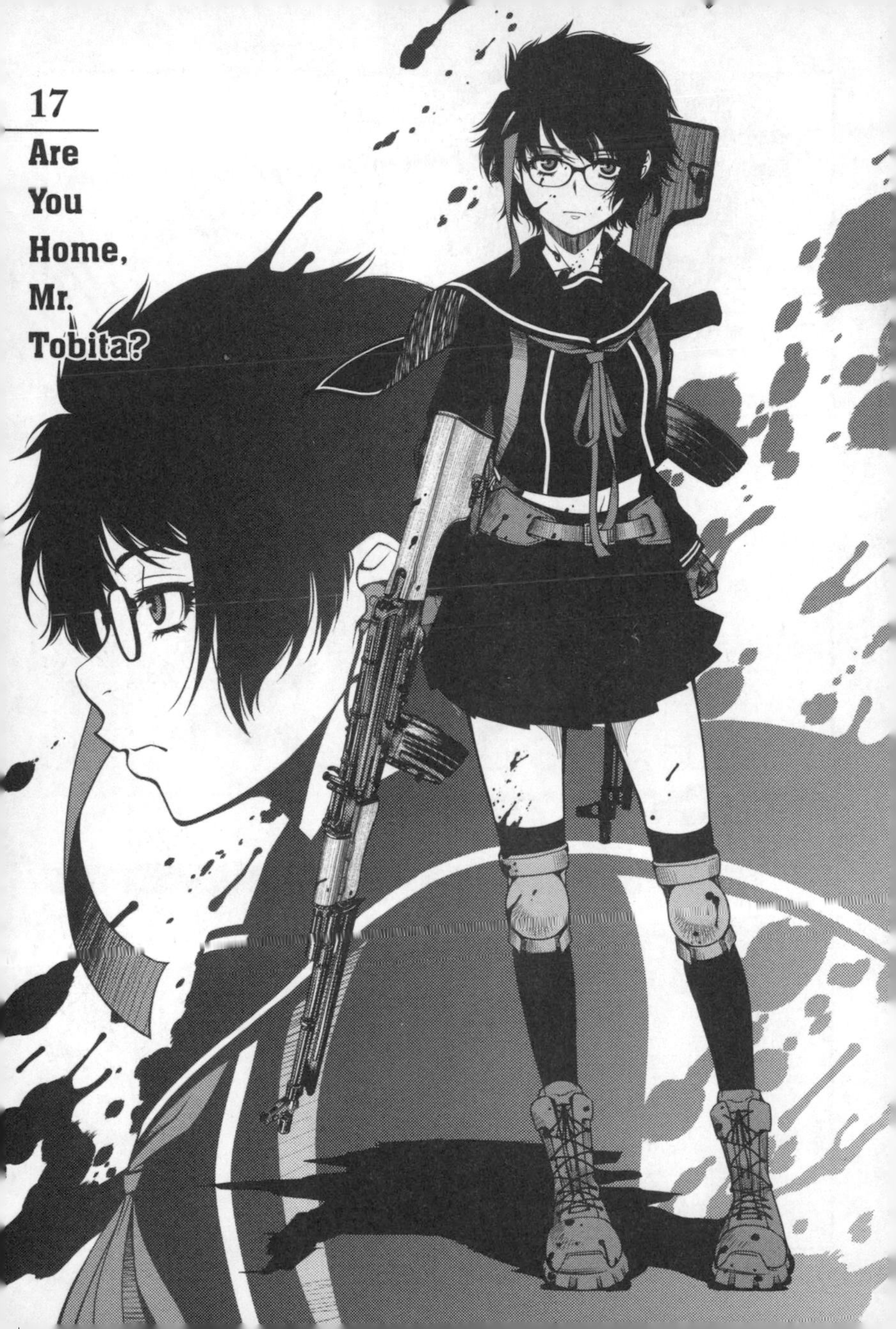

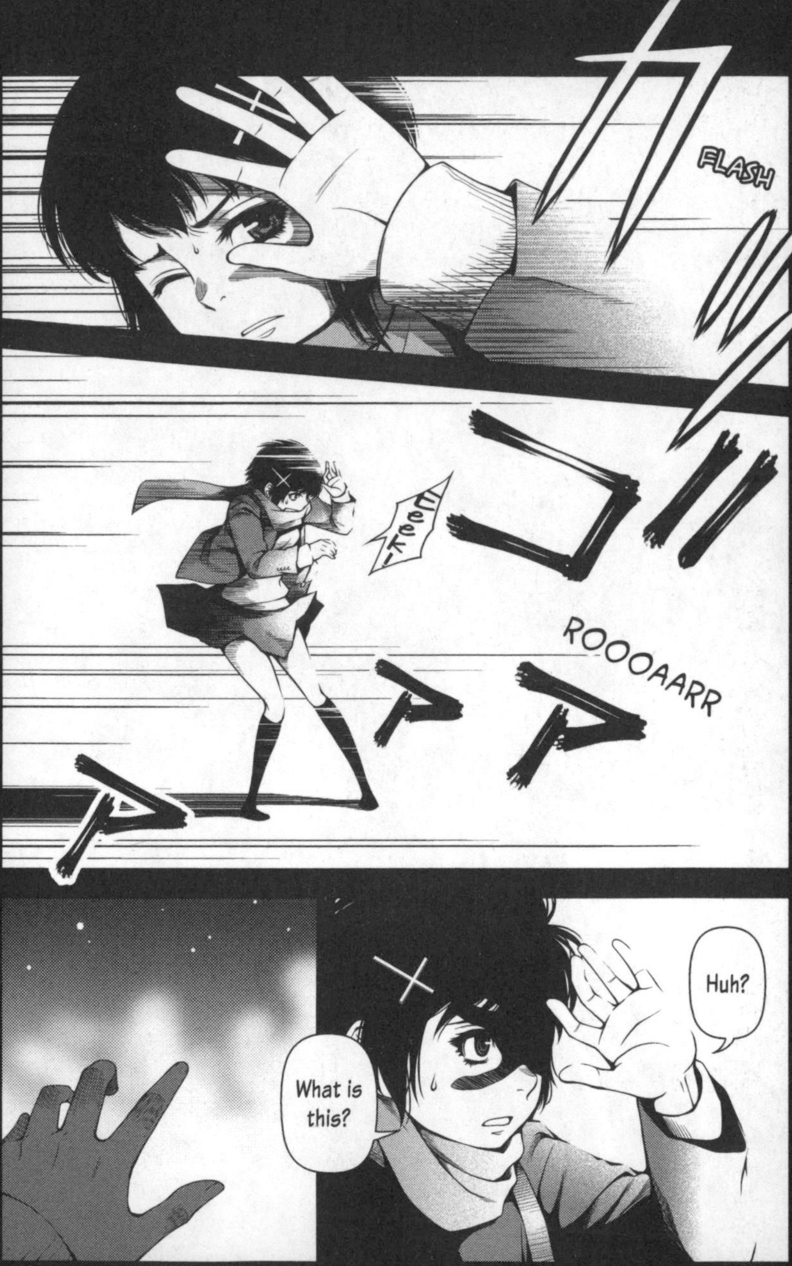
FLASH
Eeek!
ROOOAARR
Huh?
What is this?

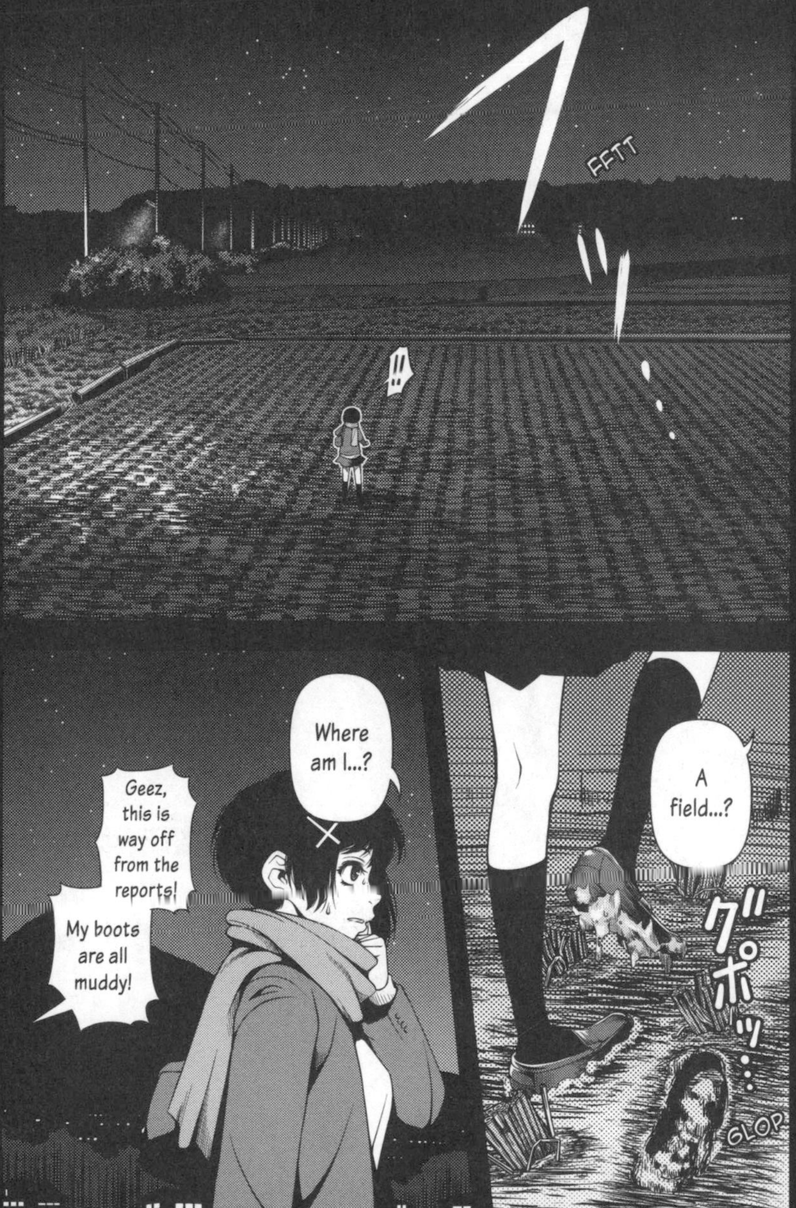
FFTT
!!
A field...?
グポッ…
GLOP
Where am I...?
Geez, this is way off from the reports!
My boots are all muddy!

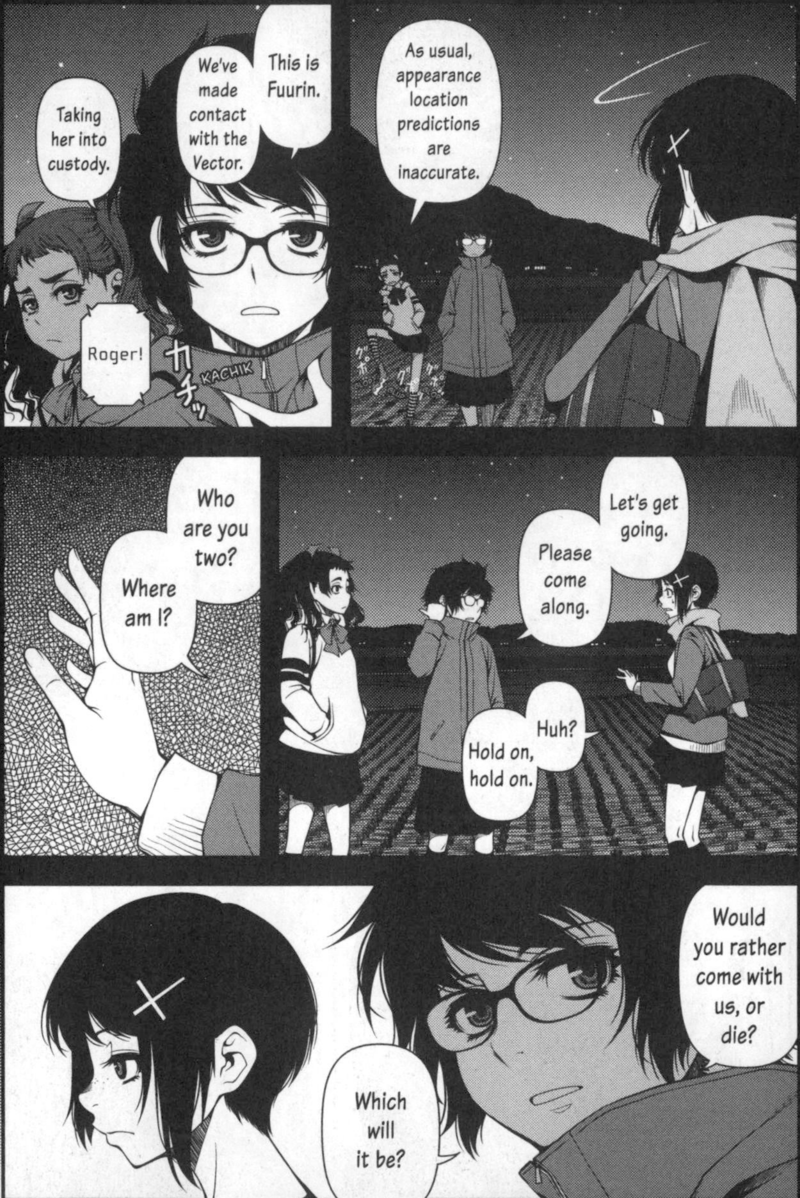

As usual, appearance location predictions are inaccurate.
This is Fuurin.
We've made contact with the Vector.
Taking her into custody.
Roger!
カチッ
KACHIK
Let's get going.
Please come along.
Huh?
Hold on, hold on.
Who are you two?
Where am I?
Would you rather come with us, or die?
Which will it be?

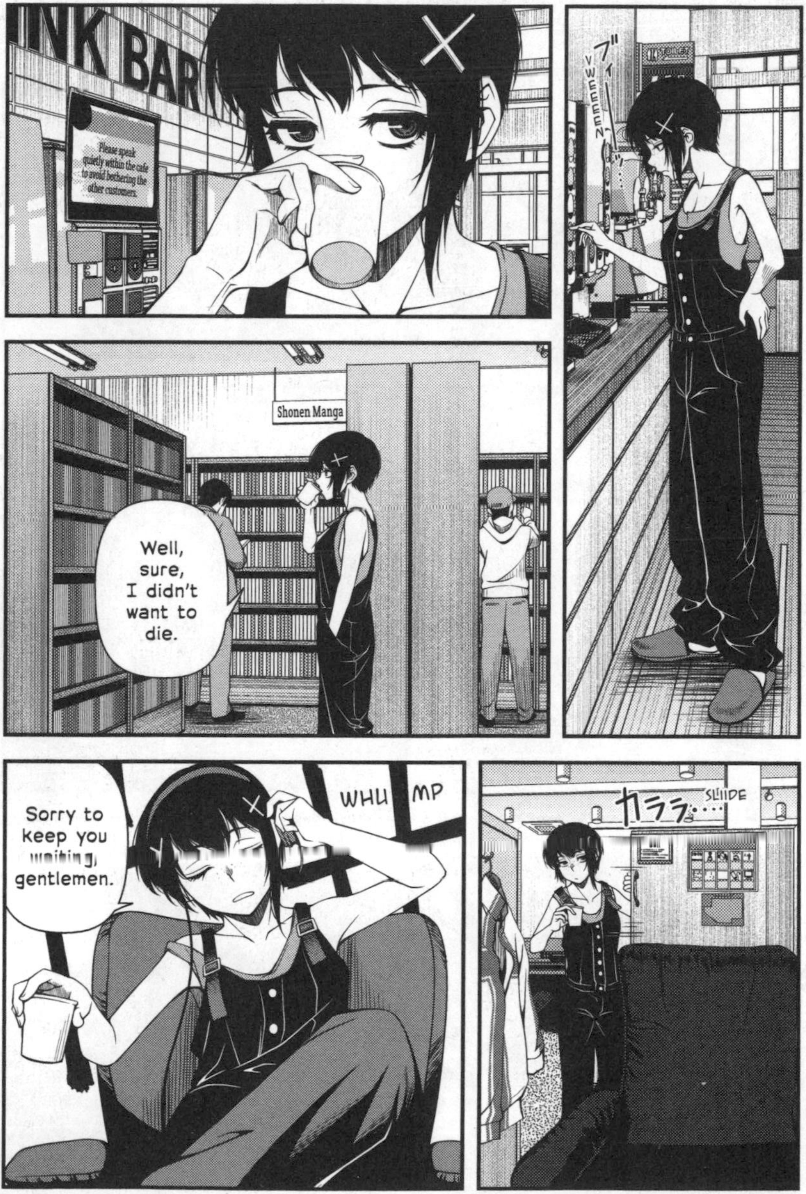
ブィー
VWEEEEN
INK BAR
Please speak quietly within the cafe to avoid bothering the other customers.
Shonen Manga
Well, sure, I didn't want to die.
カラララ…
SLIIDE
WHUMP
Sorry to keep you waiting, gentlemen.

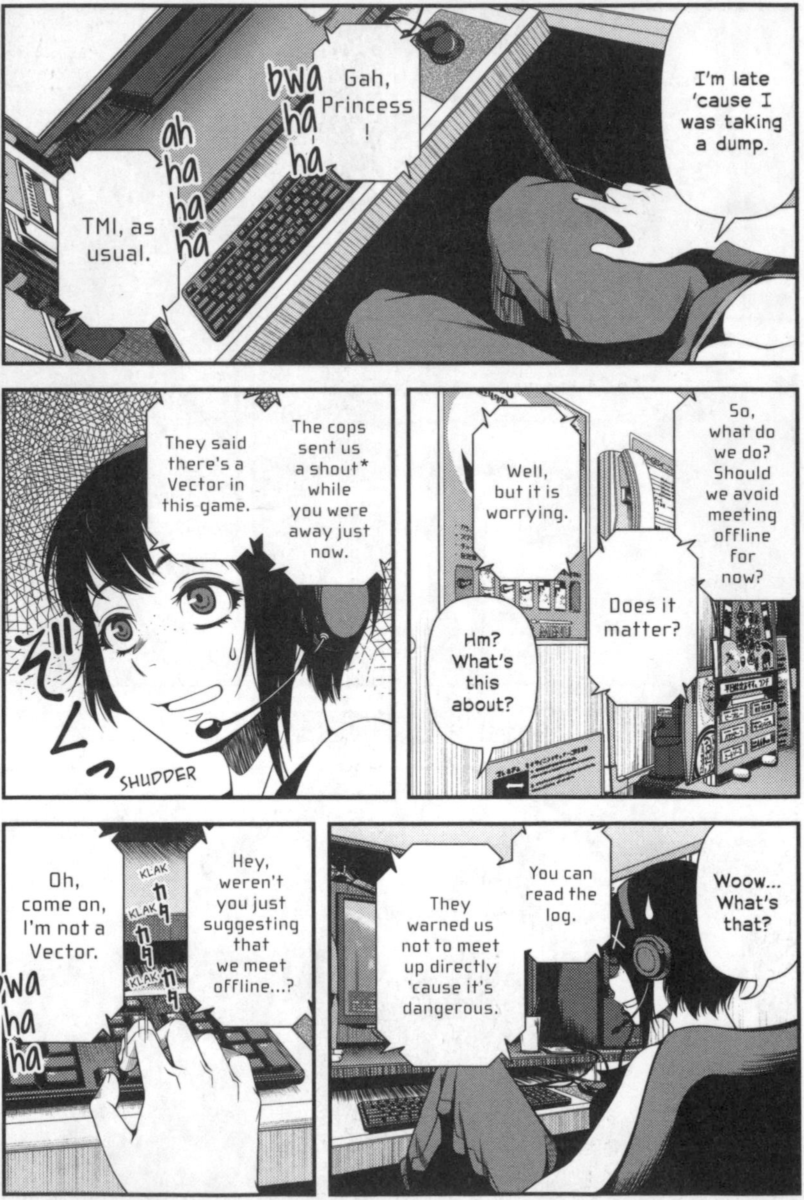
I'm late 'cause I was taking a dump.
Gah, Princess!
bwa ha ha
ah ha ha ha
TMI, as usual.
So, what do we do? Should we avoid meeting offline for now?
Well, but it is worrying.
Does it matter?
Hm? What's this about?
The cops sent us a shout* while you were away just now.
They said there's a Vector in this game.
SHUDDER
Woow... What's that?
You can read the log.
They warned us not to meet up directly 'cause it's dangerous.
Hey, weren't you just suggesting that we meet offline...?
KLAK KLAK KLAK
Oh, come on, I'm not a Vector.
bwa ha ha

*Shout = a chat that is broadcast to all players. Generally used for announcements.

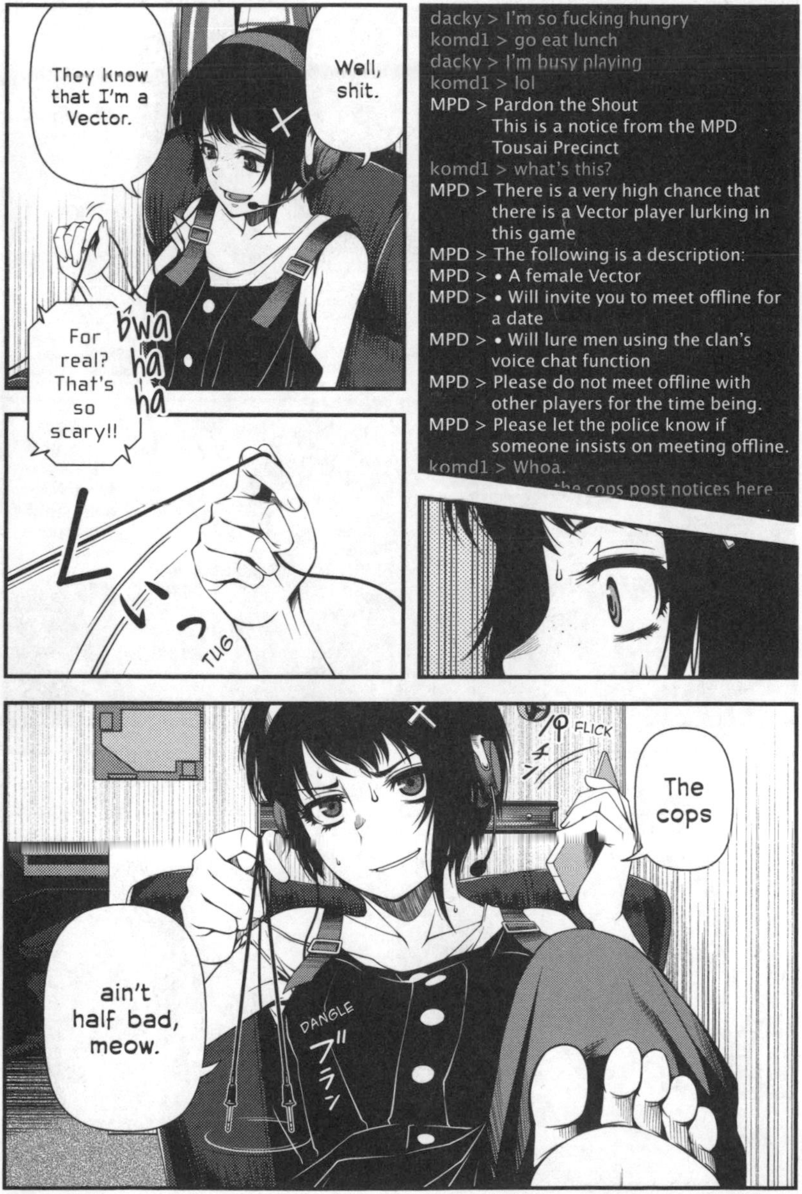
dacky > I'm so fucking hungry
komd1 > go eat lunch
dacky > I'm busy playing
komd1 > lol
MPD > Pardon the Shout
This is a notice from the MPD
Tousai Precinct
komd1 > what's this?
MPD > There is a very high chance that there is a Vector player lurking in this game
MPD > The following is a description:
MPD > • A female Vector
MPD > • Will invite you to meet offline for a date
MPD > • Will lure men using the clan's voice chat function
MPD > Please do not meet offline with other players for the time being.
MPD > Please let the police know if someone insists on meeting offline.
komd1 > Whoa.
the cops post notices here
Well, shit.
They know that I'm a Vector.
bwa ha ha
For real? That's so scary!!
TUG
FLICK
The cops
ain't half bad, meow.
DANGLE

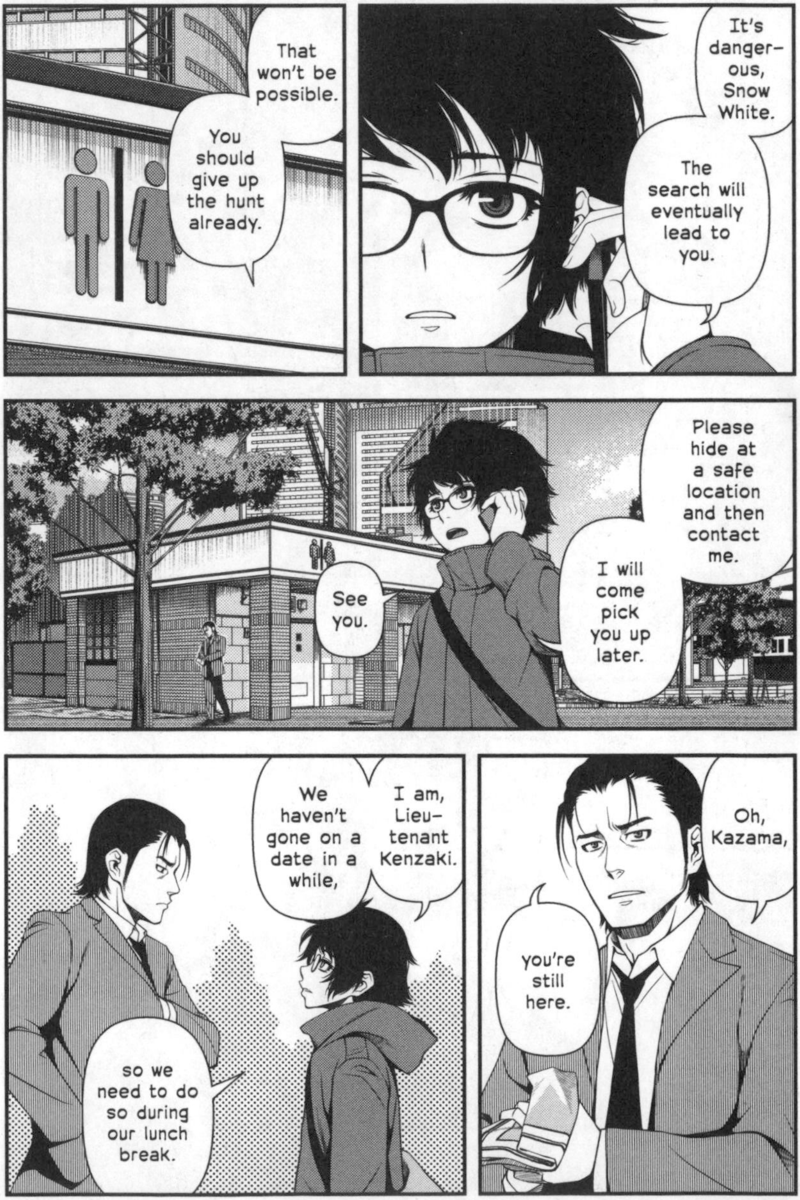
It's danger-ous, Snow White.
The search will eventually lead to you.
That won't be possible.
You should give up the hunt already.
Please hide at a safe location and then contact me.
I will come pick you up later.
See you.
Oh, Kazama,
you're still here.
I am, Lieu-tenant Kenzaki.
We haven't gone on a date in a while,
so we need to do so during our lunch break.

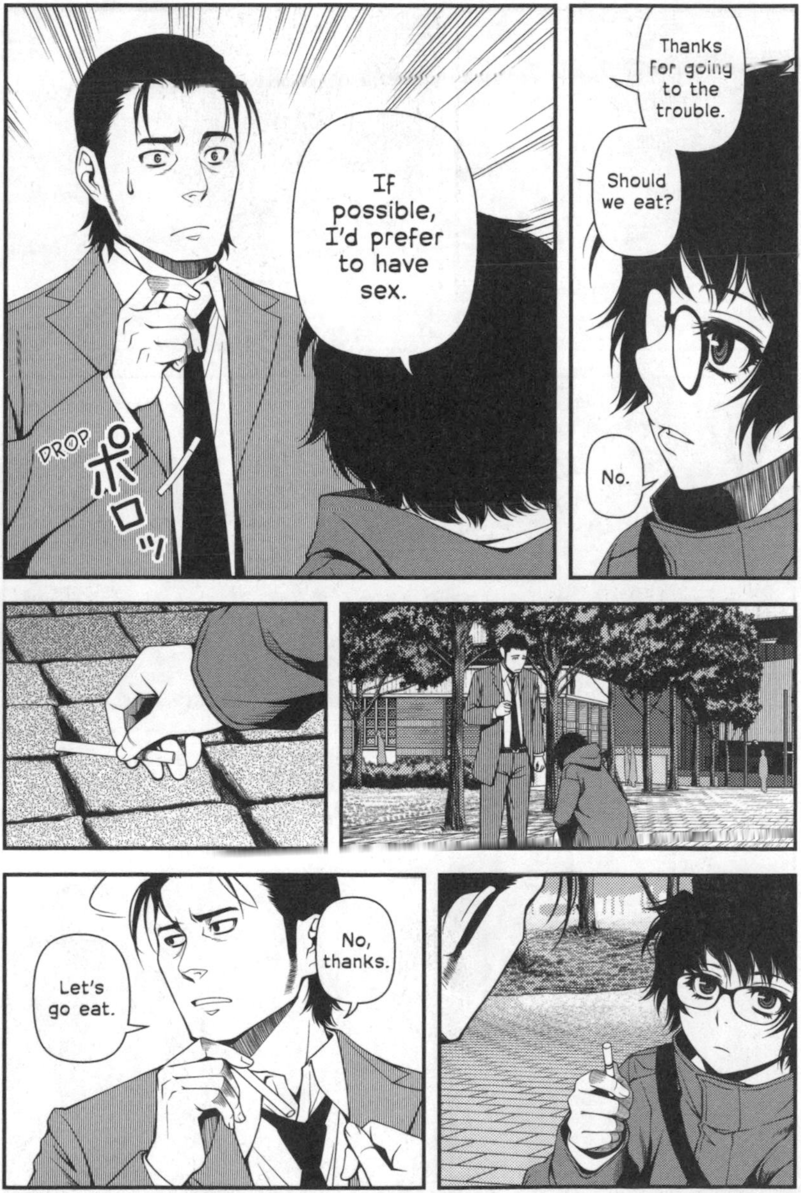
Thanks for going to the trouble.
Should we eat?
No.
If possible, I'd prefer to have sex.
DROP
ポロッ
No, thanks.
Let's go eat.

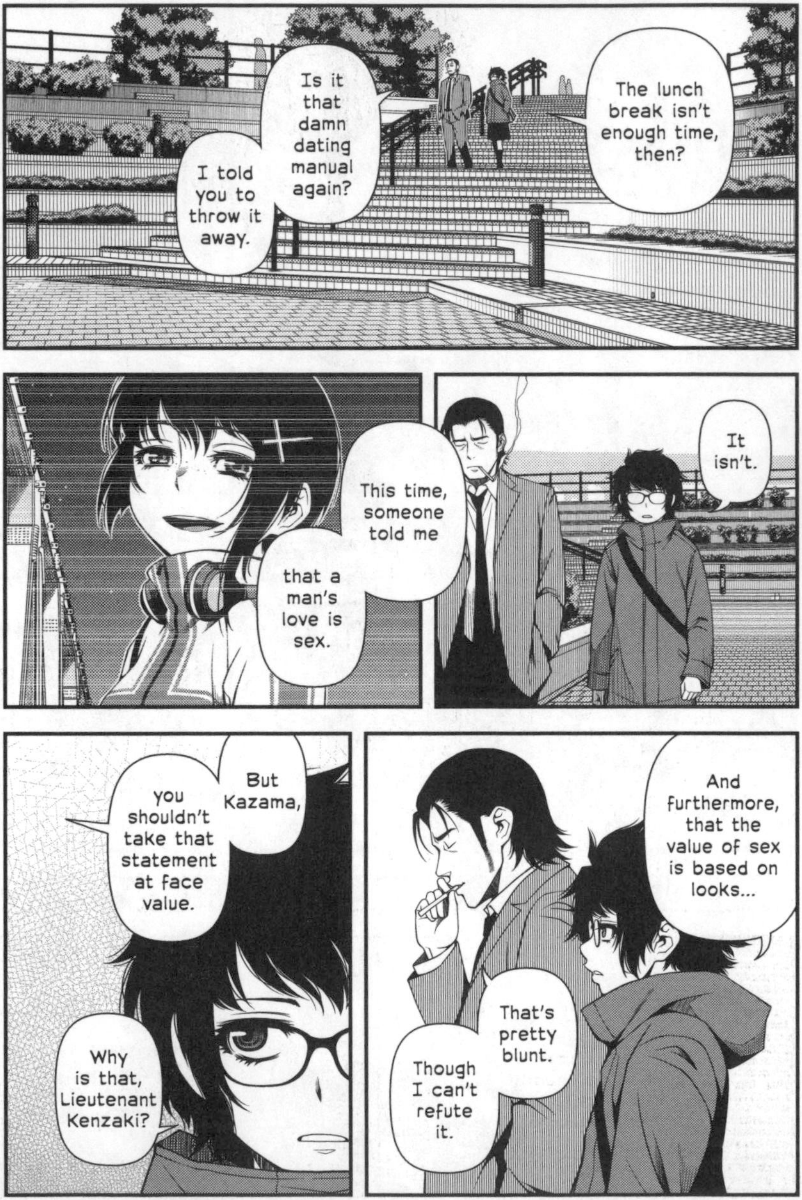

The lunch break isn't enough time, then?
Is it that damn dating manual again?
I told you to throw it away.
It isn't.
This time, someone told me
that a man's love is sex.
And furthermore, that the value of sex is based on looks...
That's pretty blunt.
Though I can't refute it.
But Kazama,
you shouldn't take that statement at face value.
Why is that, Lieutenant Kenzaki?

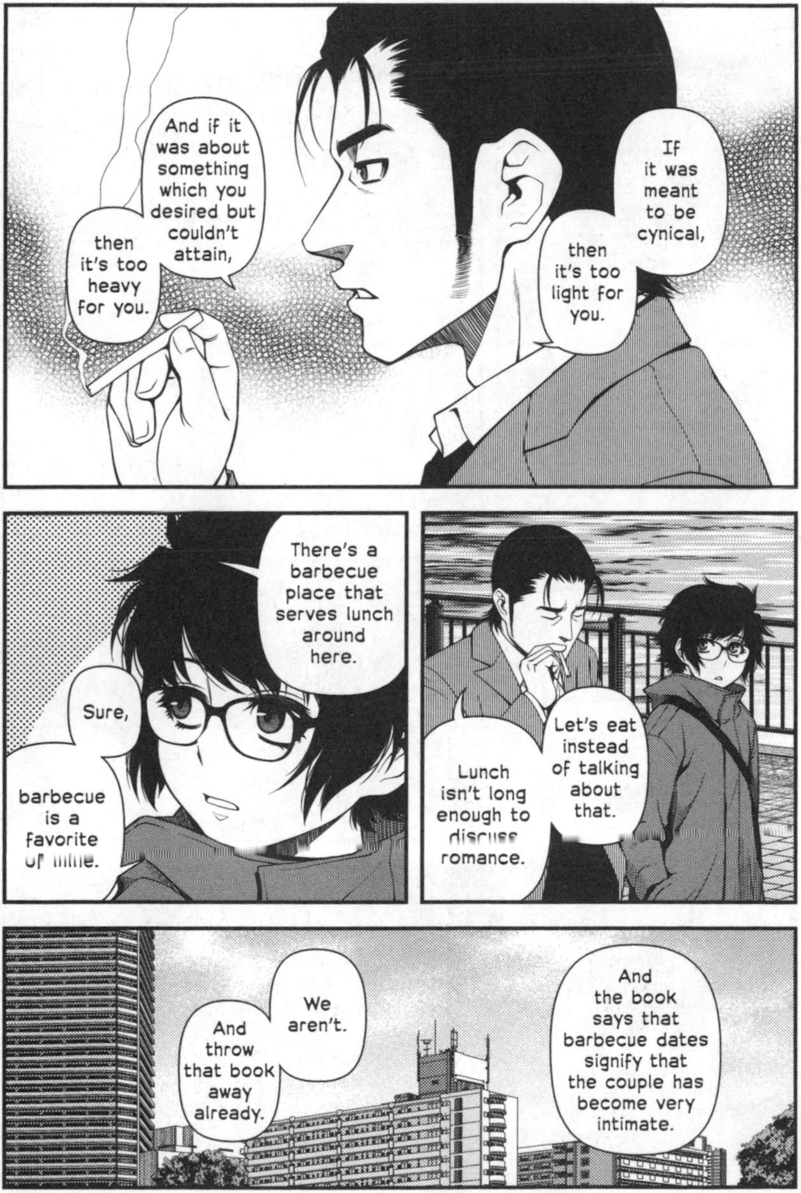
If it was meant to be cynical,
then it's too light for you.
And if it was about something which you desired but couldn't attain,
then it's too heavy for you.
Let's eat instead of talking about that.
Lunch isn't long enough to discuss romance.
There's a barbecue place that serves lunch around here.
Sure,
barbecue is a favorite of mine.
And the book says that barbecue dates signify that the couple has become very intimate.
We aren't.
And throw that book away already.

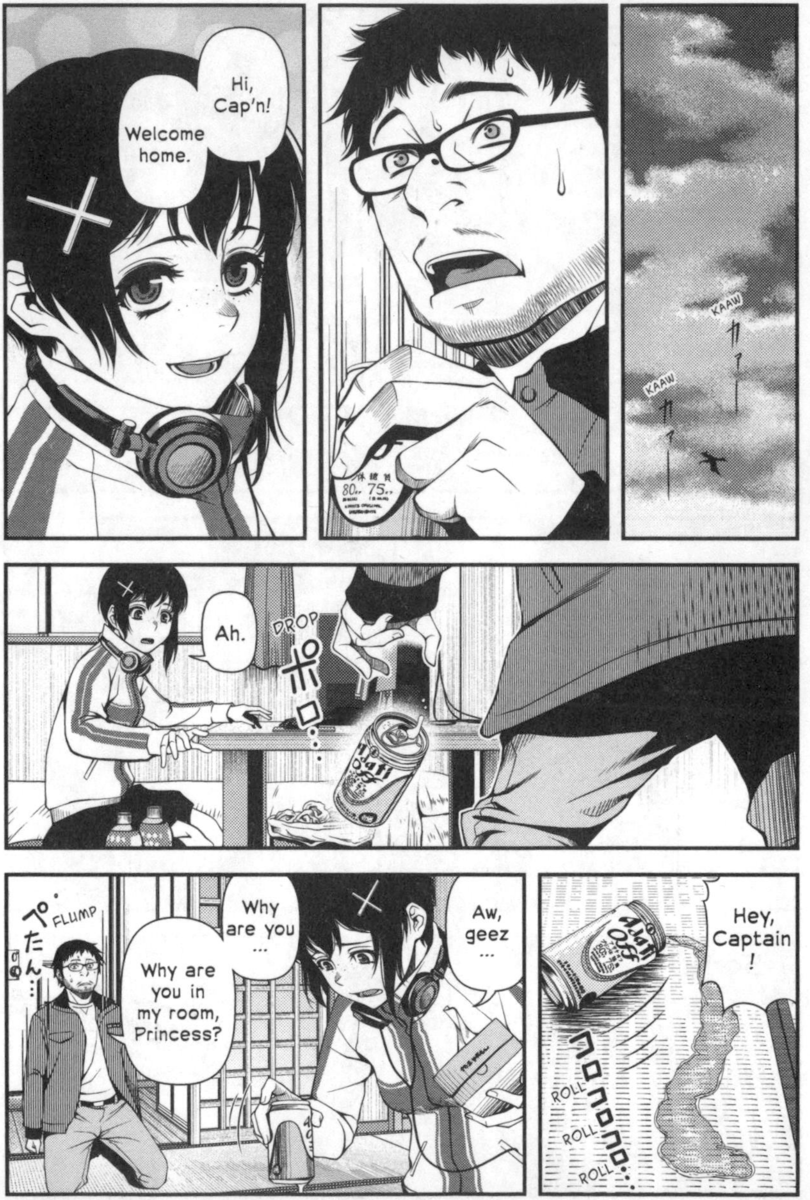
KAAW
カァー
KAAW
カァー
Hi, Cap'n!
Welcome home.
Ah.
DROP
ポロ…
Hey, Captain!
ROLL
ROLL
ROLL
コロコロコロ…
Aw, geez ...
Why are you ...
Why are you in my room, Princess?
FLUMP
ぺたん…

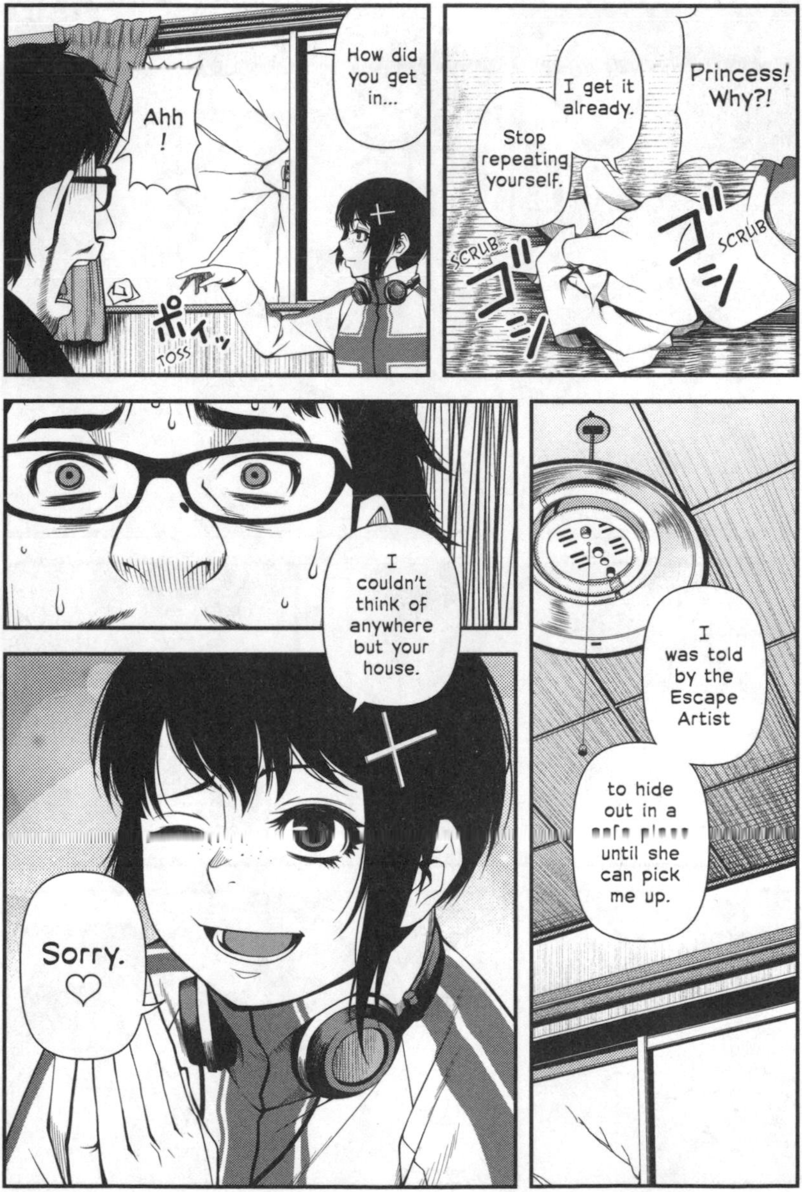
Princess! Why?!
I get it already.
Stop repeating yourself.
SCRUB ゴシ
SCRUB ゴシ
How did you get in...
Ahh!
ポイッ TOSS
I was told by the Escape Artist
to hide out in a safe place until she can pick me up.
I couldn't think of anywhere but your house.
Sorry. ♡

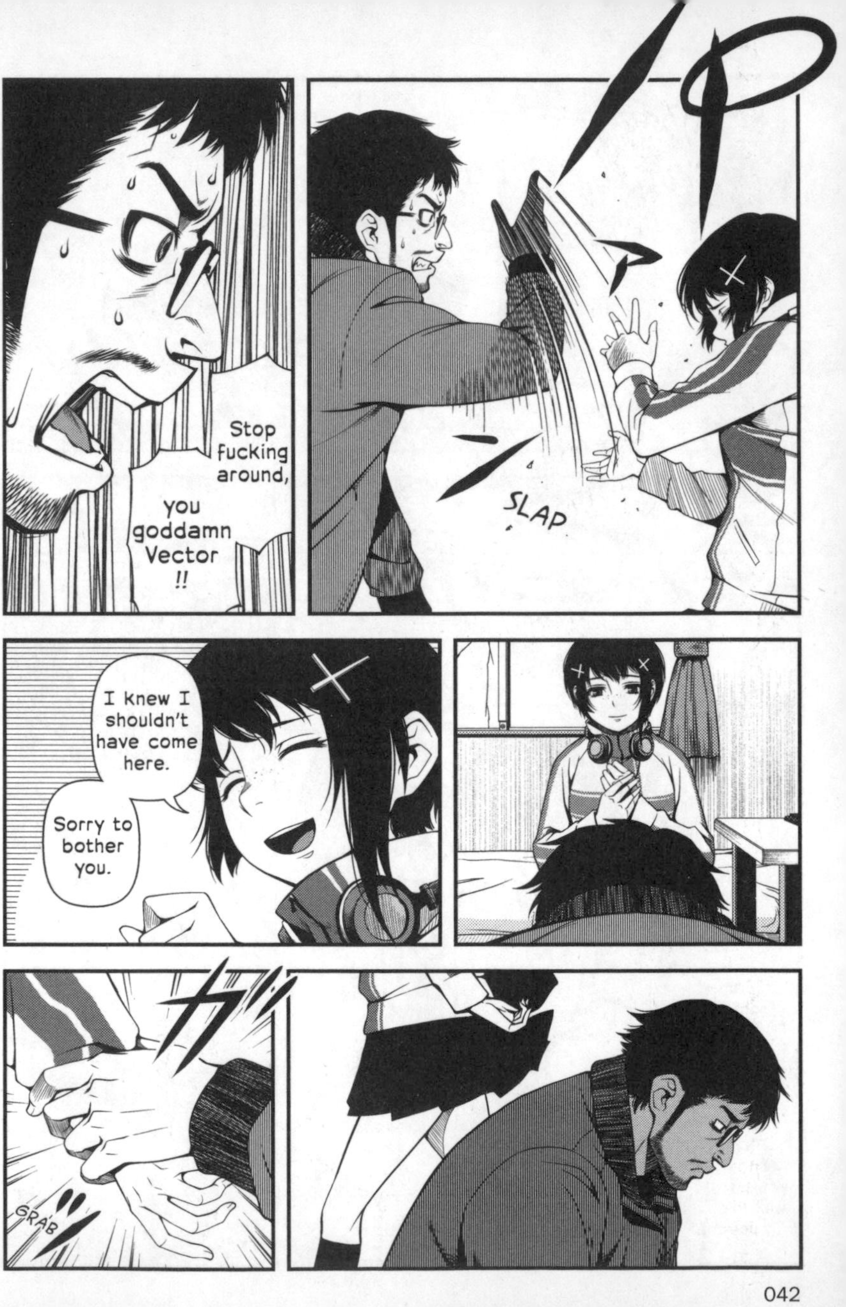
SLAP
Stop fucking around, you goddamn Vector !!
I knew I shouldn't have come here.
Sorry to bother you.
GRAB

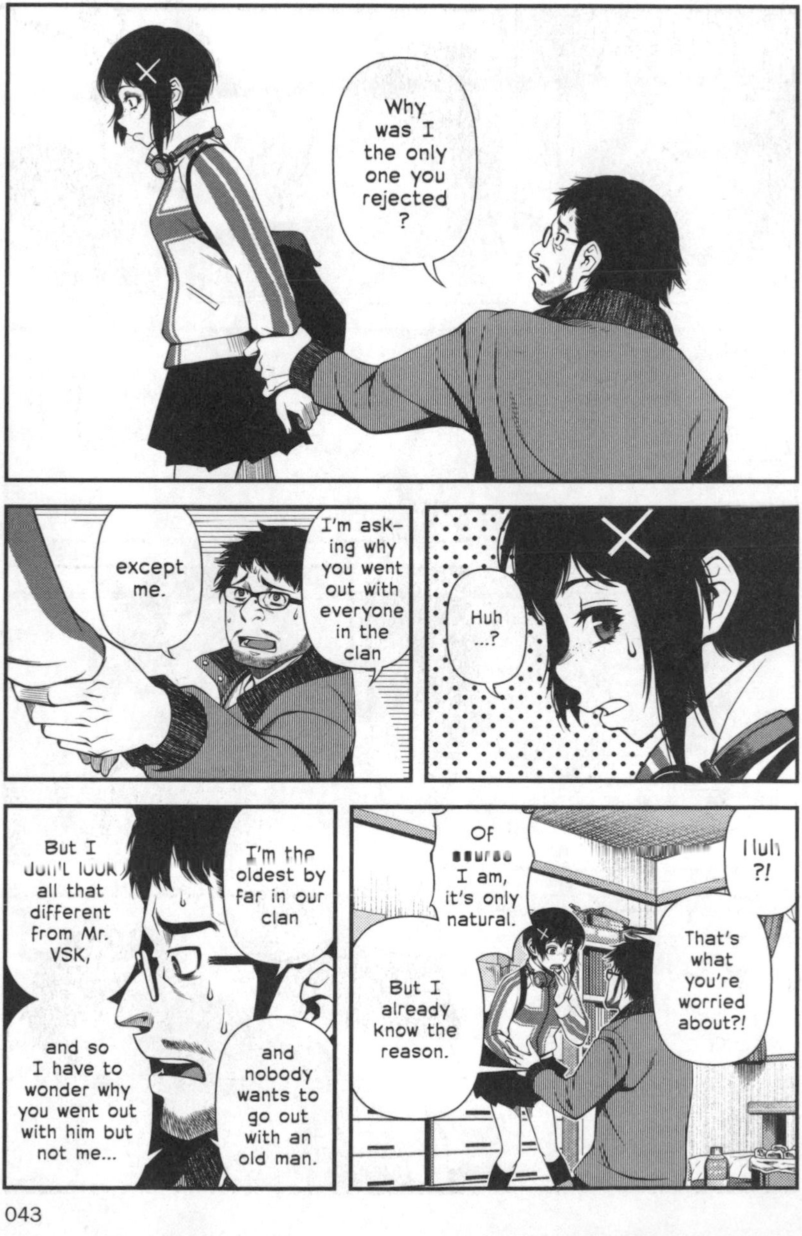
Why was I the only one you rejected ?
Huh ...?
I'm ask-ing why you went out with everyone in the clan
except me.
Huh ?!
That's what you're worried about?!
Of course I am, it's only natural.
But I already know the reason.
I'm the oldest by far in our clan
and nobody wants to go out with an old man.
But I don't look all that different from Mr. VSK,
and so I have to wonder why you went out with him but not me...

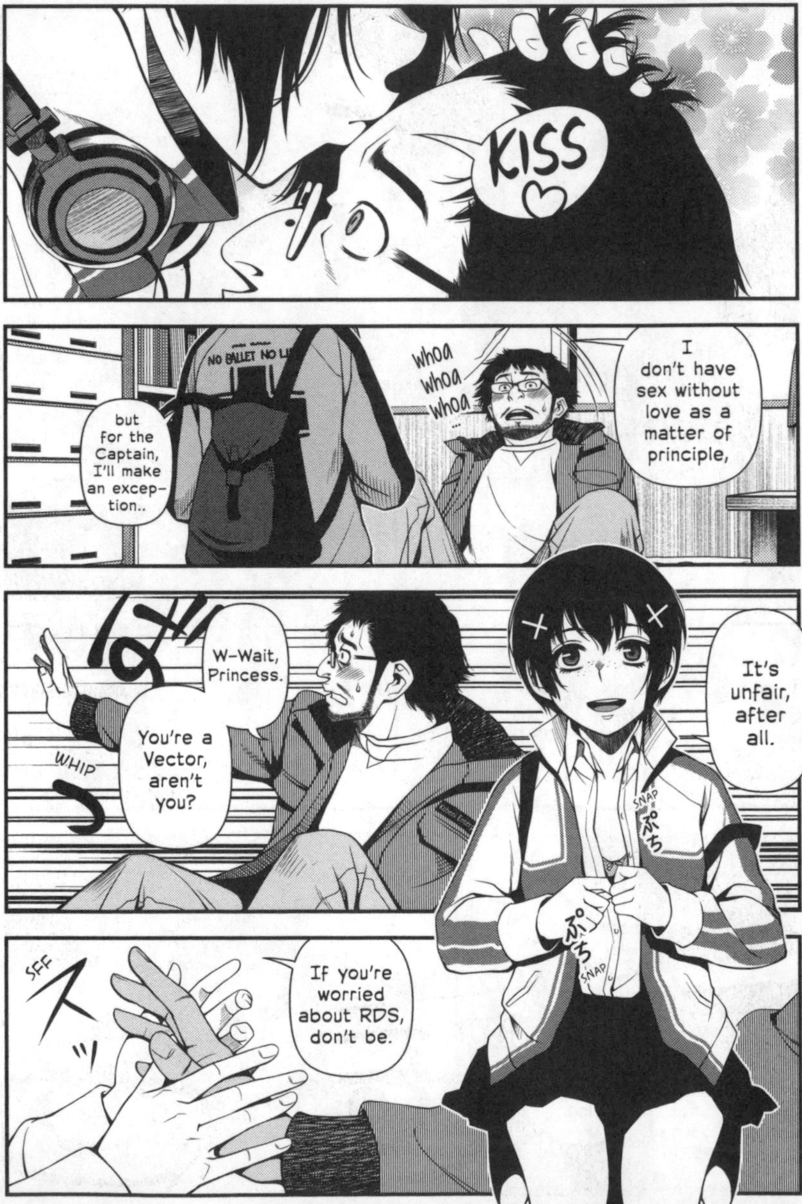
KISS
I don't have sex without love as a matter of principle,
whoa whoa whoa ...
NO BALLET NO LI
but for the Captain, I'll make an excep-tion..
It's unfair, after all.
SNAP ぷち
W-Wait, Princess.
You're a Vector, aren't you?
WHIP
ぷち SNAP
If you're worried about RDS, don't be.
SFF ス ッ

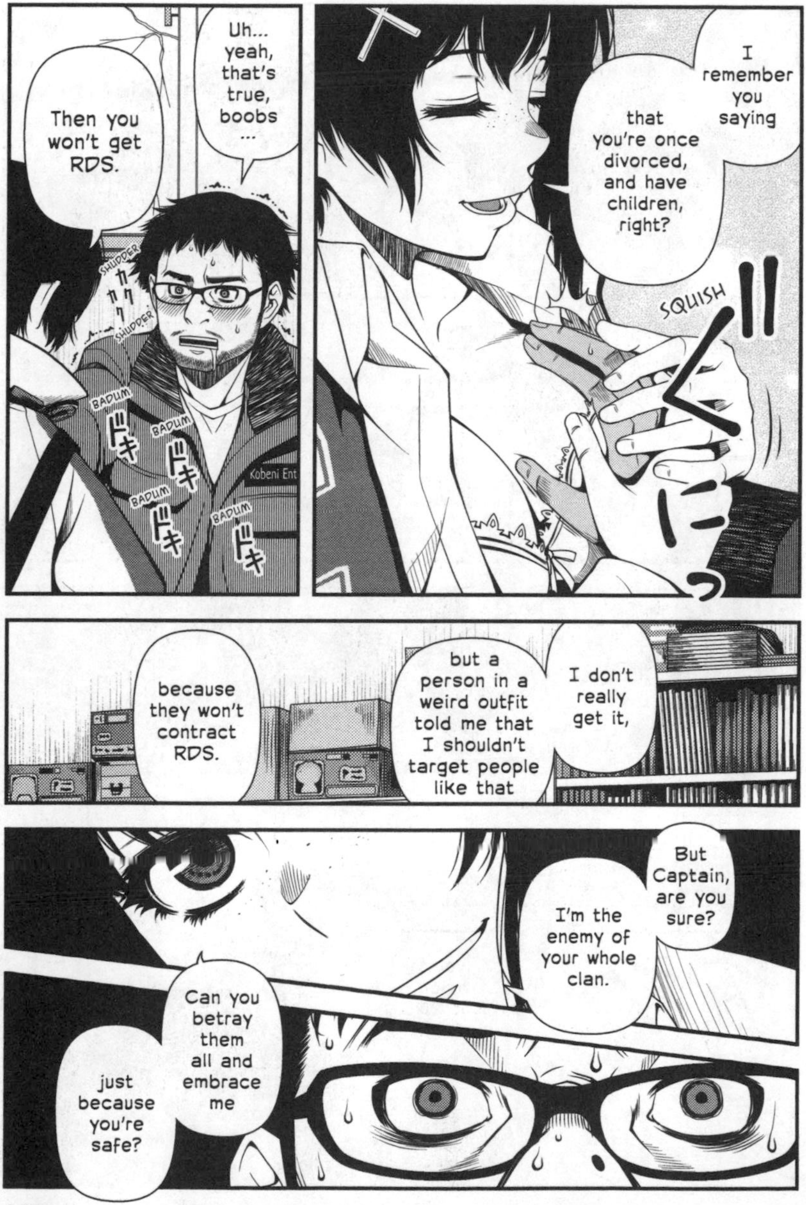
I remember you saying
that you're once divorced, and have children, right?
SQUISH
Uh... yeah, that's true, boobs ...
Then you won't get RDS.
SHUDDER
SHUDDER
BADUM
BADUM
BADUM
BADUM
Kobeni Ent
I don't really get it,
but a person in a weird outfit told me that I shouldn't target people like that
because they won't contract RDS.
But Captain, are you sure?
I'm the enemy of your whole clan.
Can you betray them all and embrace me
just because you're safe?

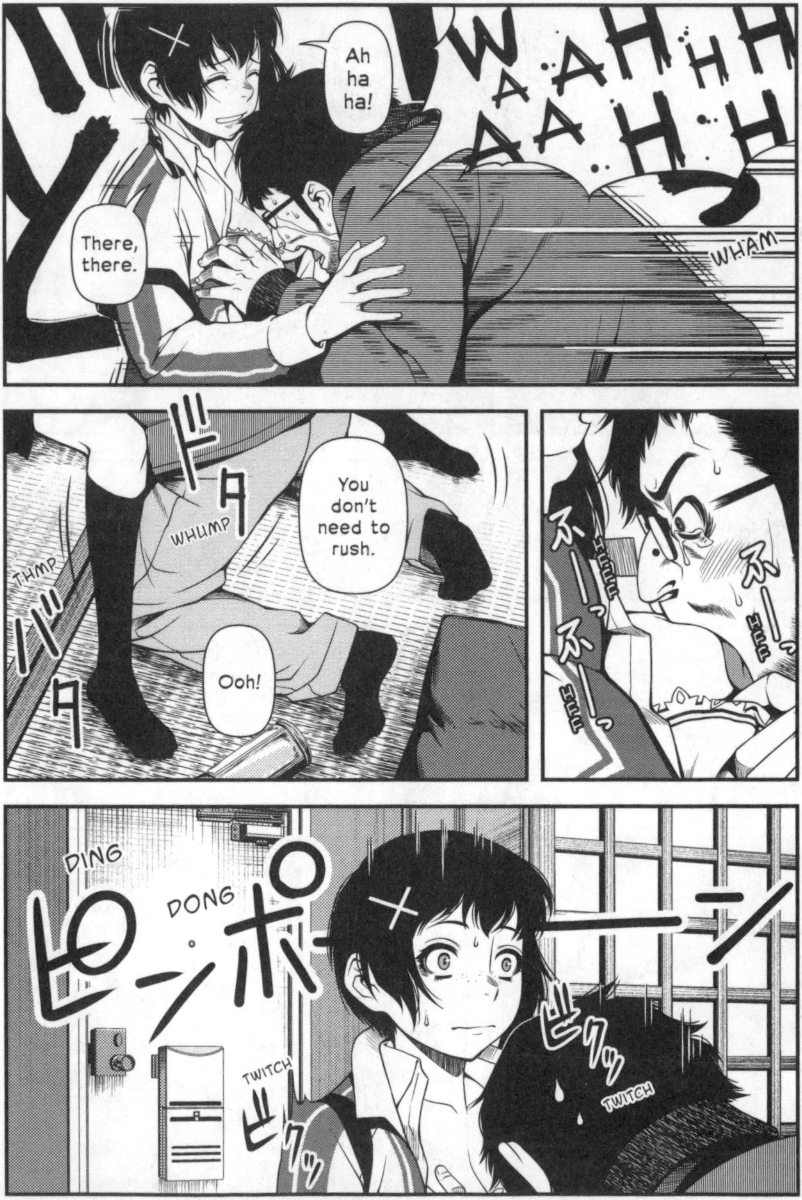
WAAAHHHHH
Ah ha ha!
WHAM
There, there.
ふーっ
HUFF
ふーっ
HUFF
ふーっ
HUFF
ドタ
WHUMP
You don't need to rush.
THMP
バタ
Ooh!
ピンポーン
DING
DONG
ビクッ
TWITCH
ビクッ
TWITCH

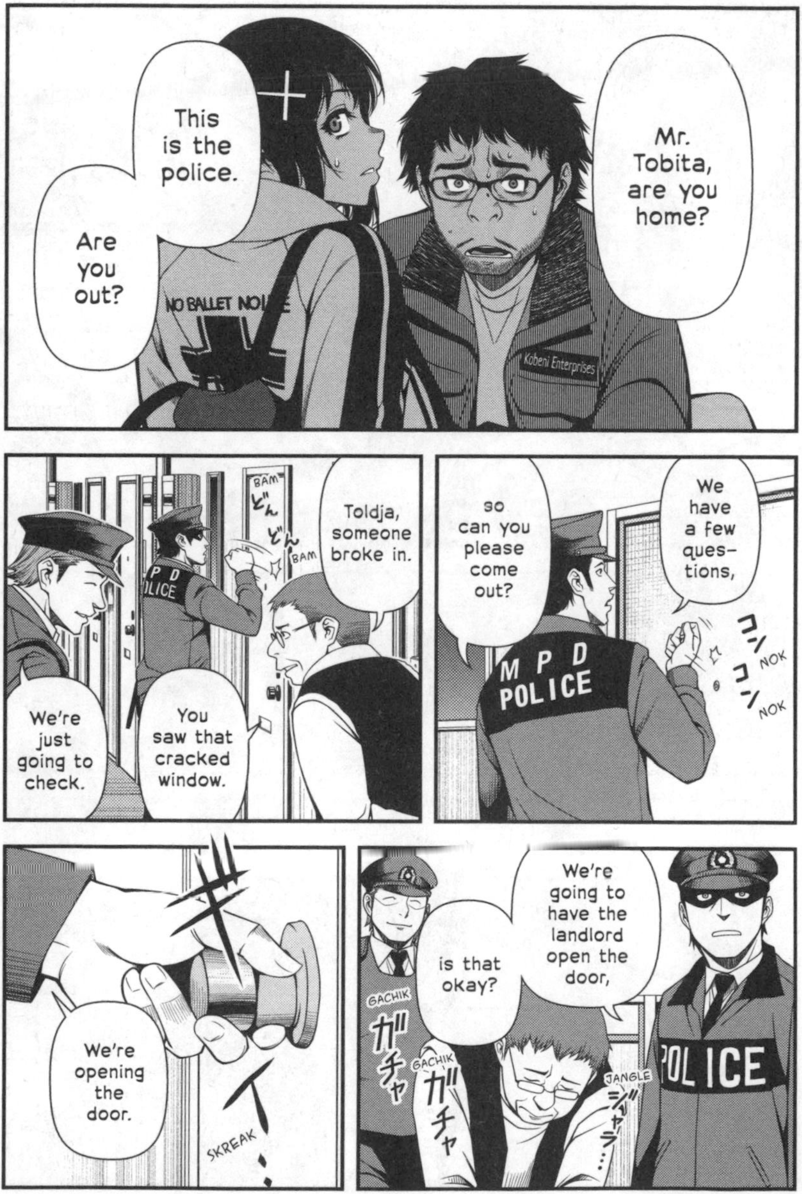
Mr. Tobita, are you home?
This is the police.
Are you out?
Kobeni Enterprises
We have a few ques-tions,
NOK
NOK
so can you please come out?
MPD POLICE
Toldja, someone broke in.
BAM
BAM
MPD POLICE
You saw that cracked window.
We're just going to check.
We're going to have the landlord open the door,
is that okay?
GACHIK
GACHIK
JANGLE
POLICE
We're opening the door.
SKREAK

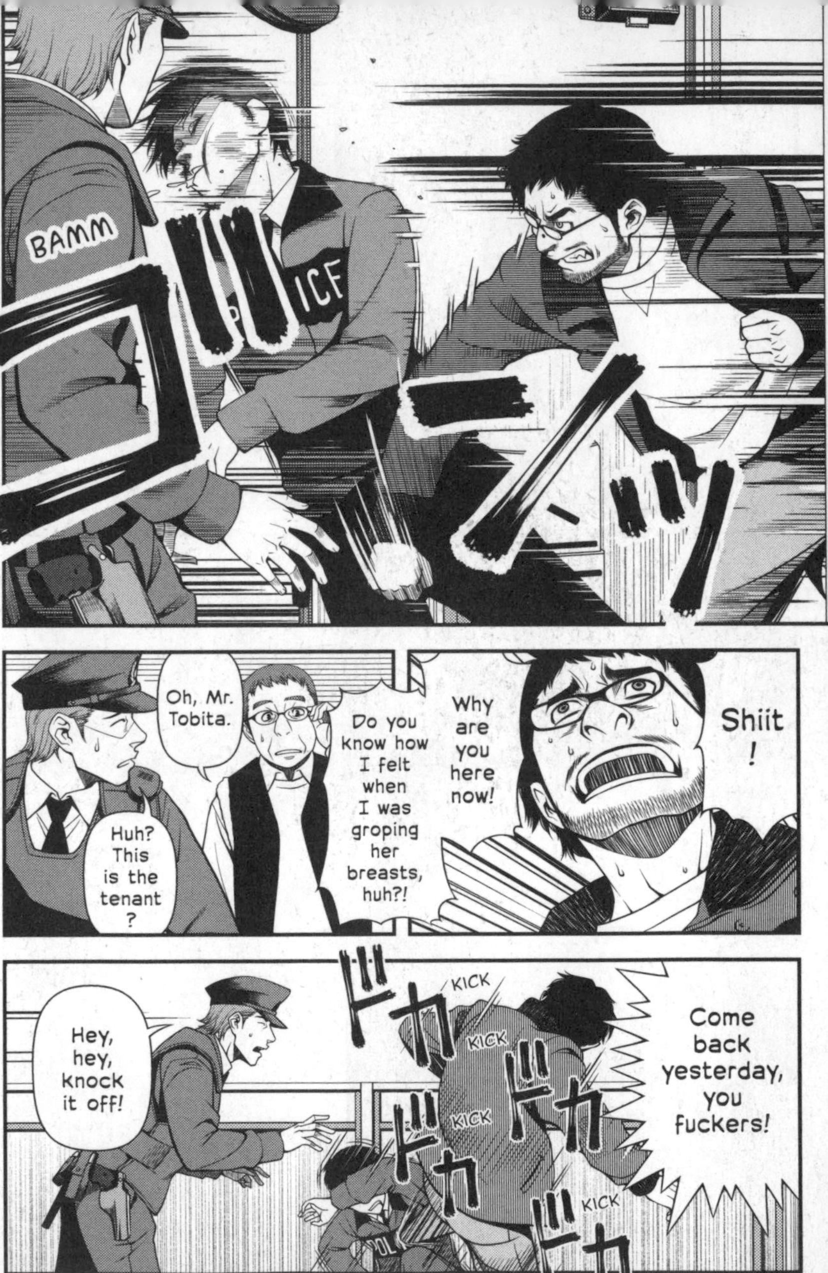
BAMM
Shiit!
Why are you here now!
Do you know how I felt when I was groping her breasts, huh?!
Oh, Mr. Tobita.
Huh? This is the tenant?
Come back yesterday, you fuckers!
KICK
ドカ
KICK
ドカ
KICK
ドカ
KICK
ドカ
Hey, hey, knock it off!

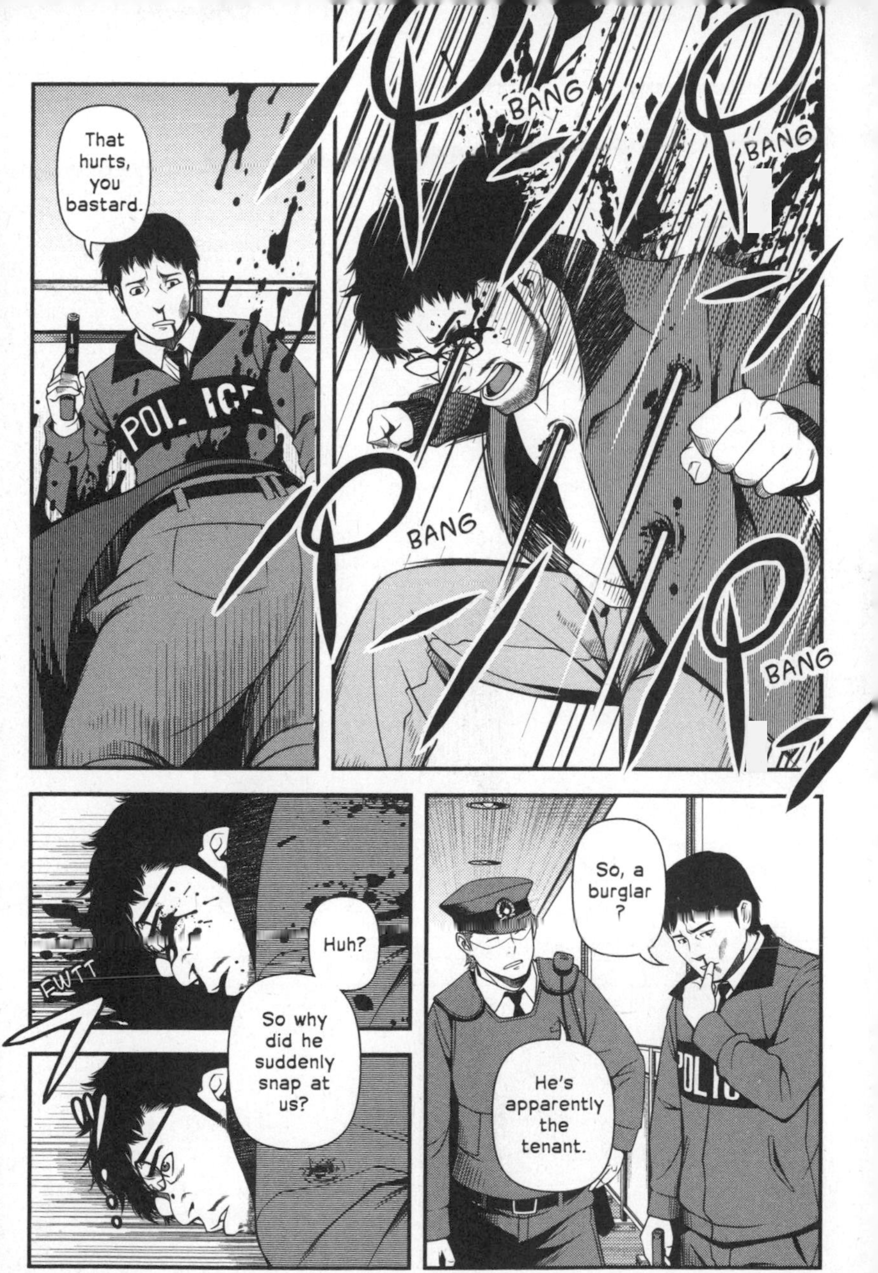
BANG
BANG
BANG
BANG
That hurts, you bastard.
POLICE
So, a burglar?
He's apparently the tenant.
POLICE
Huh?
FWTT
So why did he suddenly snap at us?

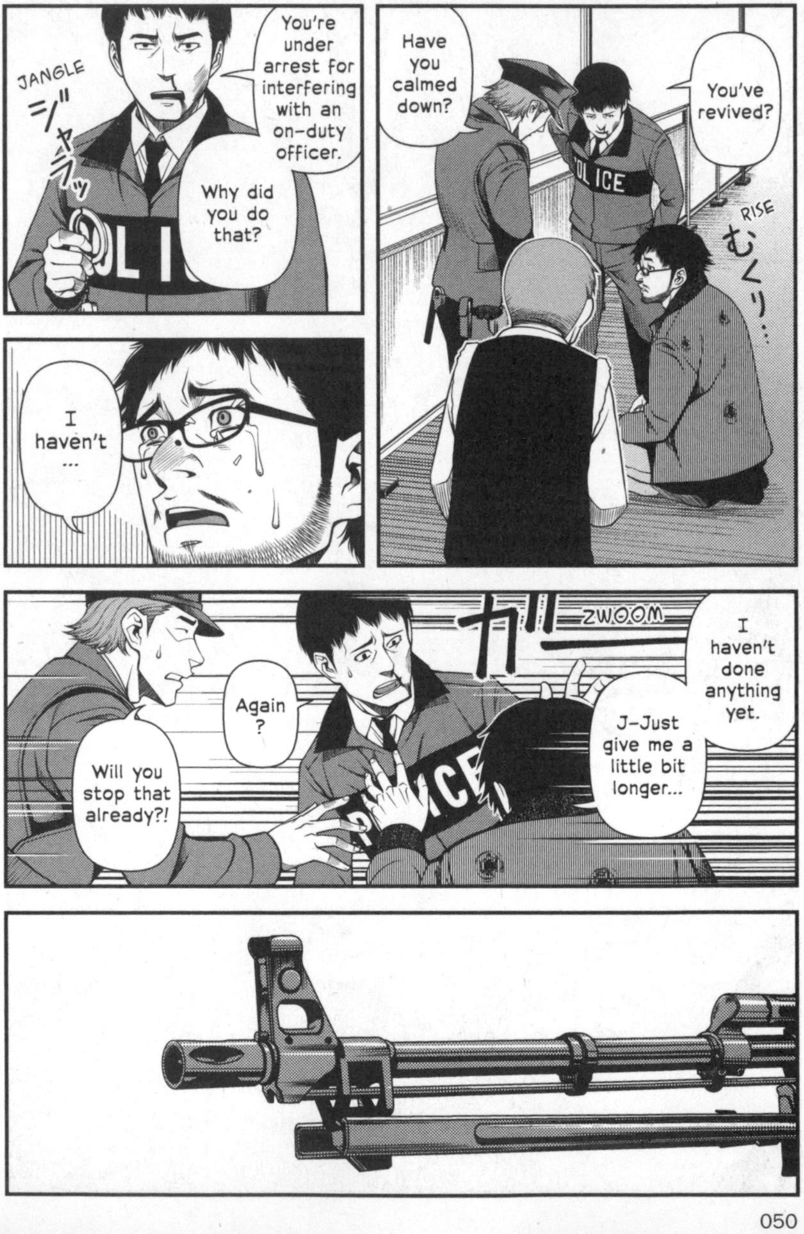
You've revived?
Have you calmed down?
RISE
むくり…
You're under arrest for interfering with an on-duty officer.
Why did you do that?
JANGLE
ジャラッ
I haven't …
ZWOOM
I haven't done anything yet.
J-Just give me a little bit longer…
Again?
Will you stop that already?!

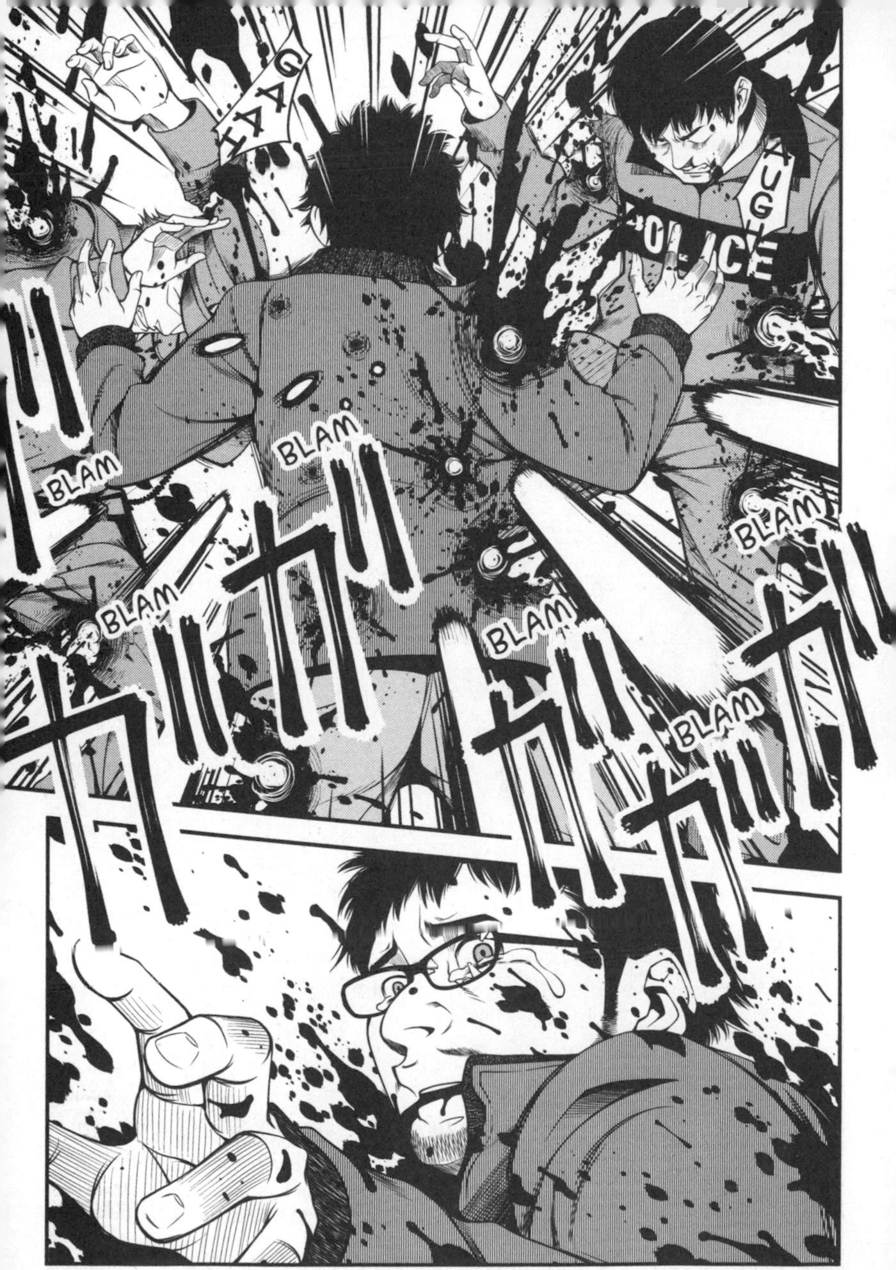
AUGH
POLICE
GAAH
BLAM
BLAM
BLAM
BLAM
BLAM
BLAM

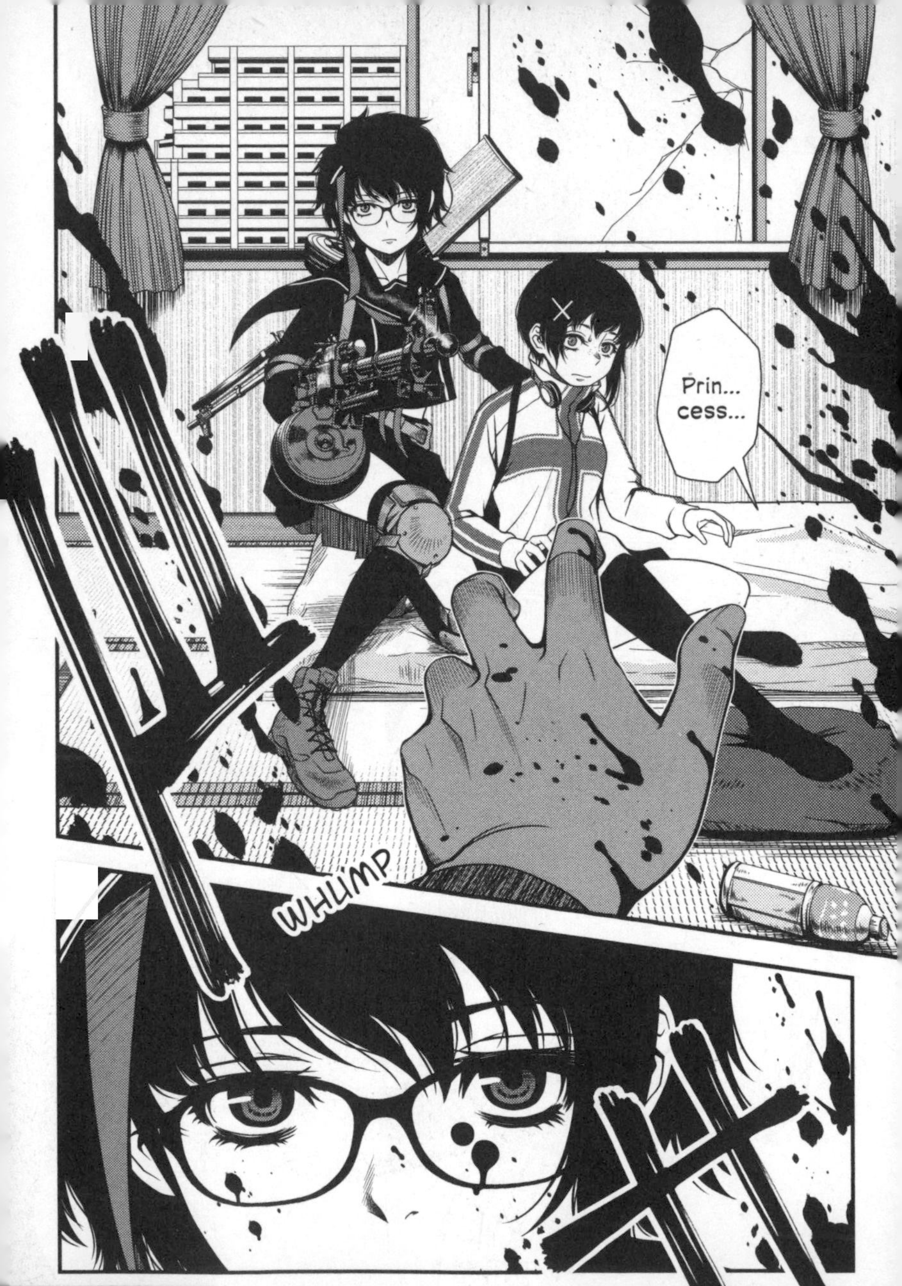
Prin... cess...
WHLIMP

End of Chapter 17

18

Creampie

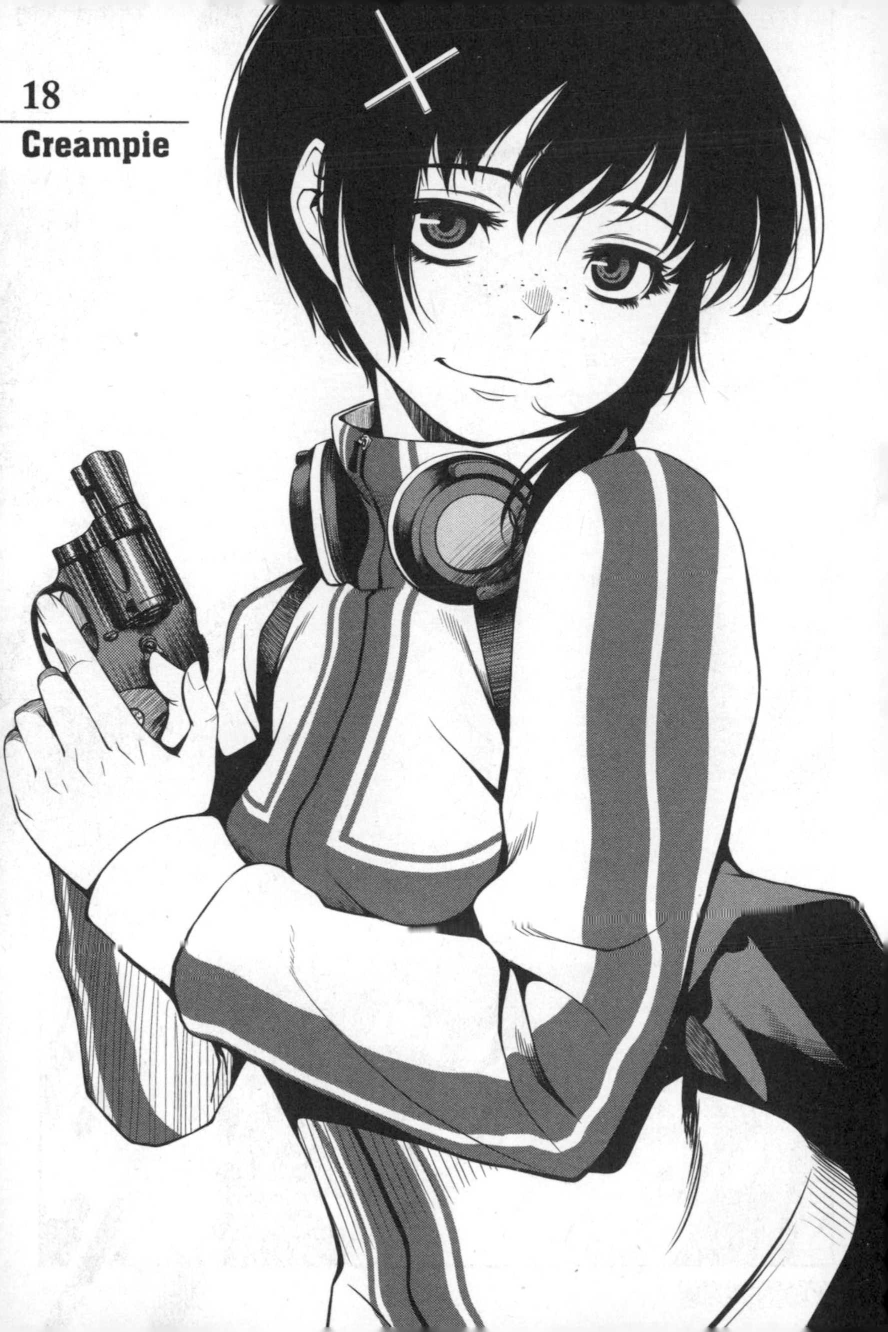

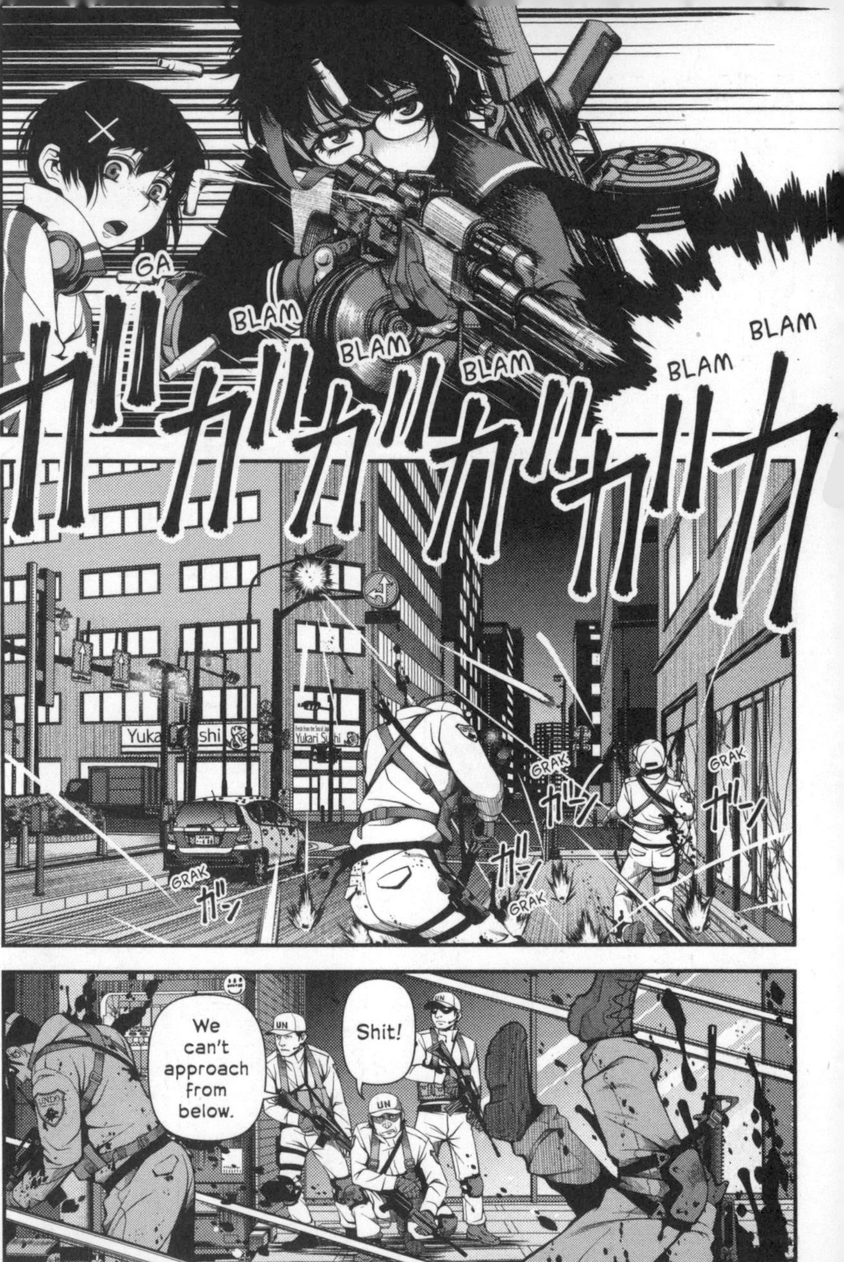
GA
BLAM
BLAM
BLAM
BLAM
BLAM
GRAK
GRAK
GRAK
GRAK
Shit!
We can't approach from below.

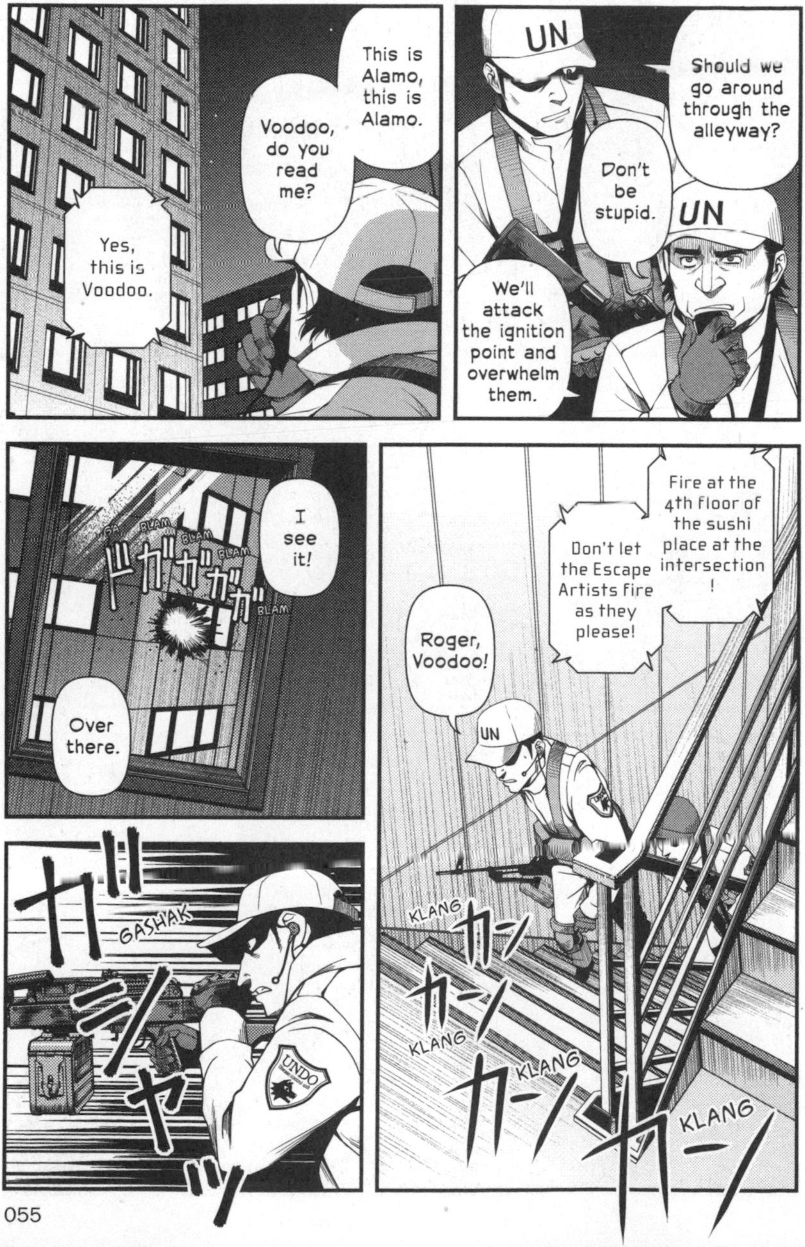
Should we go around through the alleyway?
Don't be stupid.
We'll attack the ignition point and overwhelm them.
This is Alamo, this is Alamo.
Voodoo, do you read me?
Yes, this is Voodoo.
Fire at the 4th floor of the sushi place at the intersection!
Don't let the Escape Artists fire as they please!
Roger, Voodoo!
KLANG
KLANG
KLANG
KLANG
I see it!
BLAM BLAM BLAM BLAM
Over there.
GASHAK

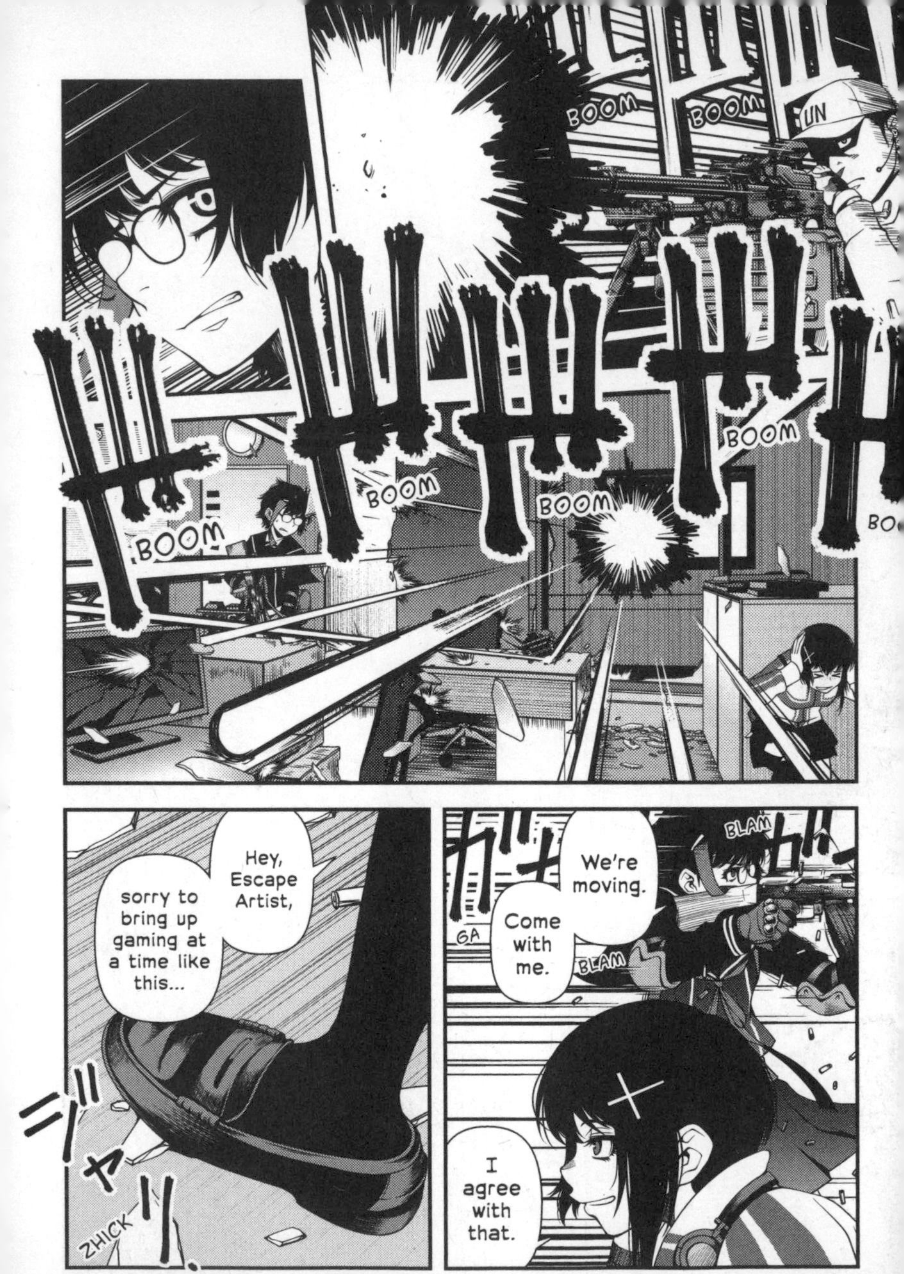
BOOM
BOOM
UN
BOOM
BOOM
BOOM
BOOM
BLAM
We're moving.
Come with me.
GA
BLAM
I agree with that.
Hey, Escape Artist,
sorry to bring up gaming at a time like this...
ZHICK

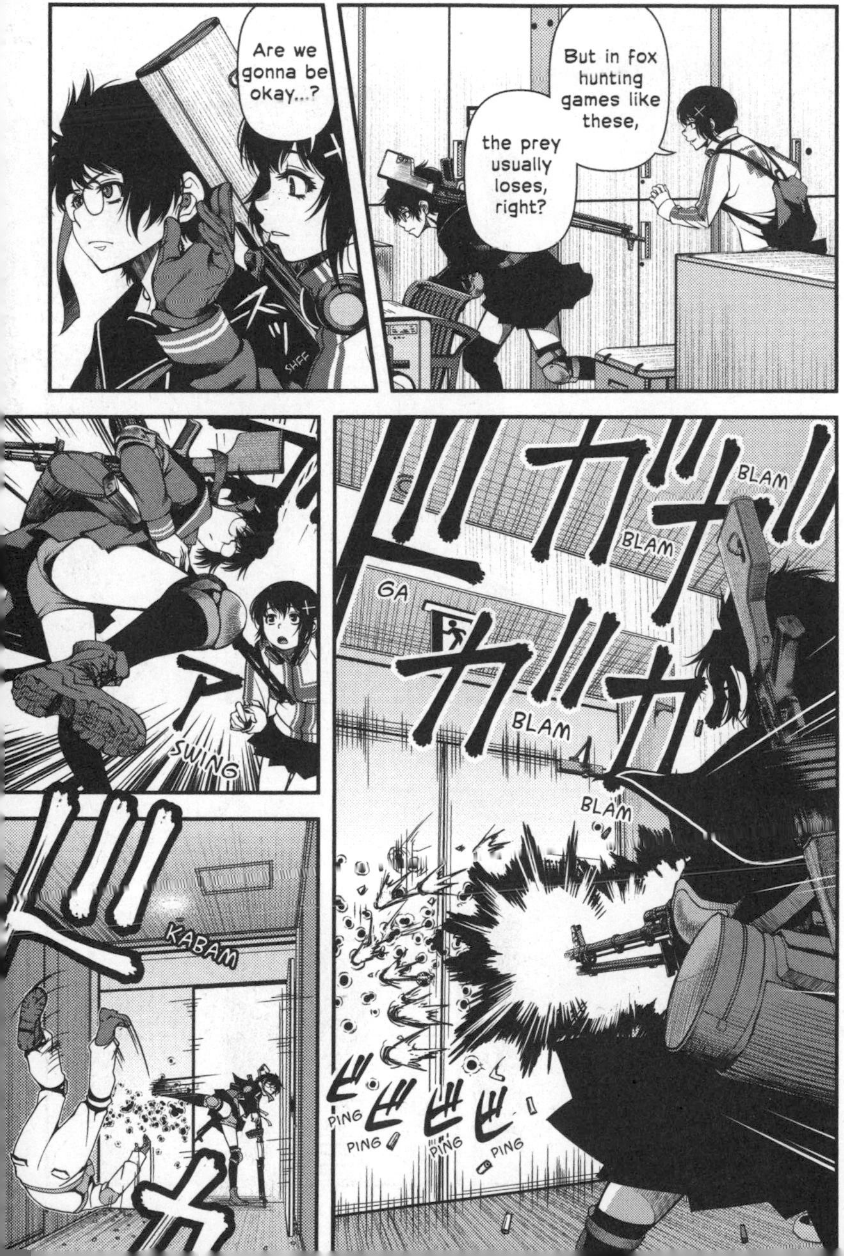
But in fox hunting games like these,
the prey usually loses, right?
Are we gonna be okay...?
SHFF
BLAM
BLAM
GA
BLAM
BLAM
PING
PING
PING
PING
SWING
KABAM

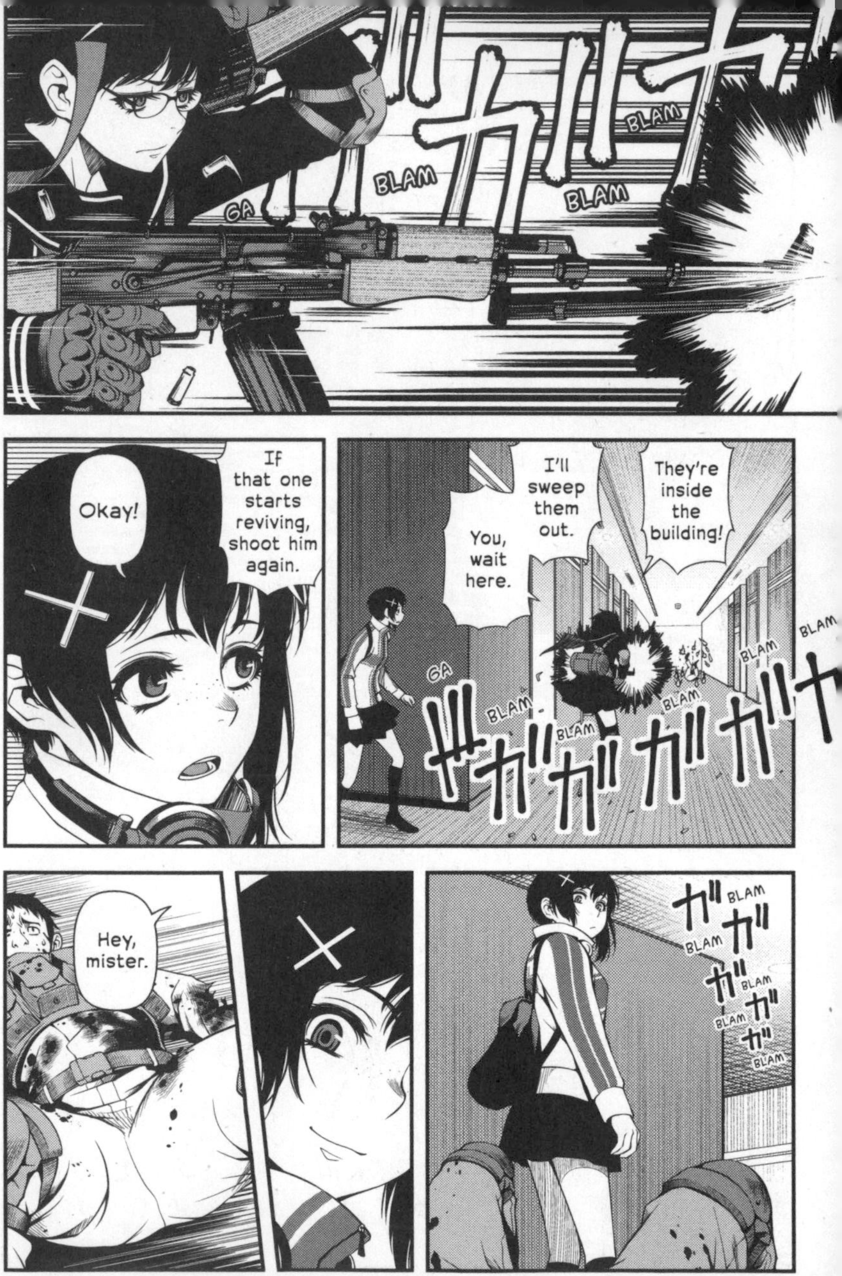
GA
BLAM
BLAM
BLAM
They're inside the building!
I'll sweep them out.
You, wait here.
GA
BLAM
BLAM
BLAM
BLAM
BLAM
If that one starts reviving, shoot him again.
Okay!
BLAM
BLAM
BLAM
BLAM
BLAM
Hey, mister.

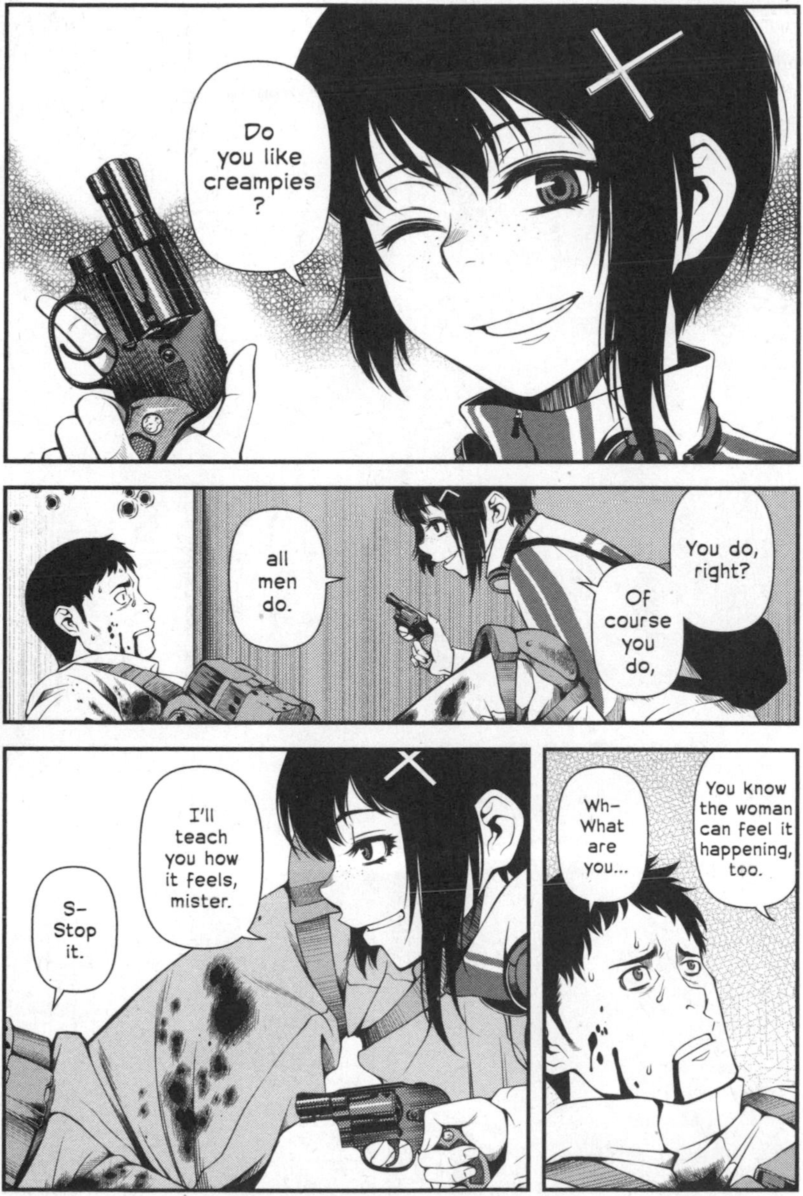
Do you like creampies?
You do, right?
Of course you do,
all men do.
You know the woman can feel it happening, too.
Wh-What are you...
I'll teach you how it feels, mister.
S-Stop it.

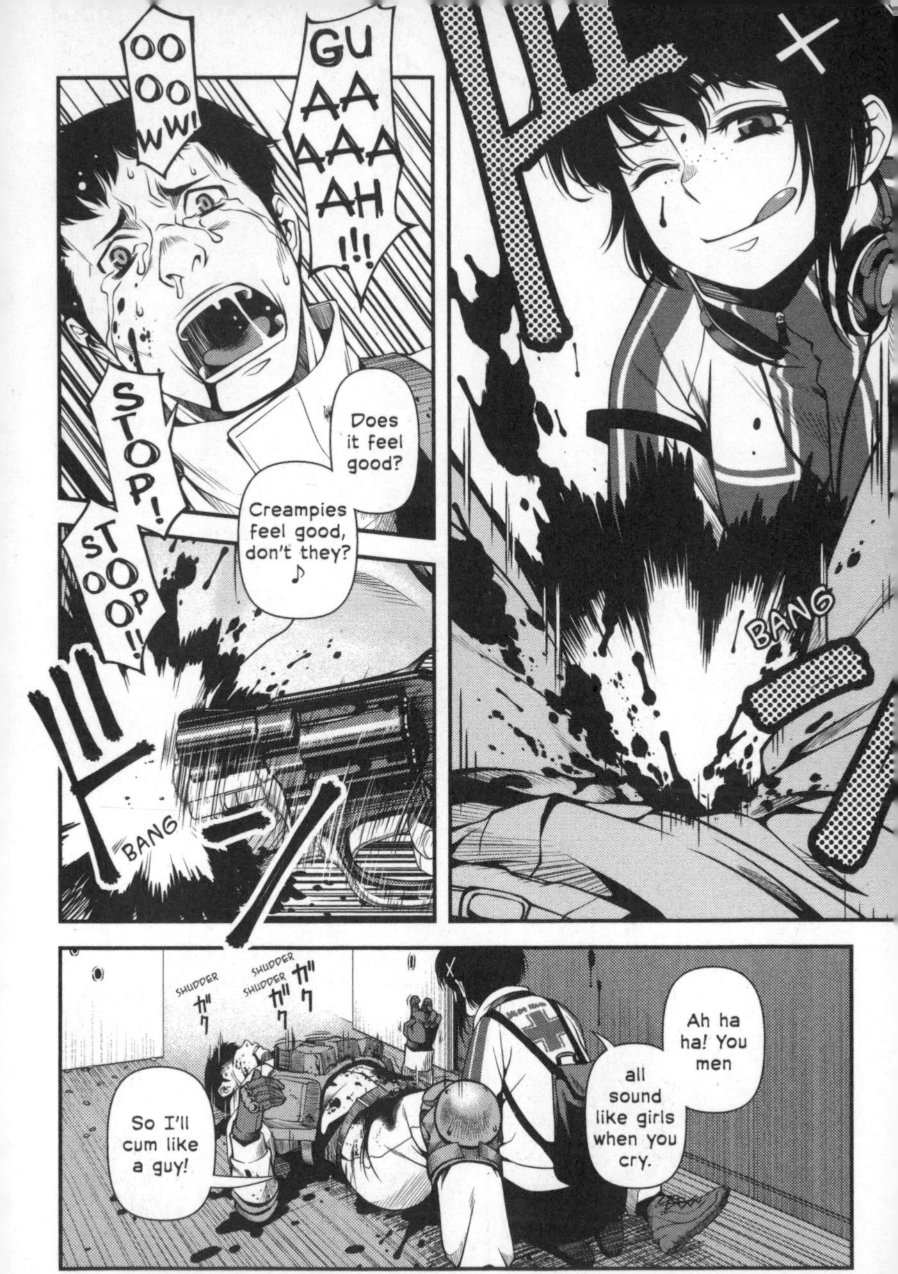
BANG
GU AAAAAAAH !!!
OOOOWW!
Does it feel good?
Creampies feel good, don't they? ♪
STOP!
STOOOOP!!
BANG
Ah ha ha! You men
all sound like girls when you cry.
SHUDDER SHUDDER
ガク ガク
SHUDDER
ガク
So I'll cum like a guy!

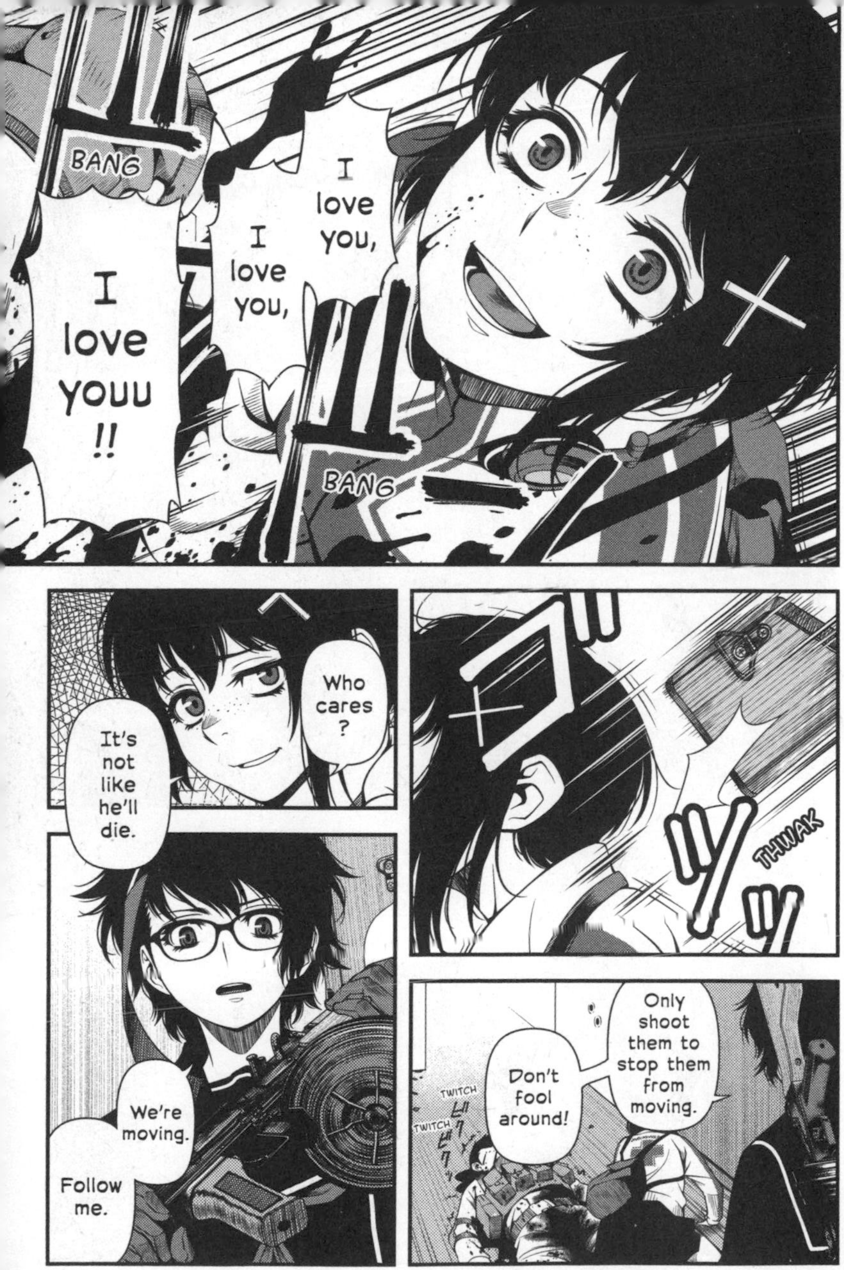
I love you,
I love you,
BANG
I love youu !!
BANG
THWAK
Who cares ?
It's not like he'll die.
Only shoot them to stop them from moving.
Don't fool around!
TWITCH
TWITCH
We're moving.
Follow me.

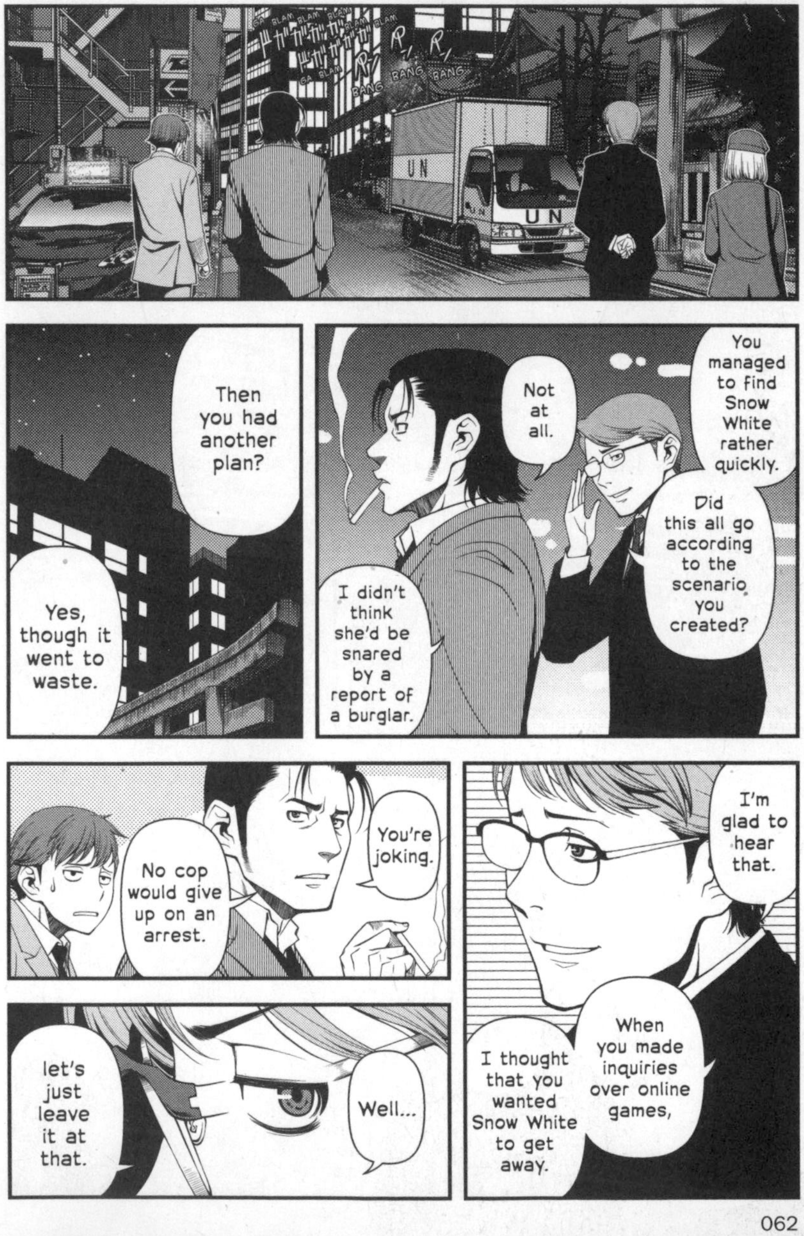
UN
UN
You managed to find Snow White rather quickly.
Did this all go according to the scenario you created?
Not at all.
I didn't think she'd be snared by a report of a burglar.
Then you had another plan?
Yes, though it went to waste.
I'm glad to hear that.
When you made inquiries over online games,
I thought that you wanted Snow White to get away.
You're joking.
No cop would give up on an arrest.
Well...
let's just leave it at that.

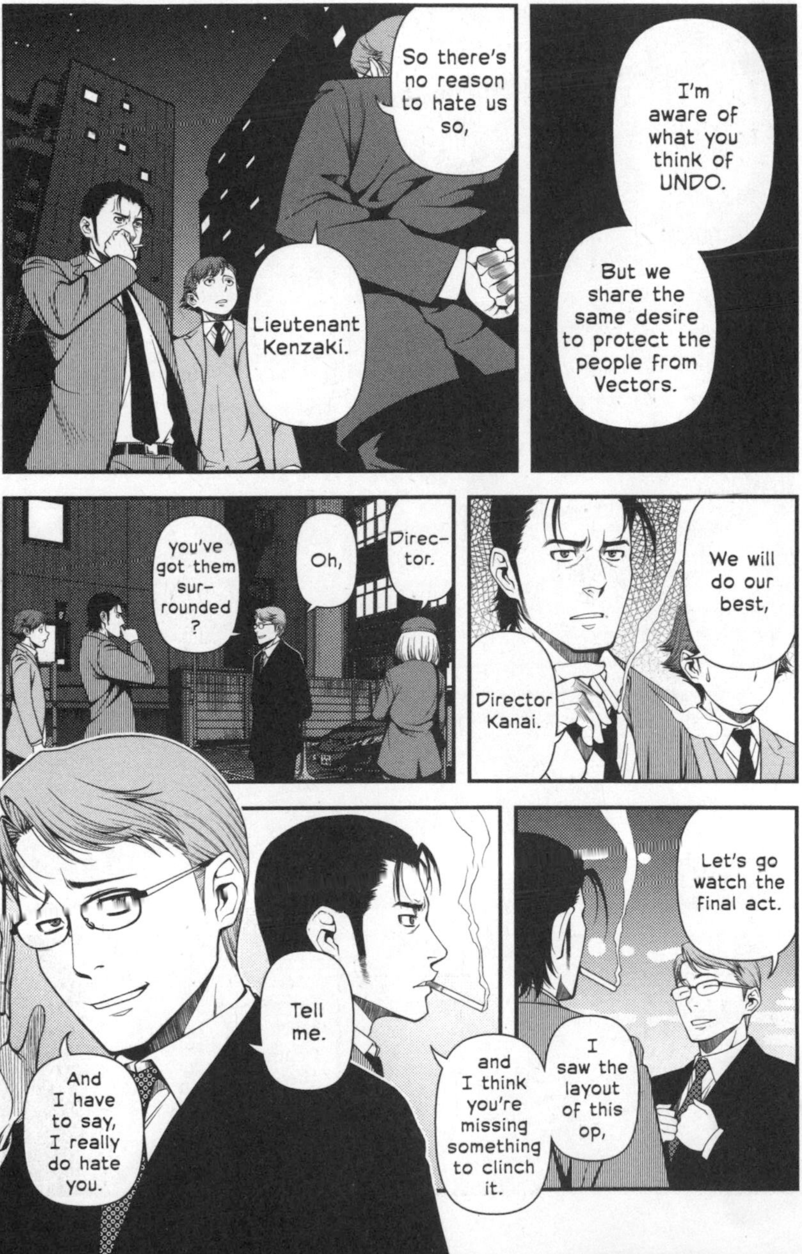
I'm aware of what you think of UNDO.
But we share the same desire to protect the people from Vectors.
So there's no reason to hate us so,
Lieutenant Kenzaki.
We will do our best,
Director Kanai.
Director.
Oh,
you've got them surrounded?
Let's go watch the final act.
I saw the layout of this op,
and I think you're missing something to clinch it.
Tell me.
And I have to say, I really do hate you.

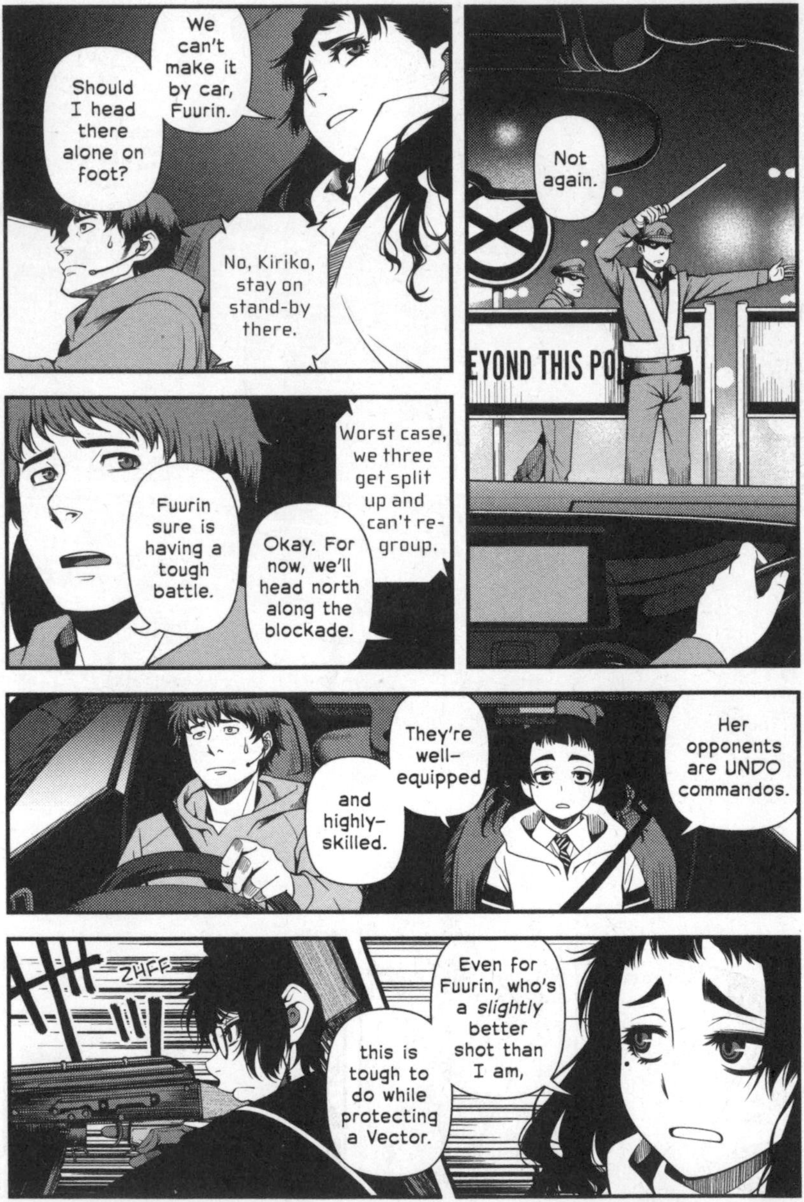
Not again.
EYOND THIS PO
We can't make it by car, Fuurin.
Should I head there alone on foot?
No, Kiriko, stay on stand-by there.
Worst case, we three get split up and can't re-group.
Okay. For now, we'll head north along the blockade.
Fuurin sure is having a tough battle.
Her opponents are UNDO commandos.
They're well-equipped
and highly-skilled.
Even for Fuurin, who's a *slightly* better shot than I am,
this is tough to do while protecting a Vector.
ZHFF

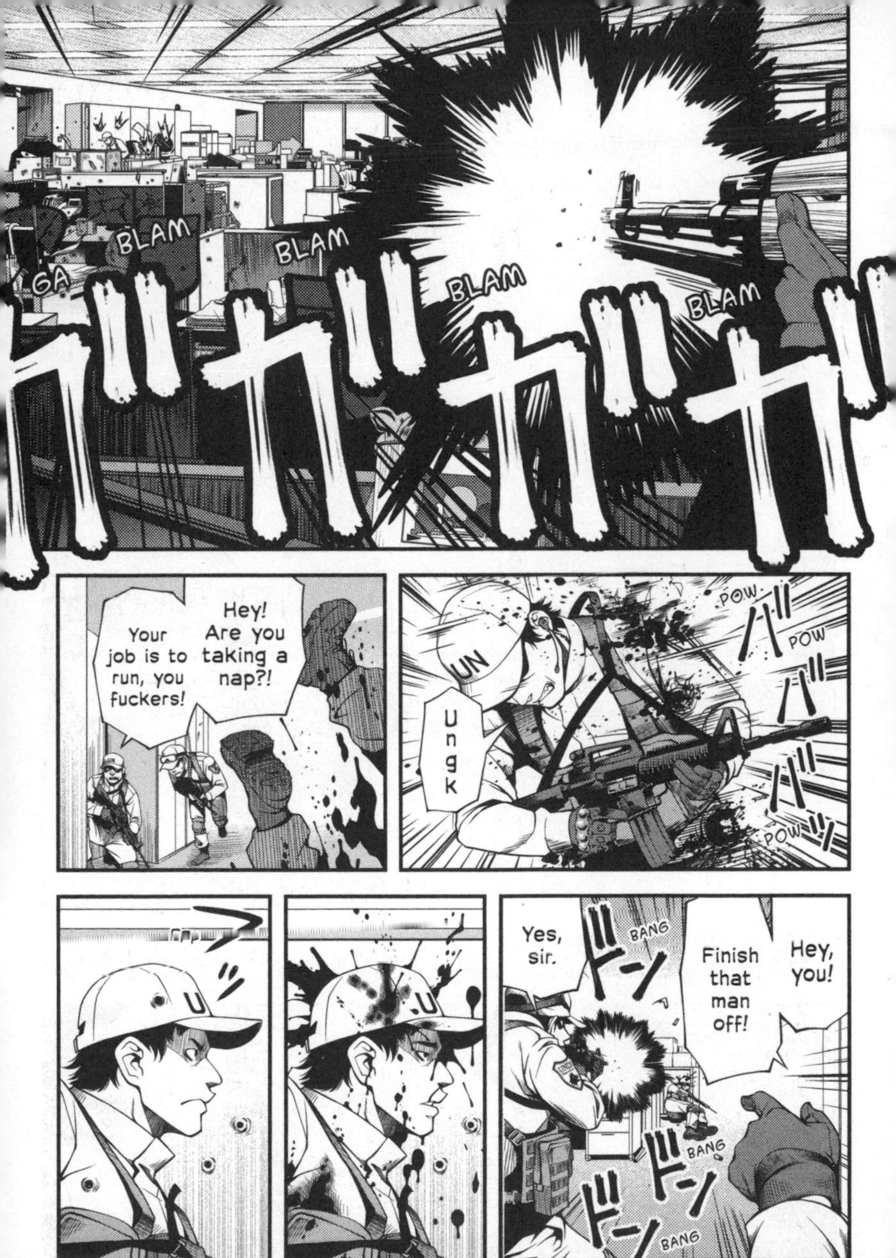
GA
BLAM
BLAM
BLAM
BLAM
Ungk
POW
POW
POW
Hey! Are you taking a nap?!
Your job is to run, you fuckers!
Hey, you!
Finish that man off!
Yes, sir.
BANG
BANG
BANG

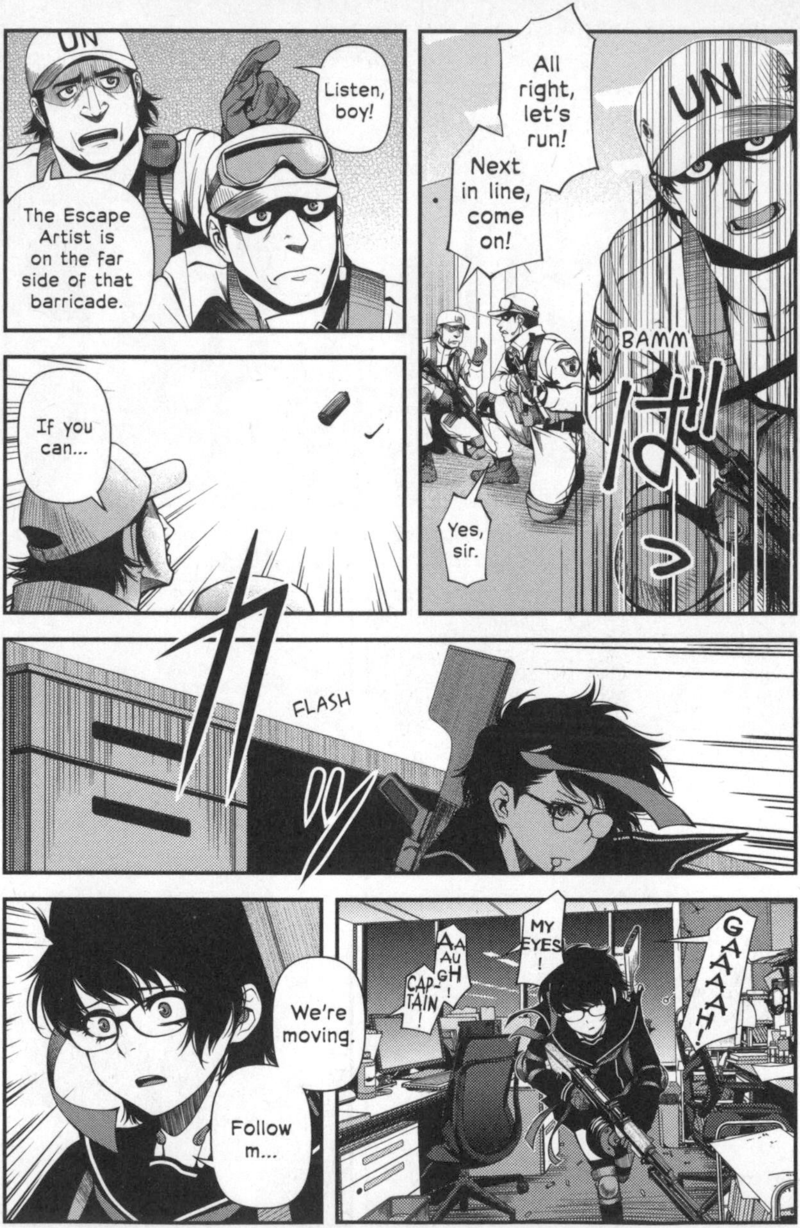

All right, let's run!
Next in line, come on!
BAMM
ばっ
Yes, sir.
Listen, boy!
The Escape Artist is on the far side of that barricade.
If you can...
FLASH
GAAAAH!
MY EYES!
AAAUGH!
CAP-TAIN!
We're moving.
Follow m...

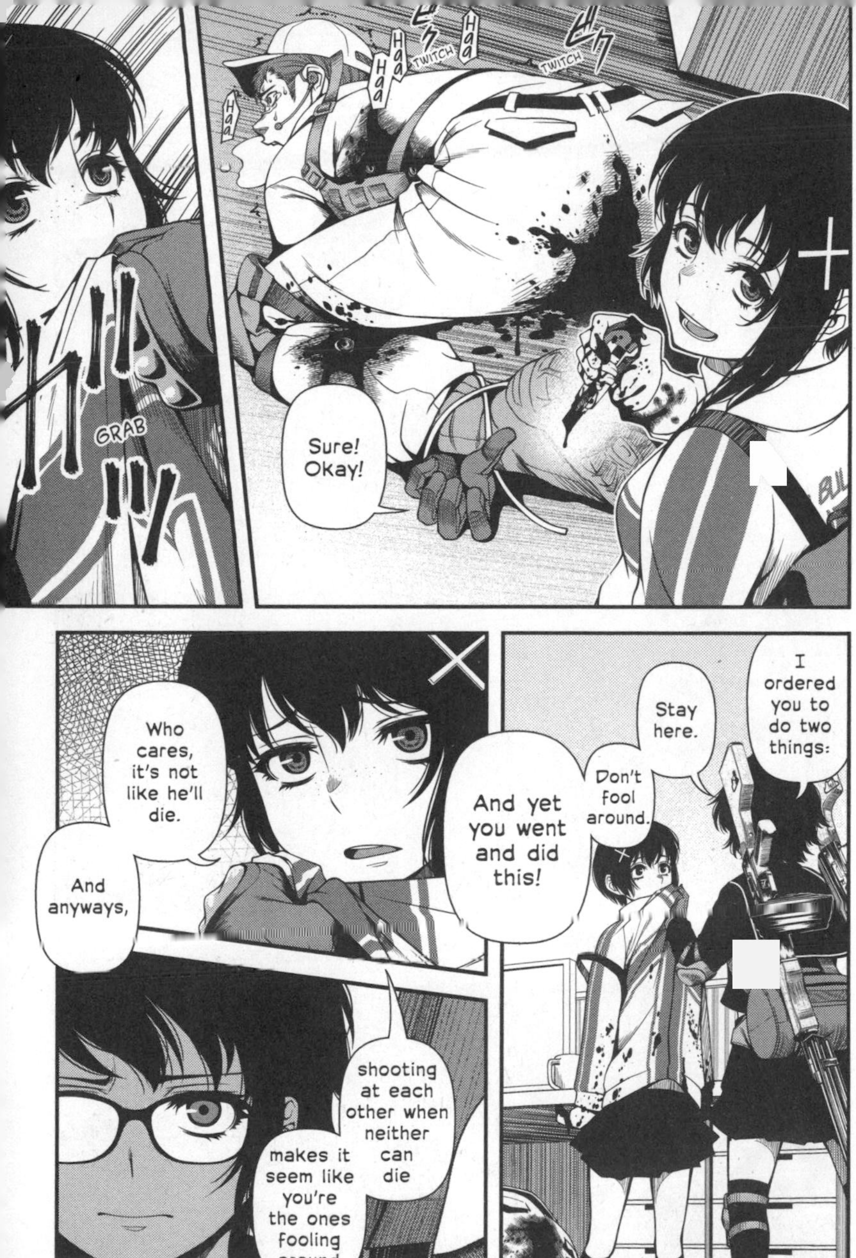

Haa
Haa
TWITCH
Haa
Haa
TWITCH
Sure! Okay!
GRAB
I ordered you to do two things:
Stay here.
Don't fool around.
And yet you went and did this!
Who cares, it's not like he'll die.
And anyways,
shooting at each other when neither can die
makes it seem like you're the ones fooling around.

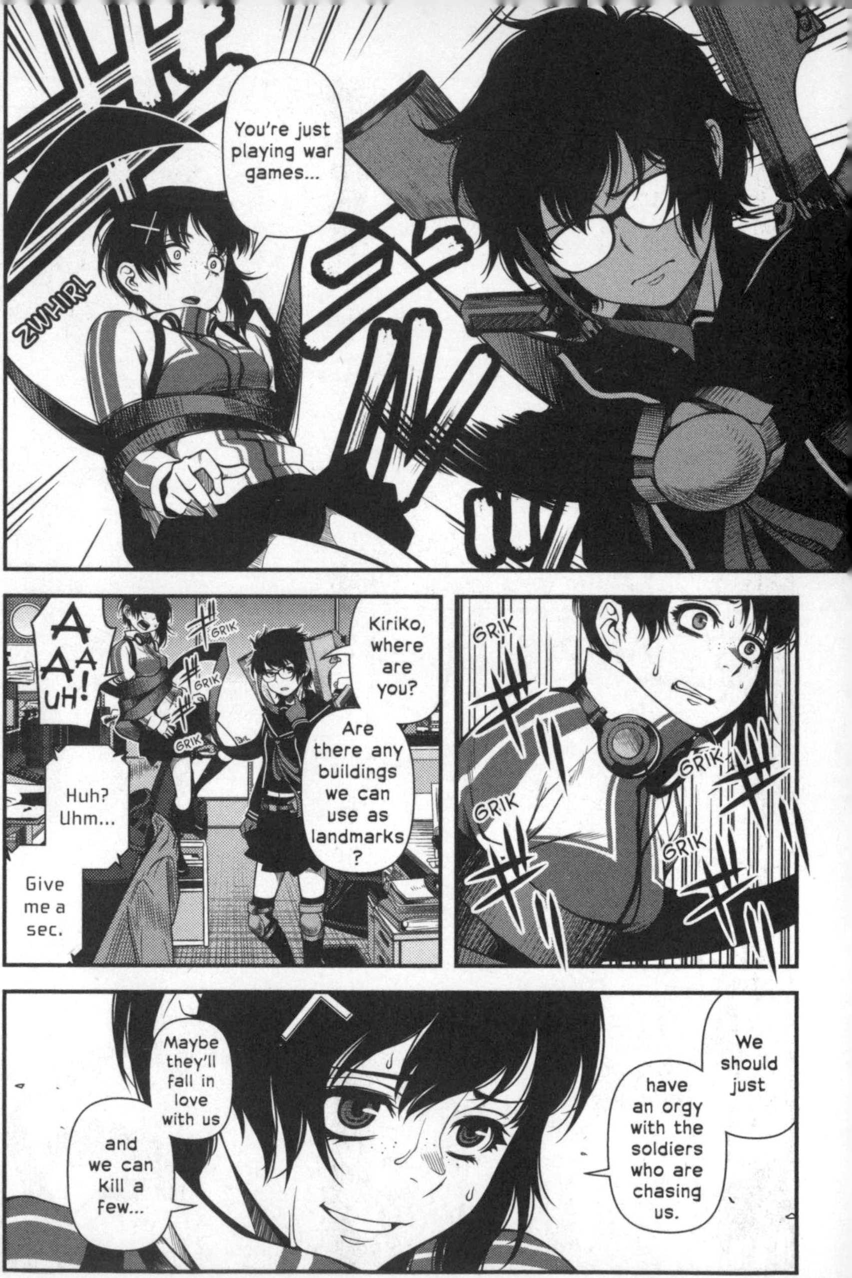
You're just playing war games...
ZWHIRL
GRIK GRIK GRIK GRIK
Kiriko, where are you?
Are there any buildings we can use as landmarks?
AAAUH!
GRIK GRIK GRIK
Huh? Uhm...
Give me a sec.
We should just have an orgy with the soldiers who are chasing us.
Maybe they'll fall in love with us
and we can kill a few...

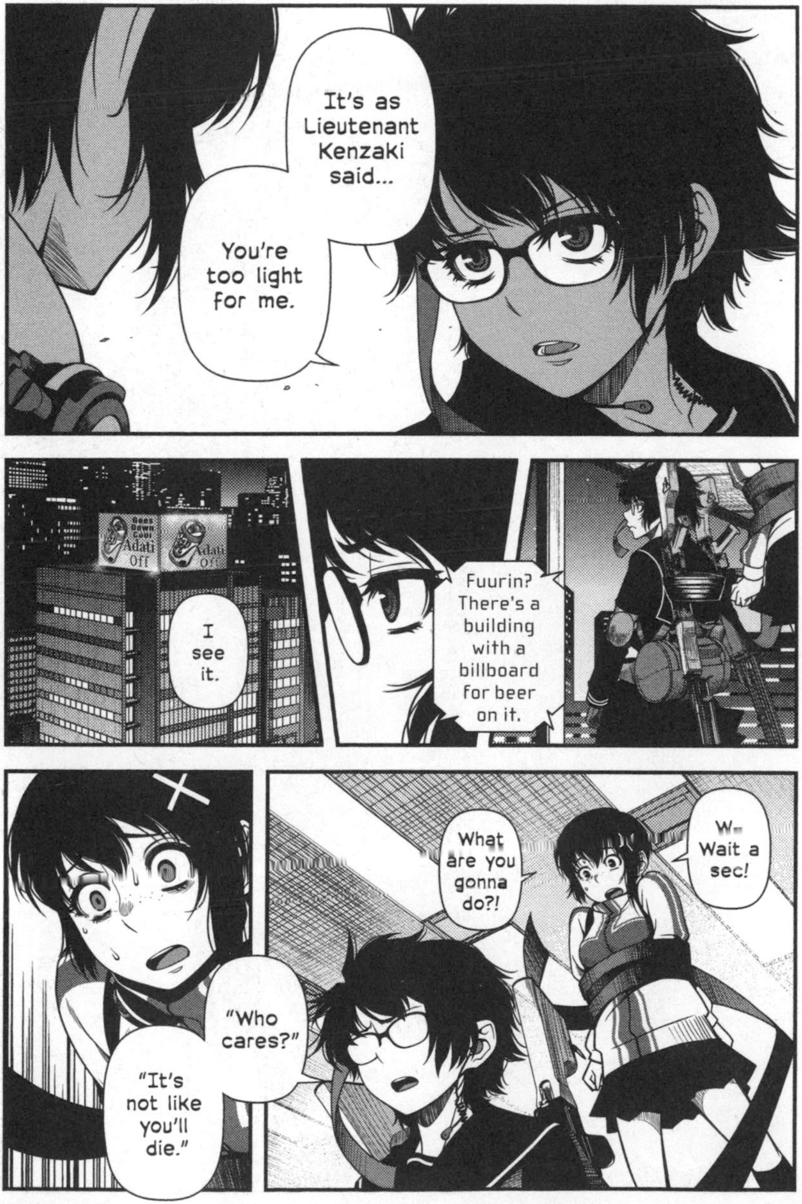
It's as Lieutenant Kenzaki said...
You're too light for me.
Fuurin? There's a building with a billboard for beer on it.
I see it.
W... Wait a sec!
What are you gonna do?!
"Who cares?"
"It's not like you'll die."

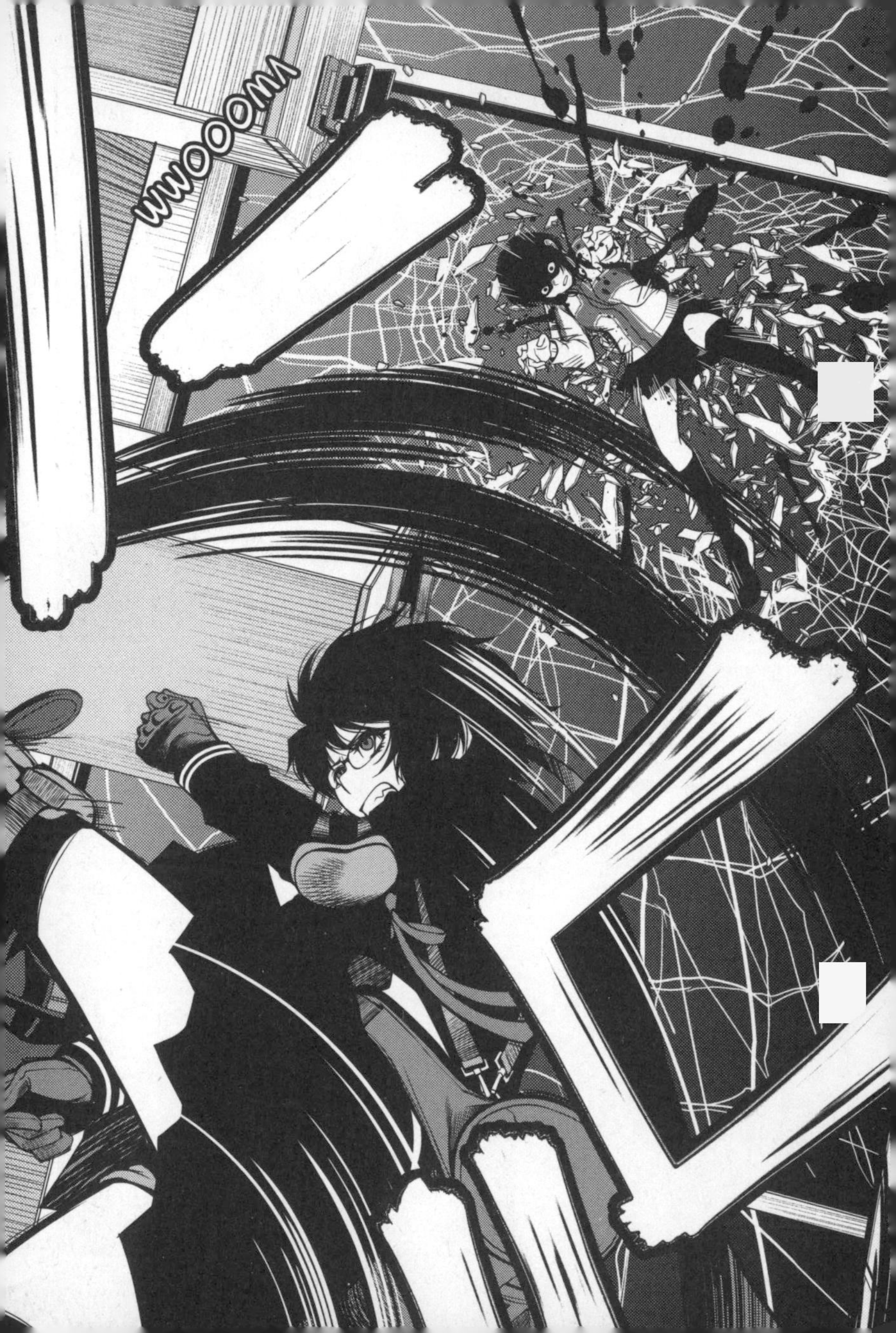
WOOOMM

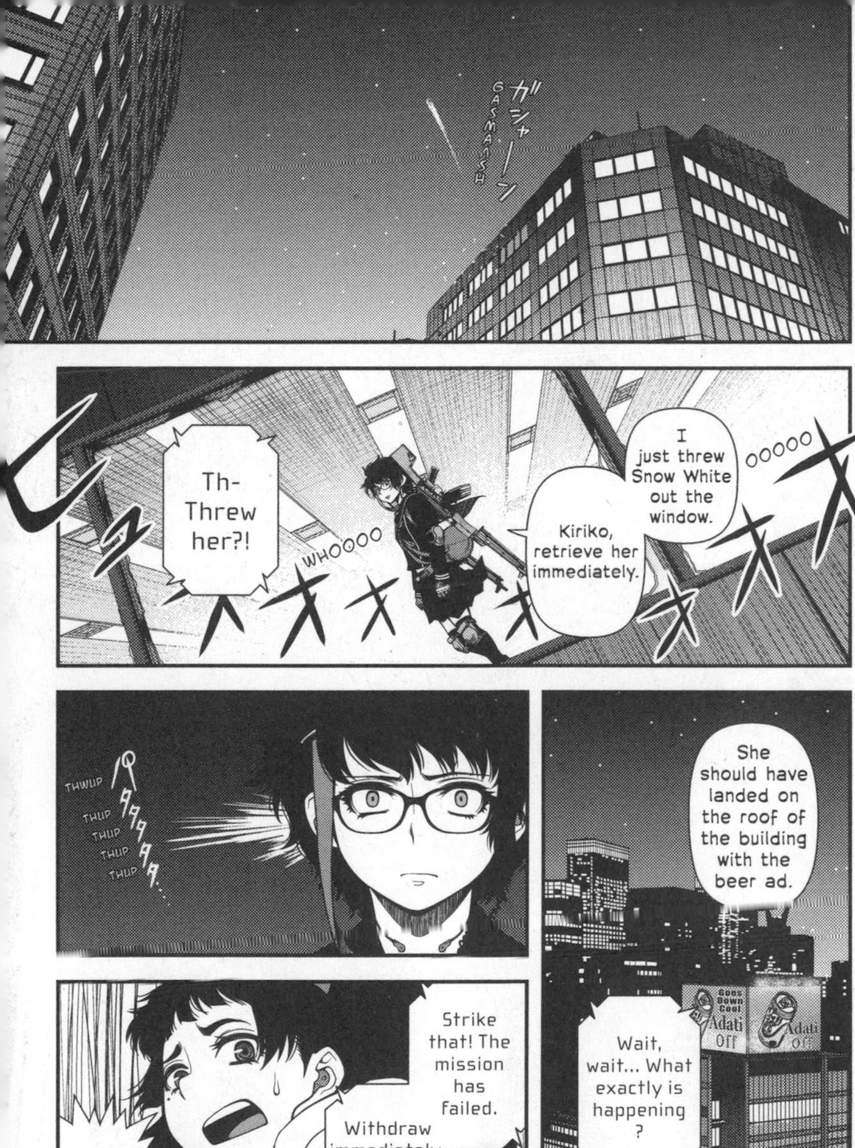
GASMAASH
I just threw Snow White out the window.
Kiriko, retrieve her immediately.
OOOOO
WHOOOO
Th- Threw her?!
She should have landed on the roof of the building with the beer ad.
Goes Down Cool
Adati Off
Wait, wait... What exactly is happening?
THWUP
THUP
THUP
THUP
THUP
Strike that! The mission has failed.
Withdraw immediately. Don't wait for me.
What's going on?!

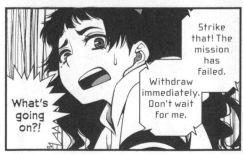

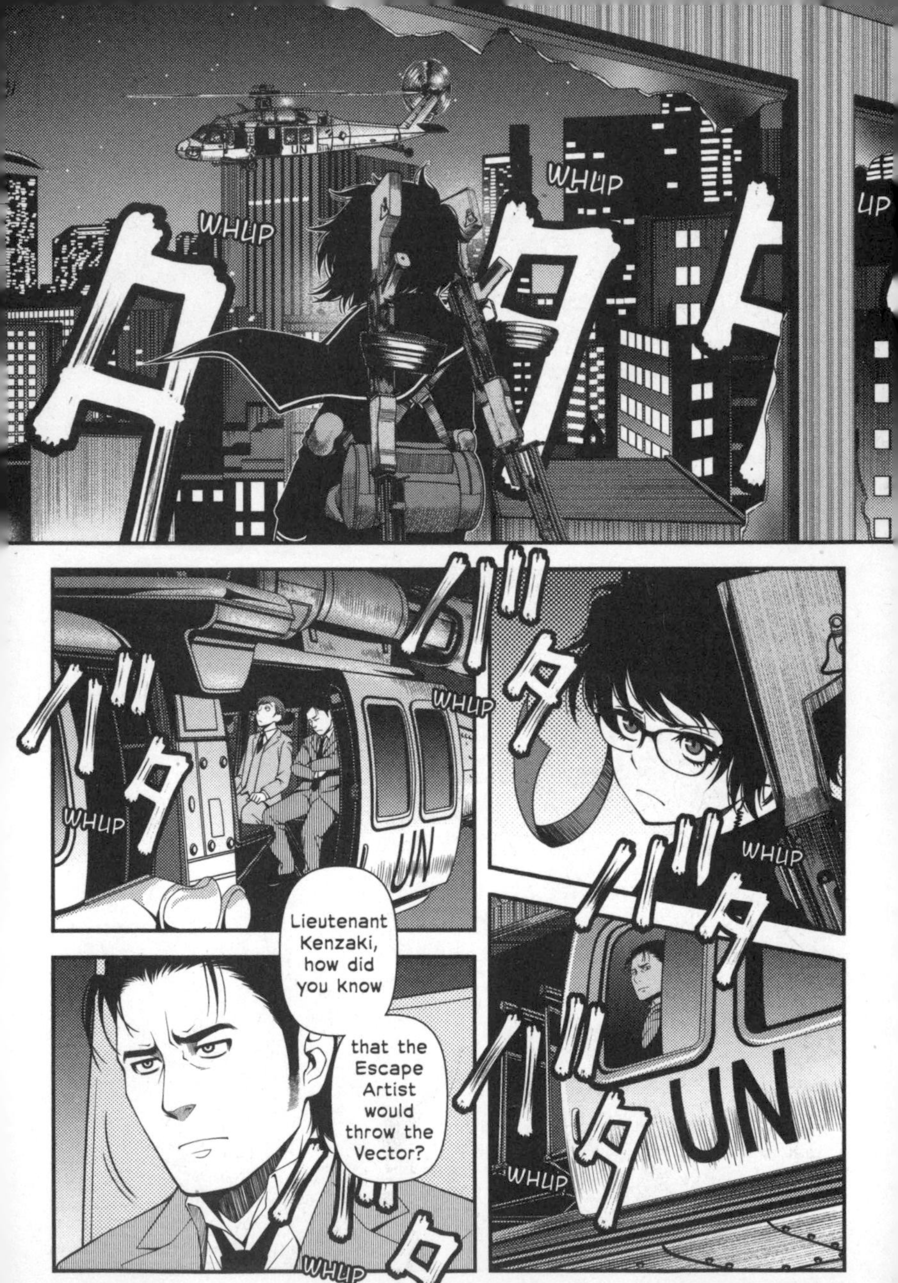
UP
WHUP
WHUP
WHUP
WHUP
WHUP
WHUP
Lieutenant Kenzaki, how did you know
that the Escape Artist would throw the Vector?
WHUP

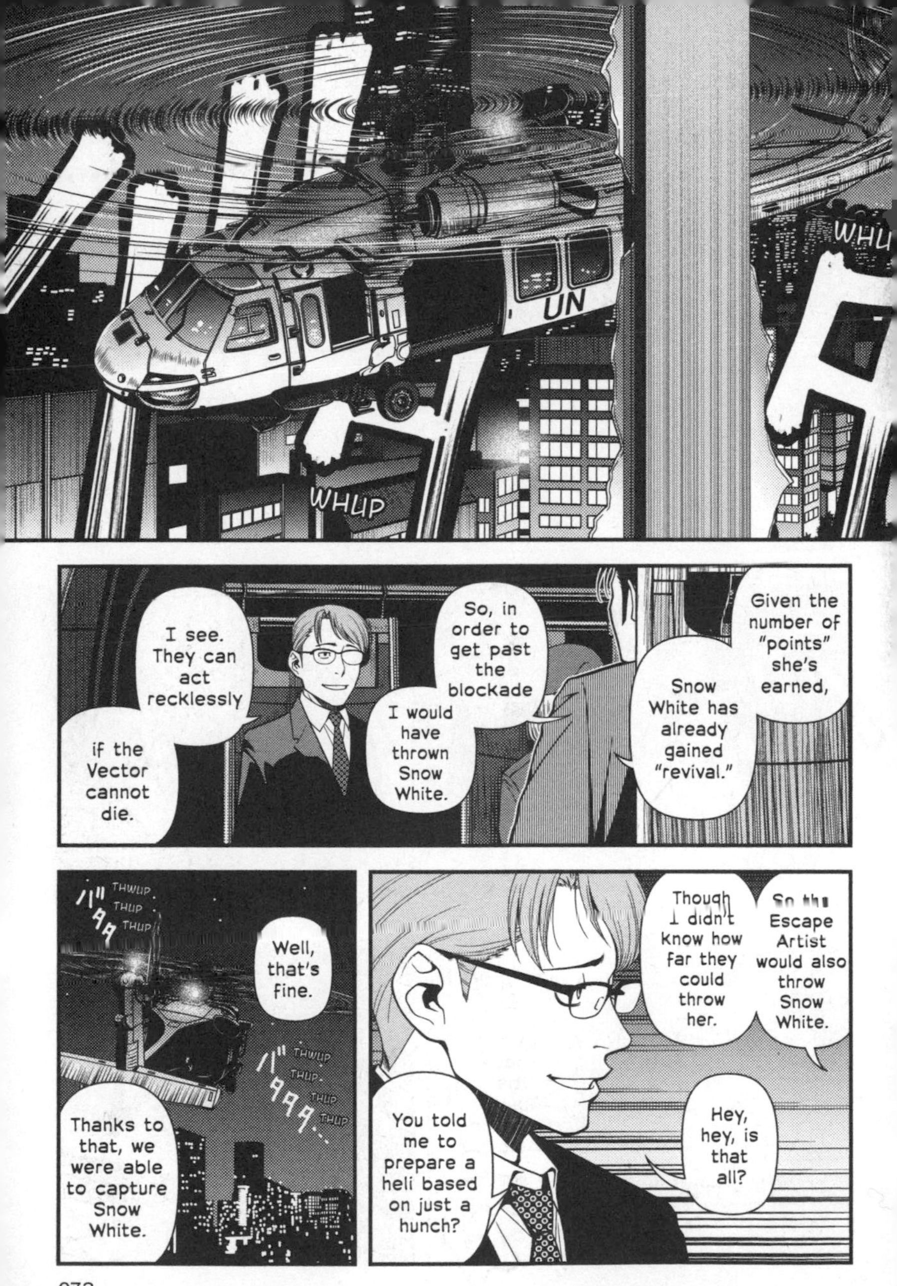
WHLU
WHUP
Given the number of "points" she's earned,
Snow White has already gained "revival."
So, in order to get past the blockade
I would have thrown Snow White.
I see. They can act recklessly
if the Vector cannot die.
So the Escape Artist would also throw Snow White.
Though I didn't know how far they could throw her.
Hey, hey, is that all?
You told me to prepare a heli based on just a hunch?
THWUP THUP THUP
Well, that's fine.
Thanks to that, we were able to capture Snow White.
THWUP THUP THUP THUP

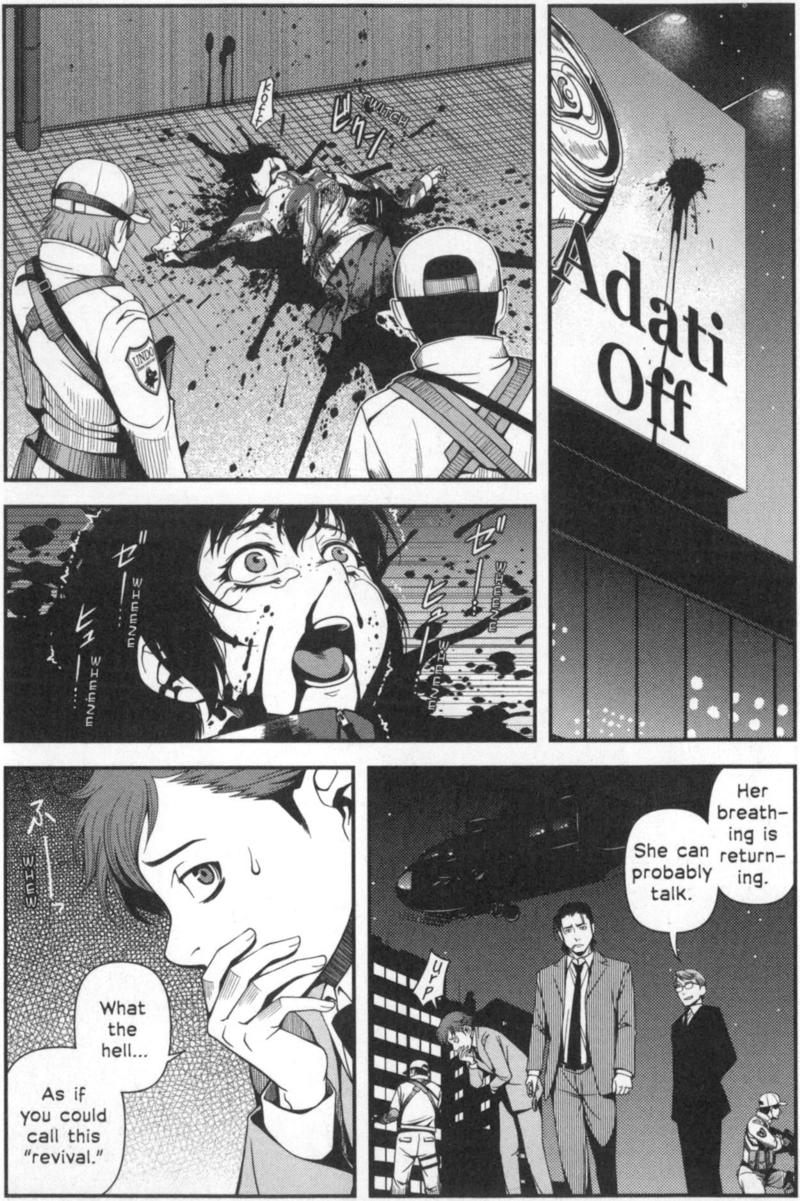
Adati
Off
KOFF
TWITCH
WHEEZE
WHEEZE
WHEEZE
WHEEZE
Her breathing is returning.
She can probably talk.
URP
WHEW
What the hell...
As if you could call this "revival."

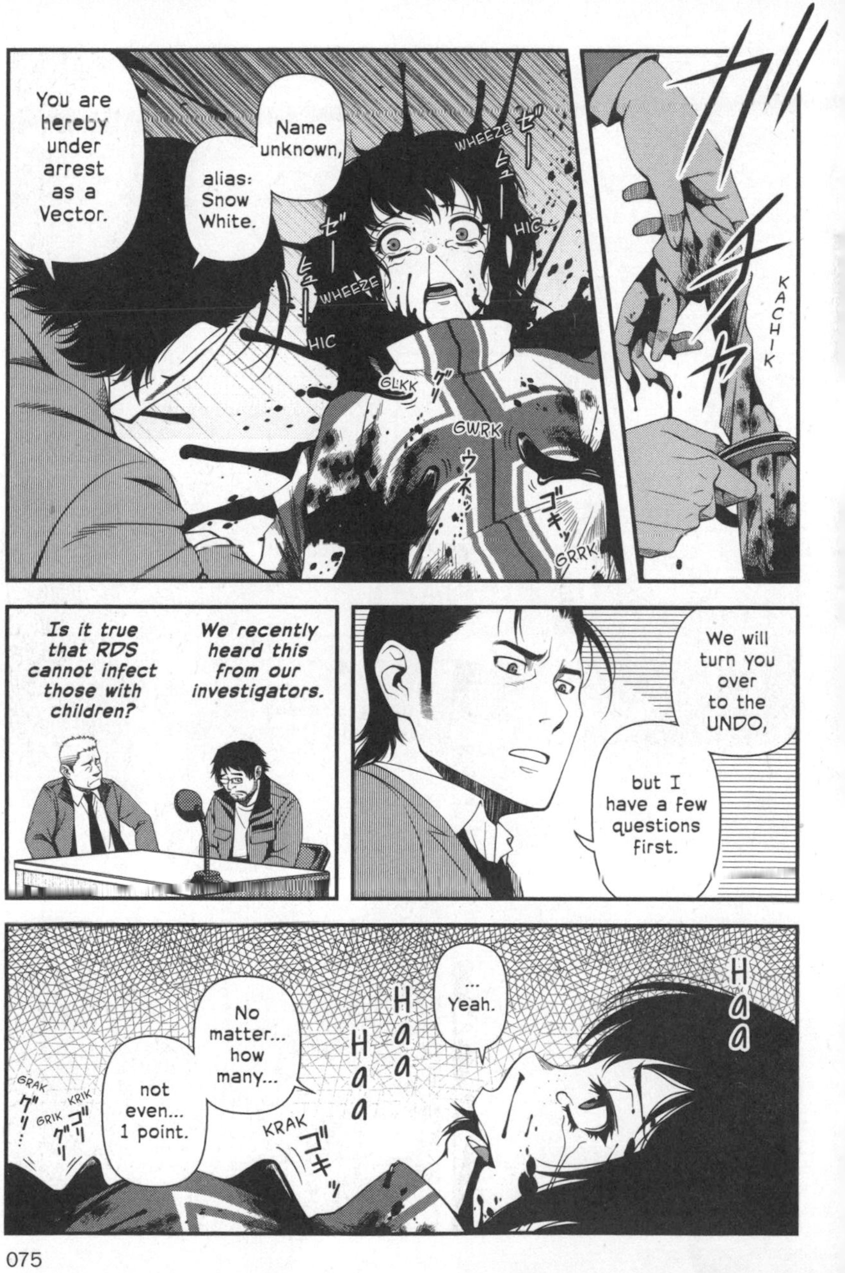
KACHIK
Name unknown,
alias: Snow White.
You are hereby under arrest as a Vector.
WHEEZE
ゼー
ヒュー
HIC
WHEEZE
ゼー
ヒュー
HIC
GLKK
グリ
GWRK
ゴキッ
GRRK
We will turn you over to the UNDO,
but I have a few questions first.
We recently heard this from our investigators.
Is it true that RDS cannot infect those with children?
Haa
... Yeah.
Haa
Haa
No matter... how many...
not even... 1 point.
KRAK
ゴキッ
GRAK
KRIK
GRIK

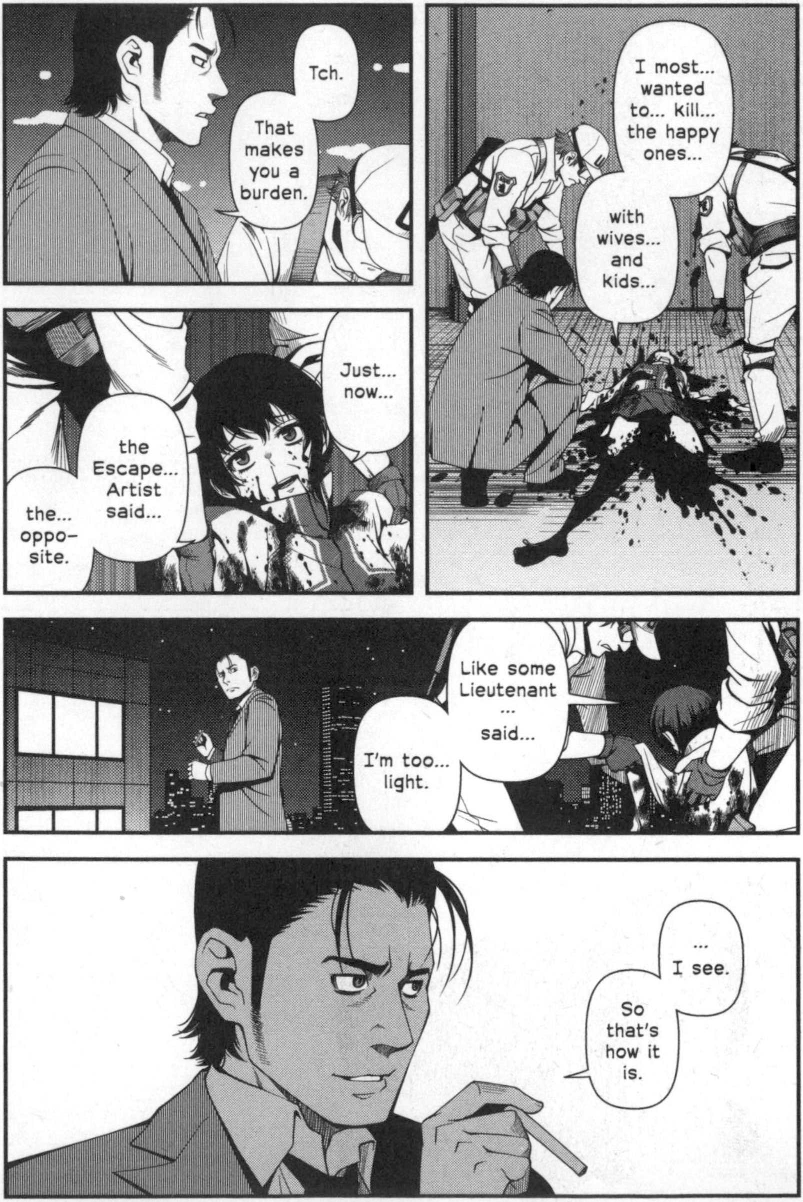
I most... wanted to... kill... the happy ones...
with wives... and kids...
Tch.
That makes you a burden.
Just... now...
the Escape... Artist said...
the... oppo- site.
Like some Lieutenant ... said...
I'm too... light.
... I see.
So that's how it is.

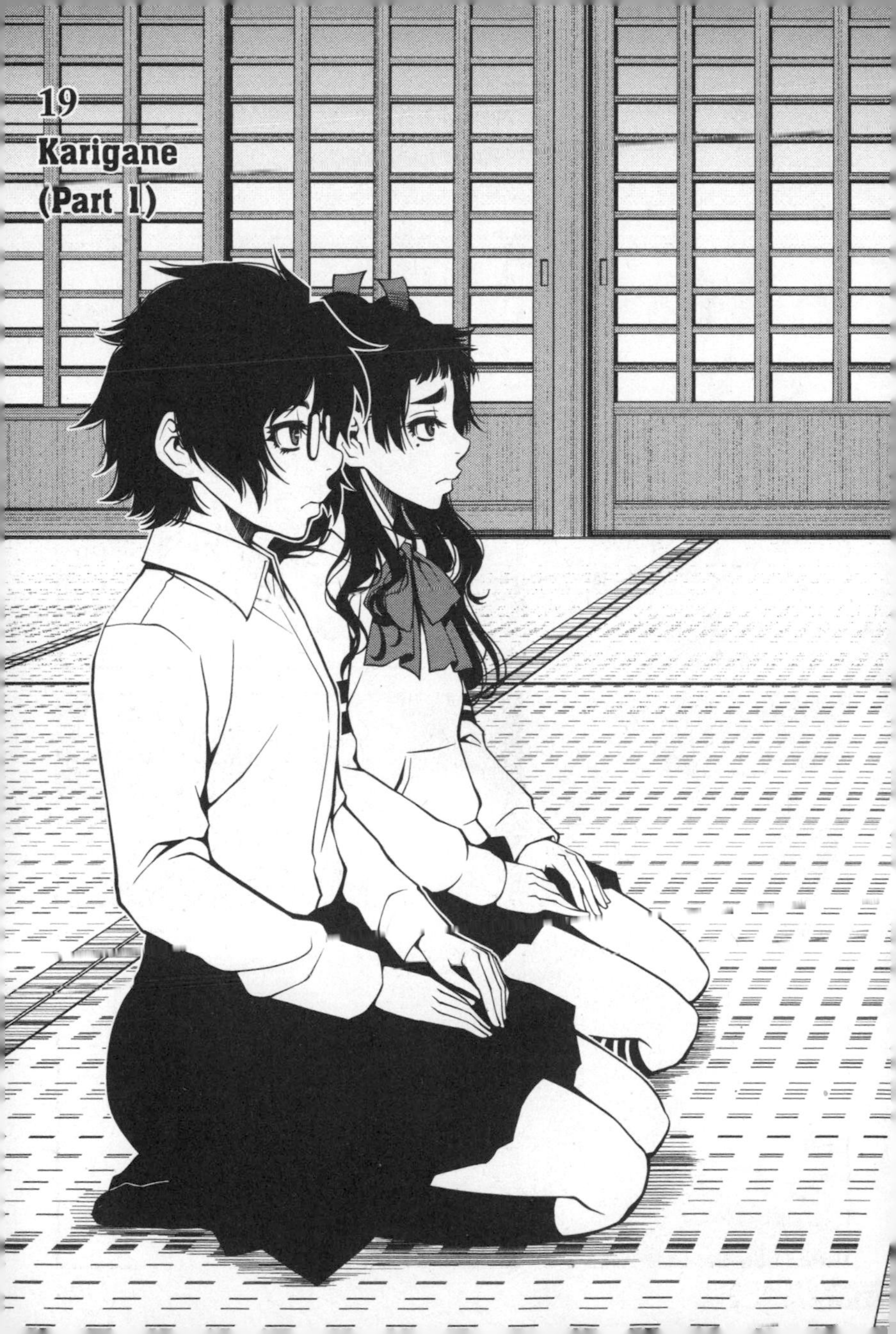
19
Karigane
(Part 1)

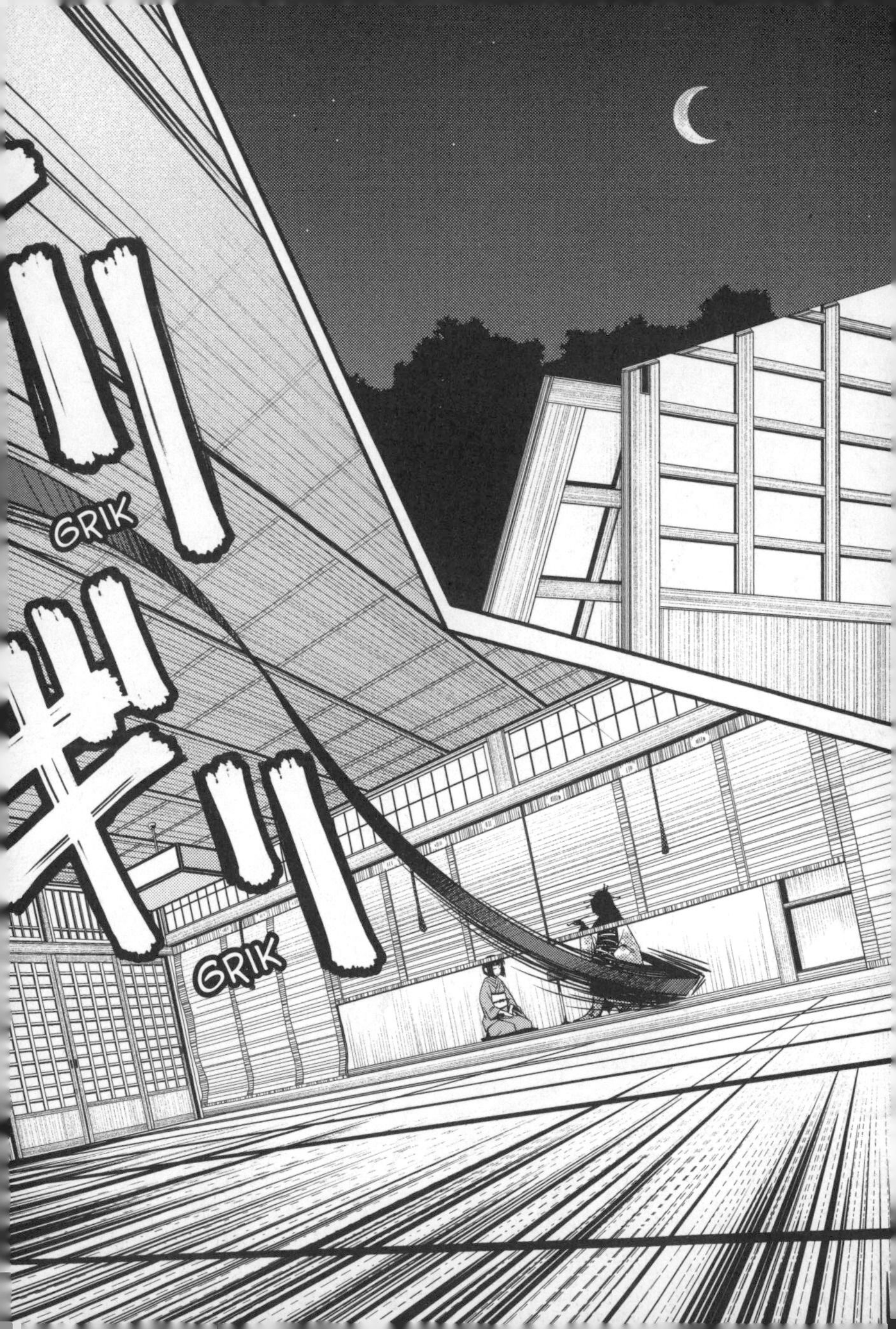
GRIK
GRIK

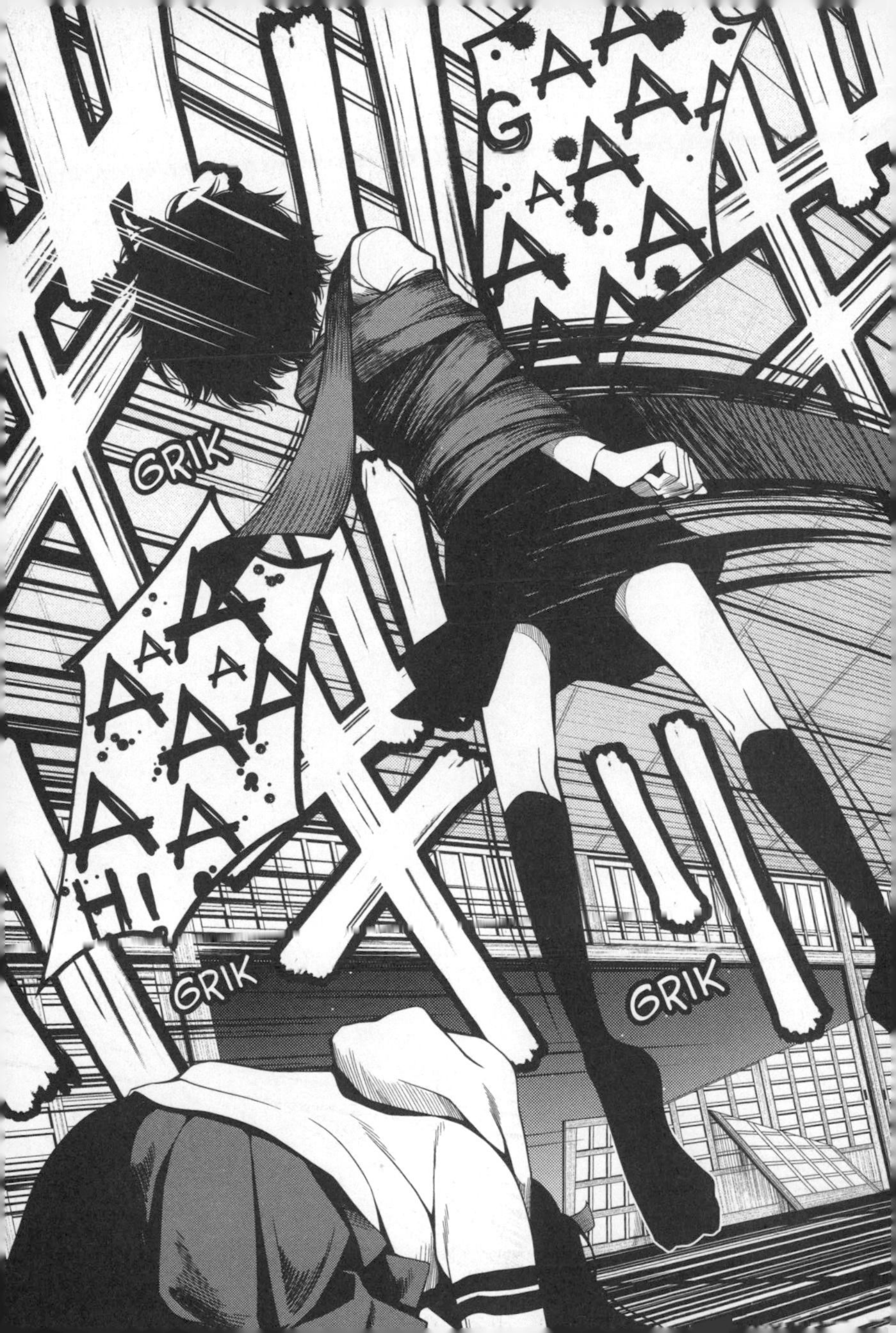
GAAAAAAAAAA
GRIK
AAAAAAAAAH!
GRIK
GRIK

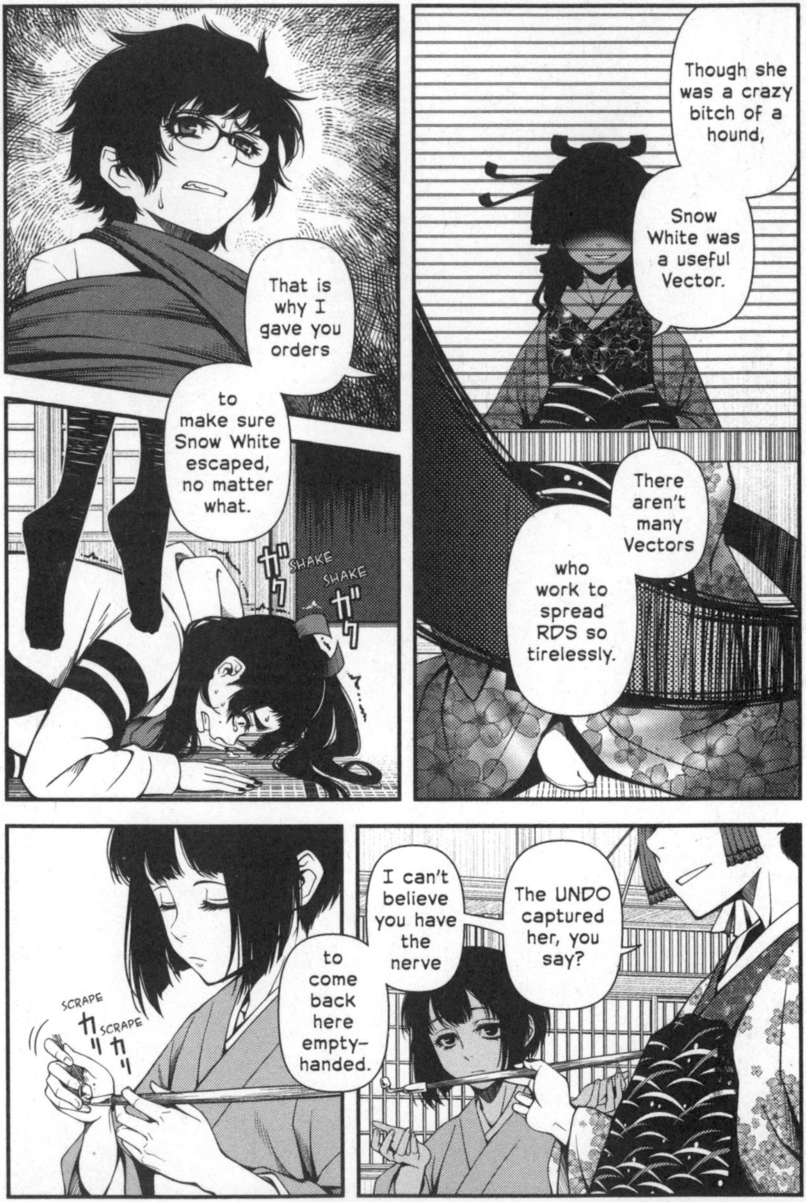
Though she was a crazy bitch of a hound,
Snow White was a useful Vector.
There aren't many Vectors
who work to spread RDS so tirelessly.
That is why I gave you orders
to make sure Snow White escaped, no matter what.
ガク SHAKE
ガク SHAKE
The UNDO captured her, you say?
I can't believe you have the nerve
to come back here empty-handed.
カリ SCRAPE
カリ SCRAPE

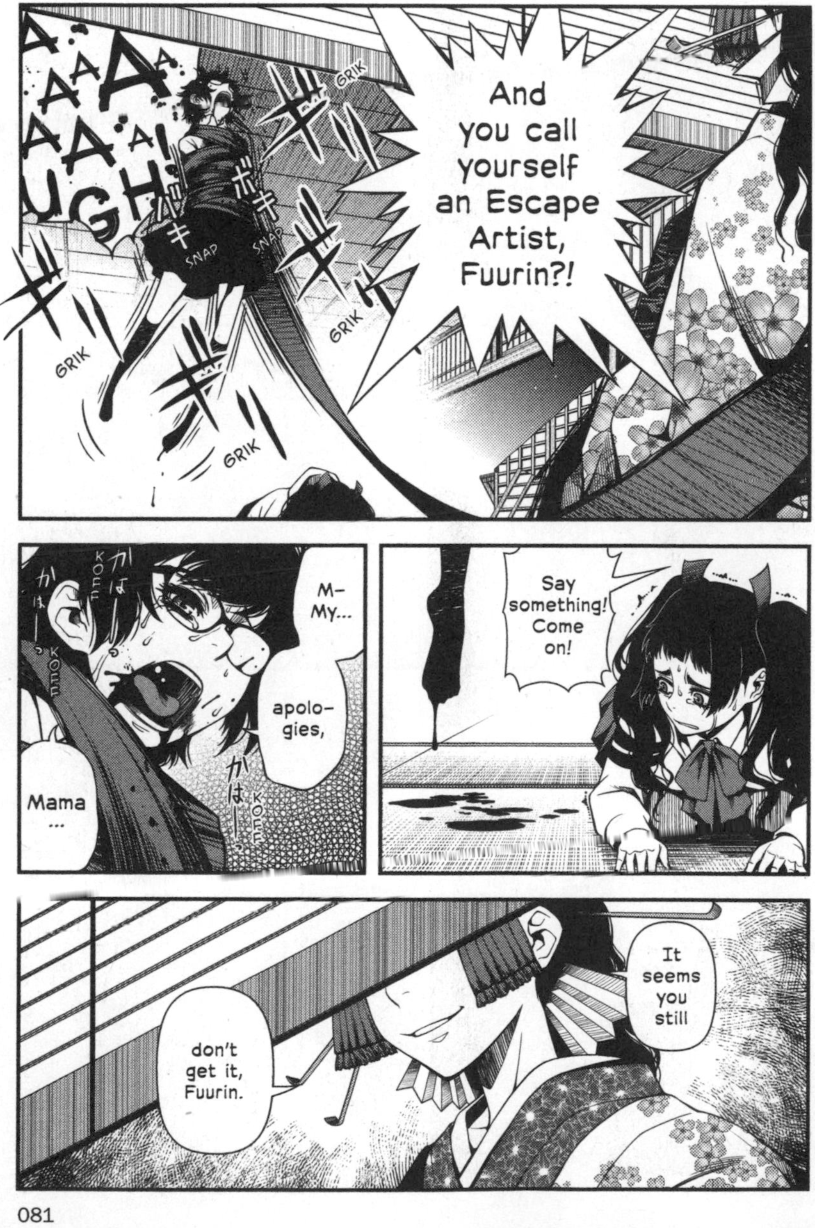
And you call yourself an Escape Artist, Fuurin?!
GRIK
SNAP
SNAP
GRIK
GRIK
GRIK
AAAAAAAAAAUGH!
Say something! Come on!
M-My...
KOFF
apologies,
KOFF
KOFF
Mama ...
It seems you still
don't get it, Fuurin.

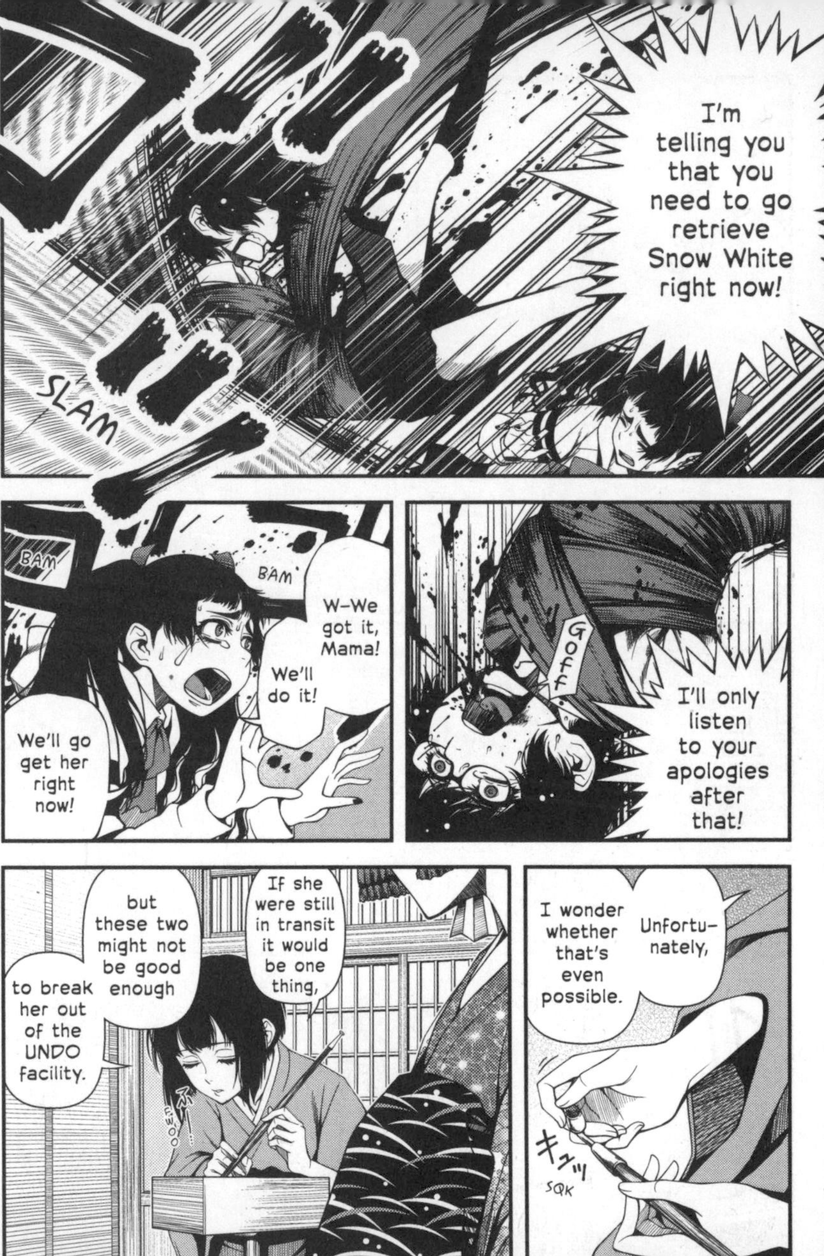
I'm telling you that you need to go retrieve Snow White right now!
SLAM
GOFF
I'll only listen to your apologies after that!
BAM
BAM
W-We got it, Mama!
We'll do it!
We'll go get her right now!
Unfortunately,
I wonder whether that's even possible.
SQK
If she were still in transit it would be one thing,
but these two might not be good enough
to break her out of the UNDO facility.
FWOO

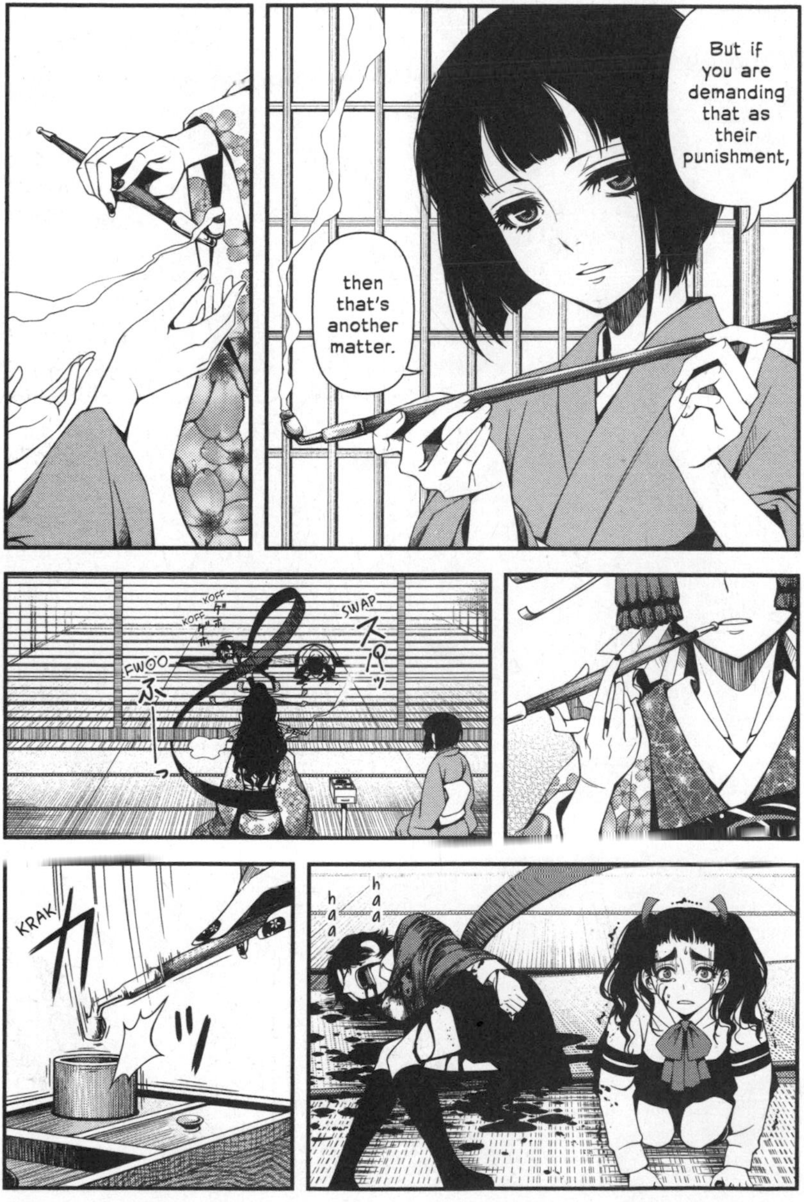
But if you are demanding that as their punishment,
then that's another matter.
SWAP
スパッ
KOFF
ゲホ
KOFF
ゲホ
FWOO
ふーーっ
haa
haa
KRAK
カッ

Fine.

WHUMP

SSWIP

I'm adding Karigane to your unit.

Retrieve Snow White from UNDO.

Karigane ...?

You mean ...

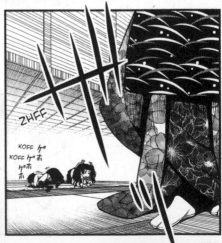

ZHFF

KOFF ゲホ
KOFF ゲホ
ゲホ

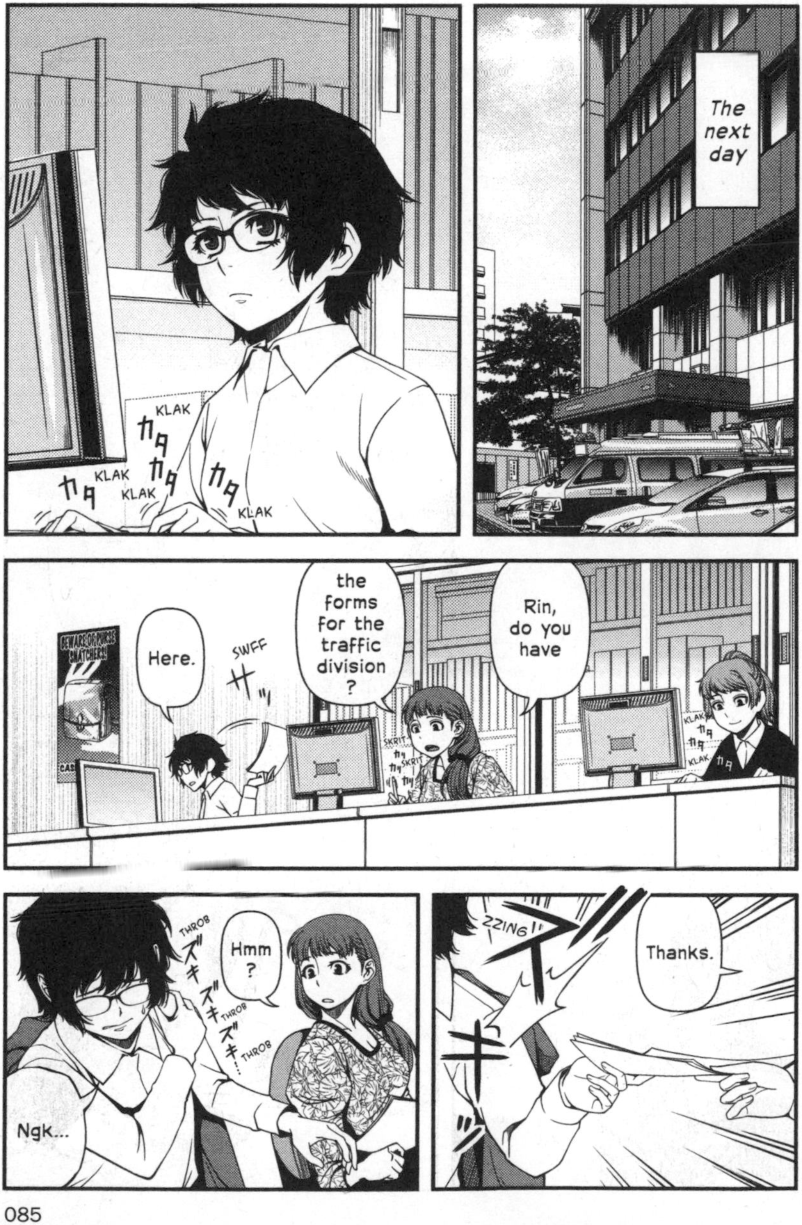
The next day
KLAK
カタ
KLAK
カタ
KLAK
カタ
KLAK
カタ
Rin, do you have
the forms for the traffic division?
KLAK
カタ
KLAK
カタ
SKRIT
カリ
SKRIT
カリ
SWFF
サッ
Here.
BEWARE OF PURSE SNATCHERS!
Thanks.
ZZING
Hmm?
THROB
ズキ
THROB
ズキ
THROB
ズキ...
Ngk...

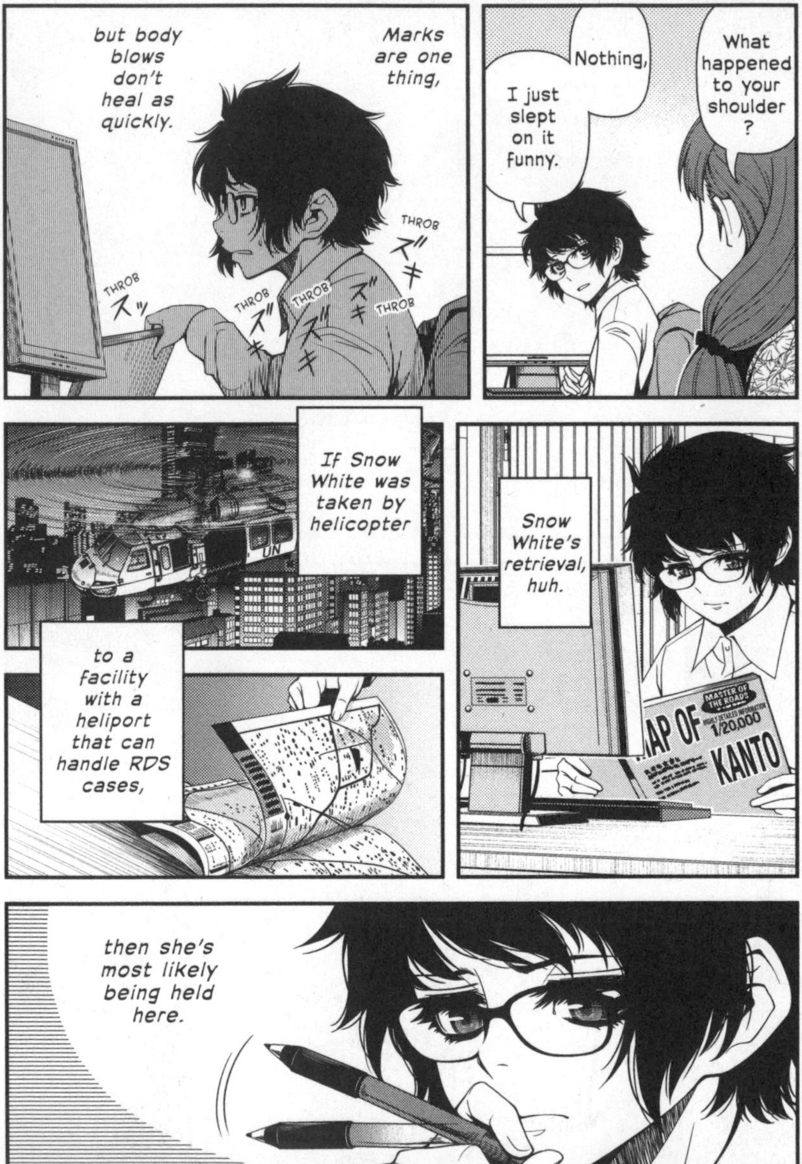
What happened to your shoulder?
Nothing,
I just slept on it funny.
Marks are one thing,
but body blows don't heal as quickly.
THROB
THROB
THROB
THROB
THROB
Snow White's retrieval, huh.
MASTER OF THE ROADS
HIGHLY DETAILED INFORMATION
1/20,000
AP OF
KANTO
If Snow White was taken by helicopter
UN
to a facility with a heliport that can handle RDS cases,
then she's most likely being held here.

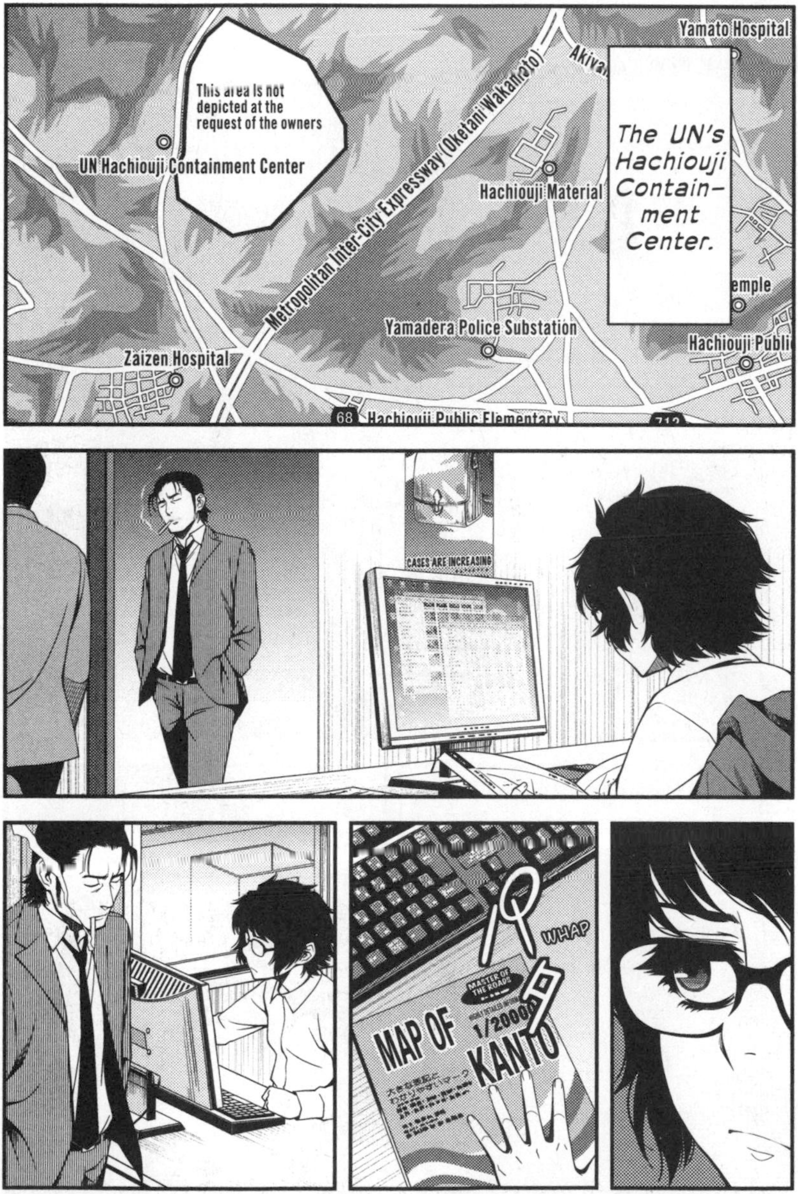
The UN's Hachiouji Contain-ment Center.
Yamato Hospital
This area is not depicted at the request of the owners
UN Hachiouji Containment Center
Metropolitan Inter-City Expressway (Oketani Wakamato)
Hachiouji Material
Yamadera Police Substation
Zaizen Hospital
68
Hachiouji Public Elementary
CASES ARE INCREASING
WHAP
MASTER OF THE ROADS
MAP OF KANTO
1/2000

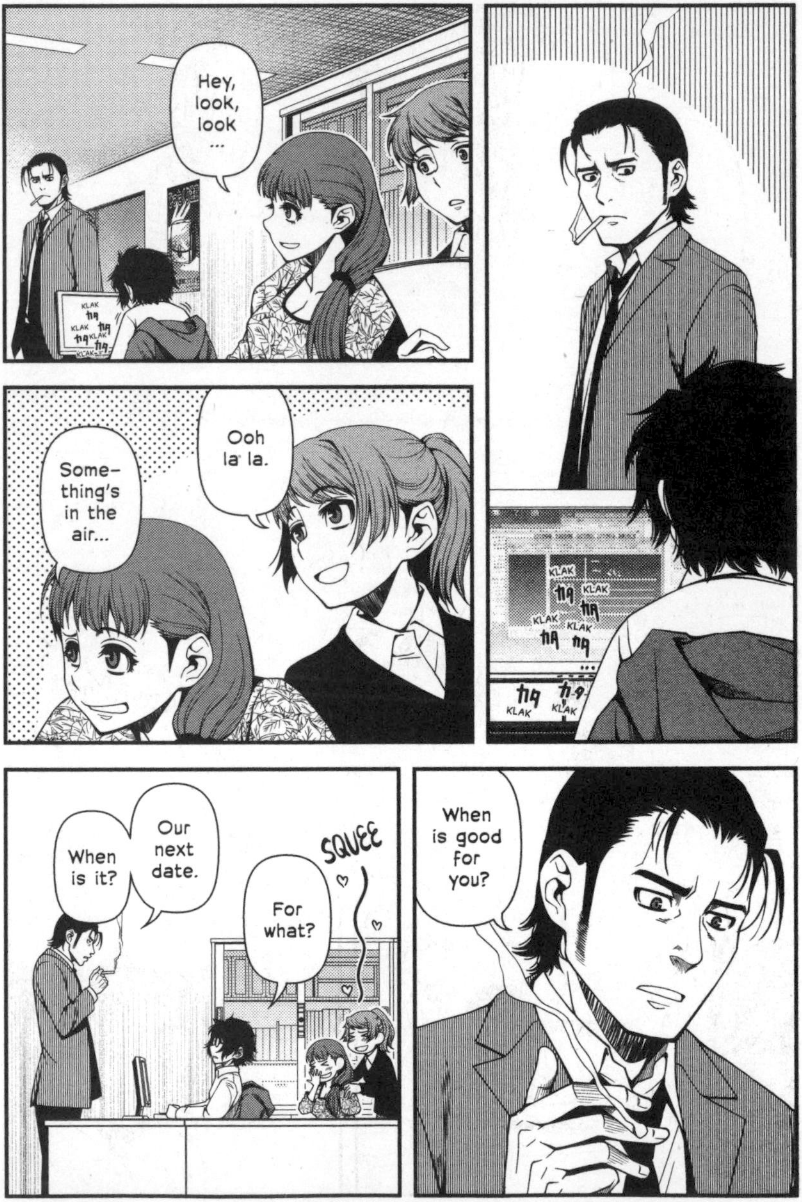
KLAK
KLAK
KLAK
KLAK
KLAK
KLAK
Hey, look, look ...
KLAK
KLAK
KLAK
KLAK
Ooh la la.
Some-thing's in the air...
When is good for you?
SQUEE
Our next date.
When is it?
For what?

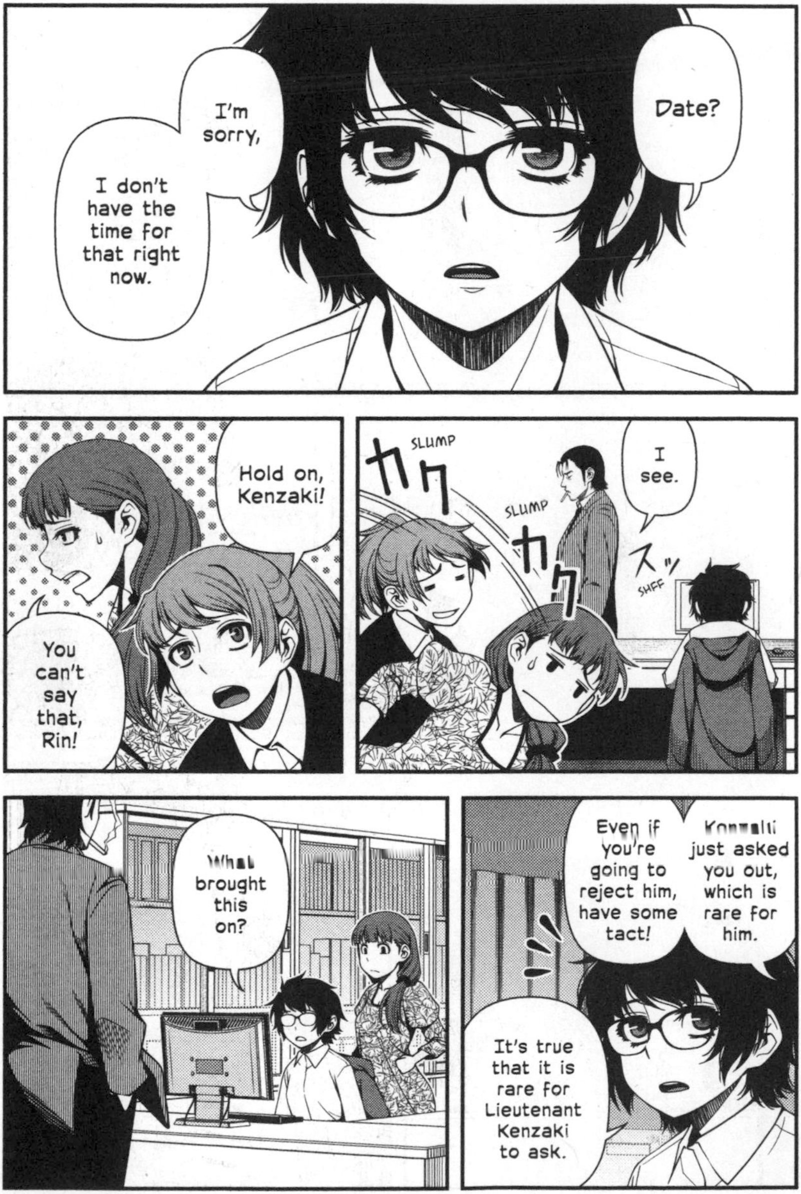
Date?
I'm sorry,
I don't have the time for that right now.
I see.
SLUMP
SLUMP
SHFF
Hold on, Kenzaki!
You can't say that, Rin!
Kenzaki just asked you out, which is rare for him.
Even if you're going to reject him, have some tact!
It's true that it is rare for Lieutenant Kenzaki to ask.
What brought this on?

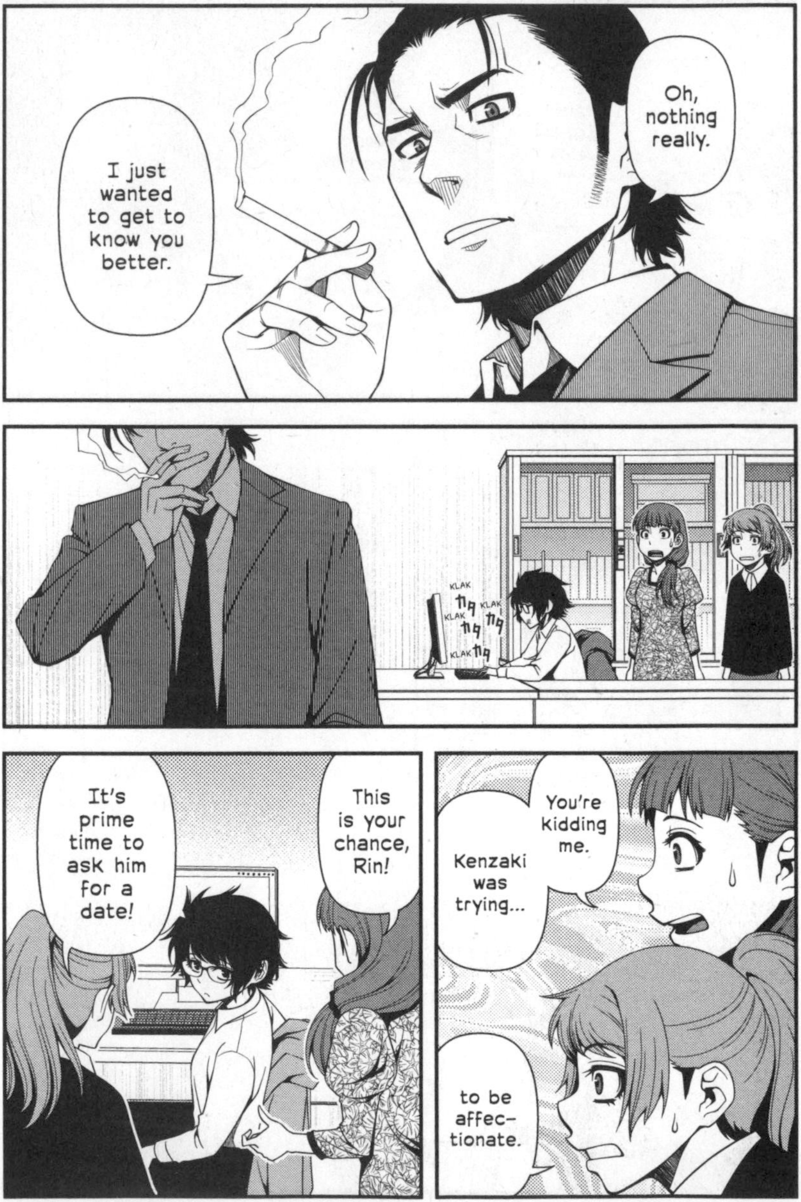
Oh, nothing really.
I just wanted to get to know you better.
KLAK
KLAK
KLAK
KLAK
You're kidding me.
Kenzaki was trying...
to be affectionate.
This is your chance, Rin!
It's prime time to ask him for a date!

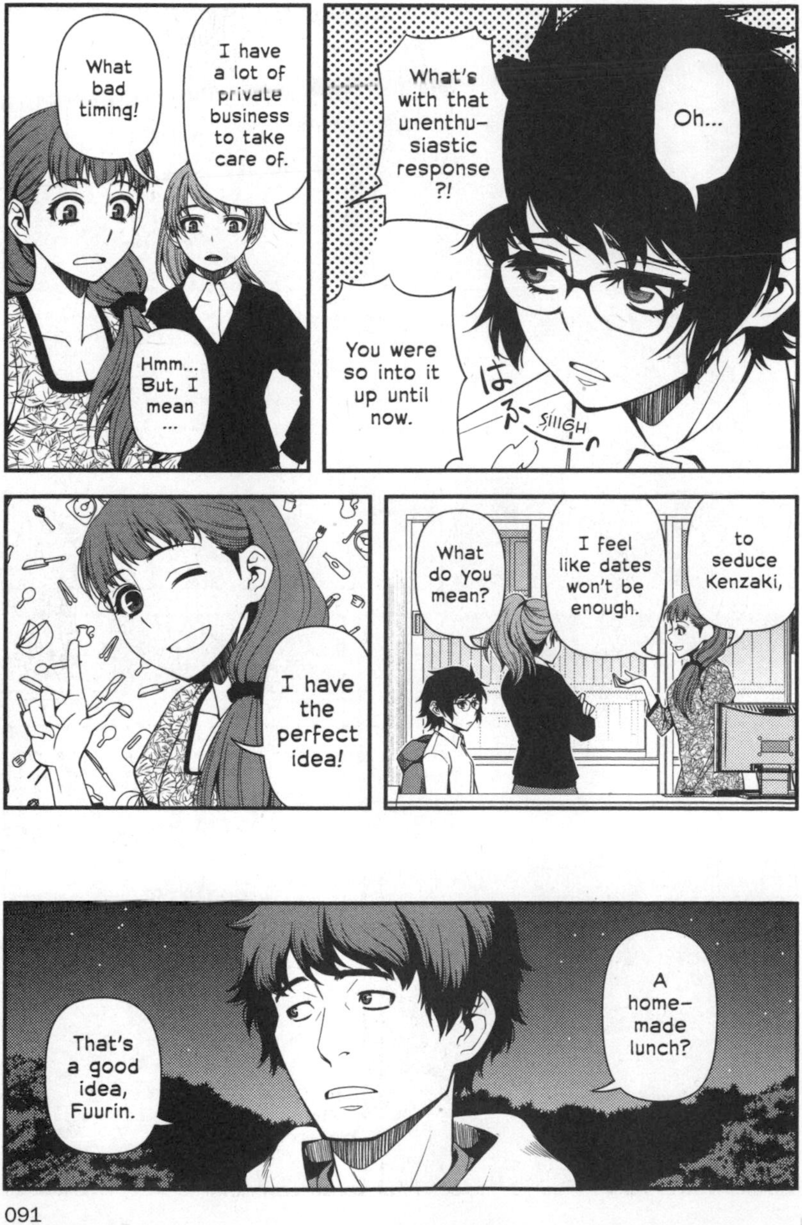
Oh...
What's with that unenthu-siastic response?!
You were so into it up until now.
SIIIGH
I have a lot of private business to take care of.
What bad timing!
Hmm... But, I mean ...
to seduce Kenzaki,
I feel like dates won't be enough.
What do you mean?
I have the perfect idea!
A home-made lunch?
That's a good idea, Fuurin.

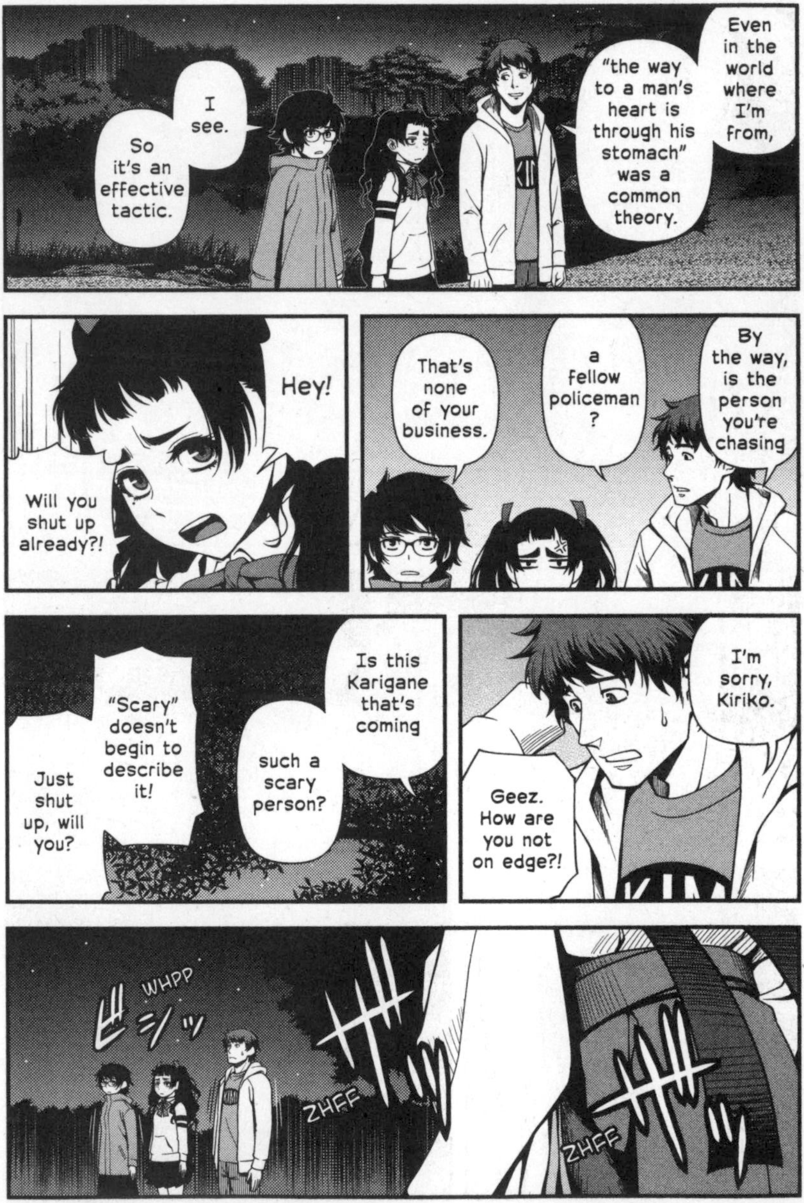
Even in the world where I'm from,
“the way to a man's heart is through his stomach” was a common theory.
I see.
So it's an effective tactic.
By the way, is the person you're chasing
a fellow policeman?
That's none of your business.
Hey!
Will you shut up already?!
I'm sorry, Kiriko.
Geez. How are you not on edge?!
Is this Karigane that's coming
such a scary person?
“Scary” doesn't begin to describe it!
Just shut up, will you?
ZHFF
ZHFF
WHPP
ビシッ

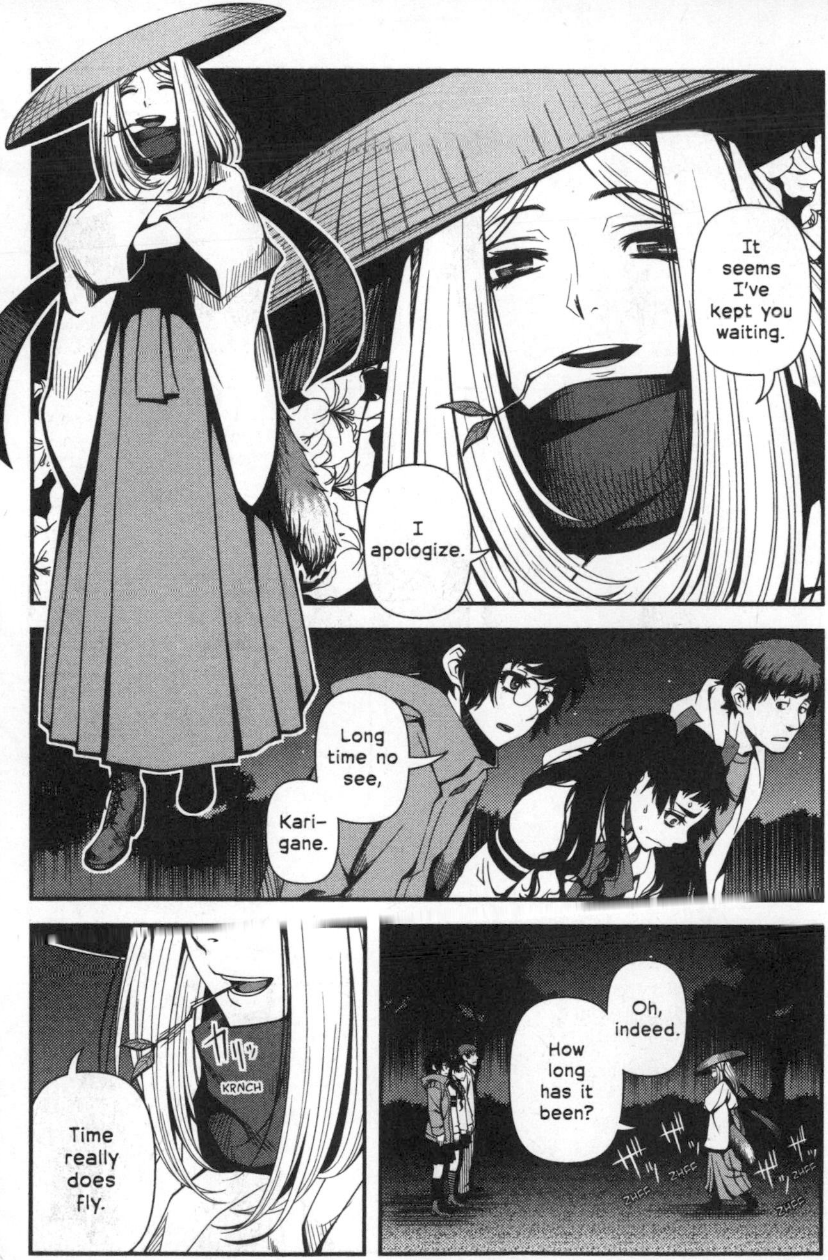
It seems I've kept you waiting.
I apologize.
Long time no see,
Kari-gane.
Oh, indeed.
How long has it been?
ZHFF
ZHFF
ZHFF
ZHFF
KRNCH
Time really does fly.

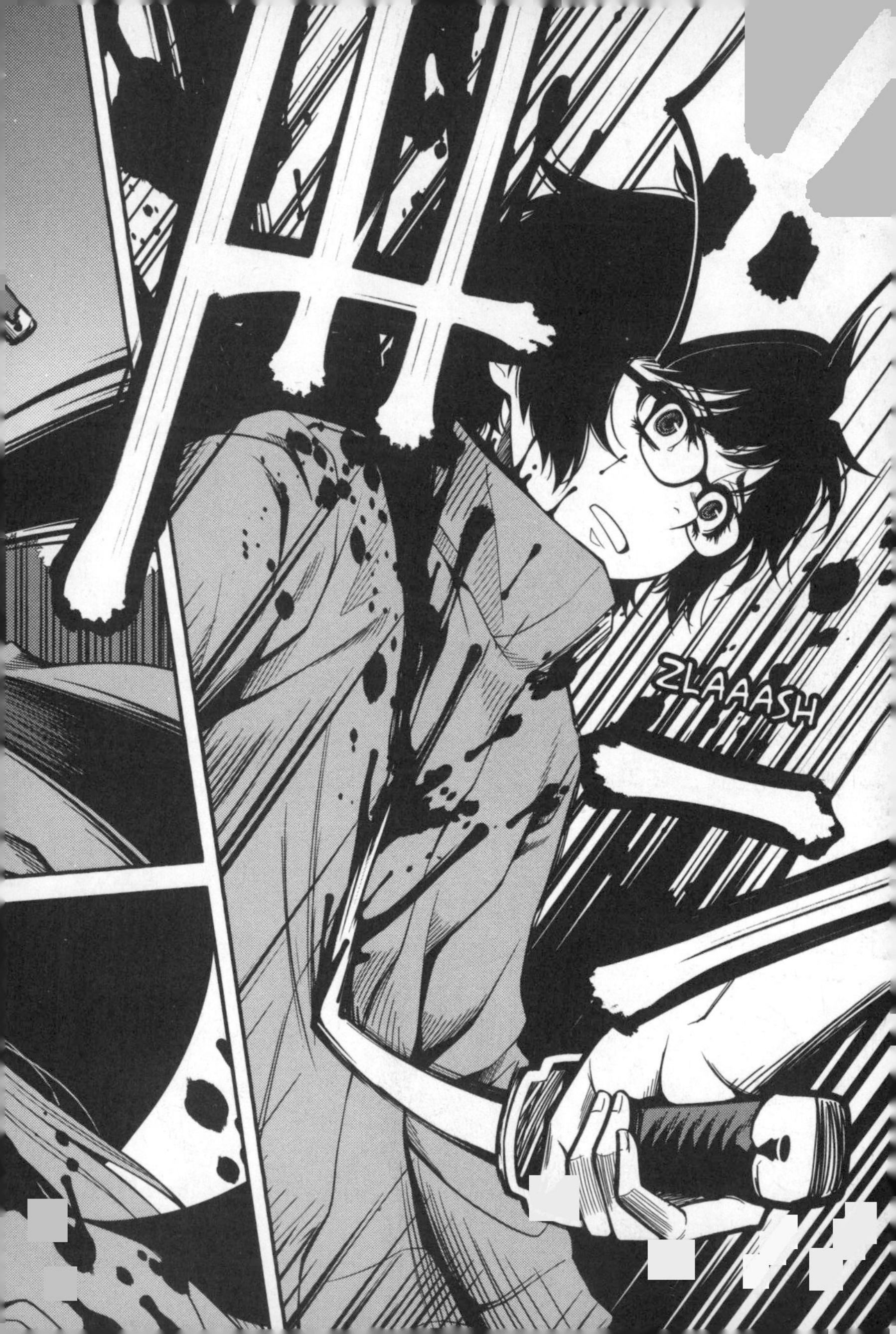
ZLAAASH

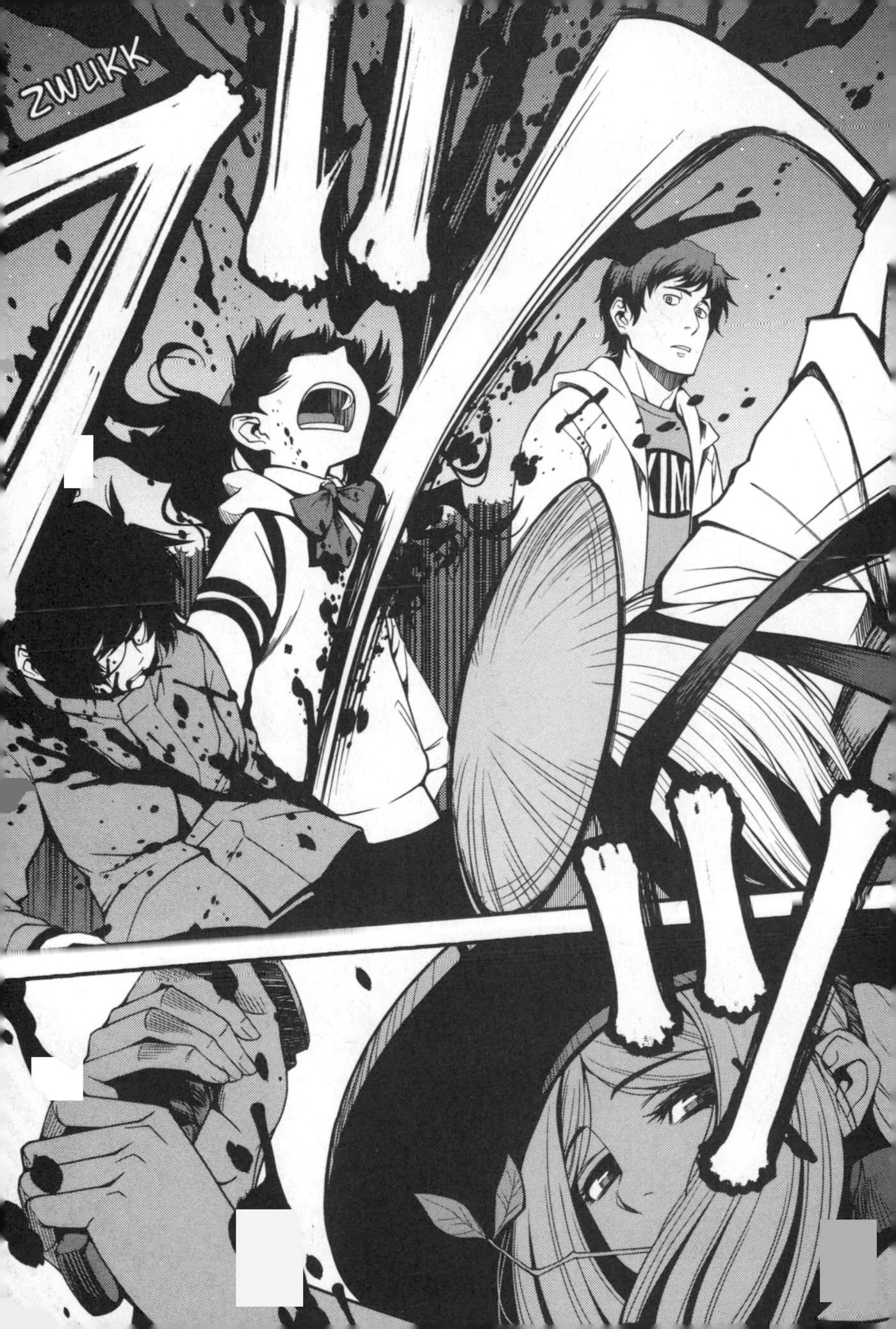
ZWUKK

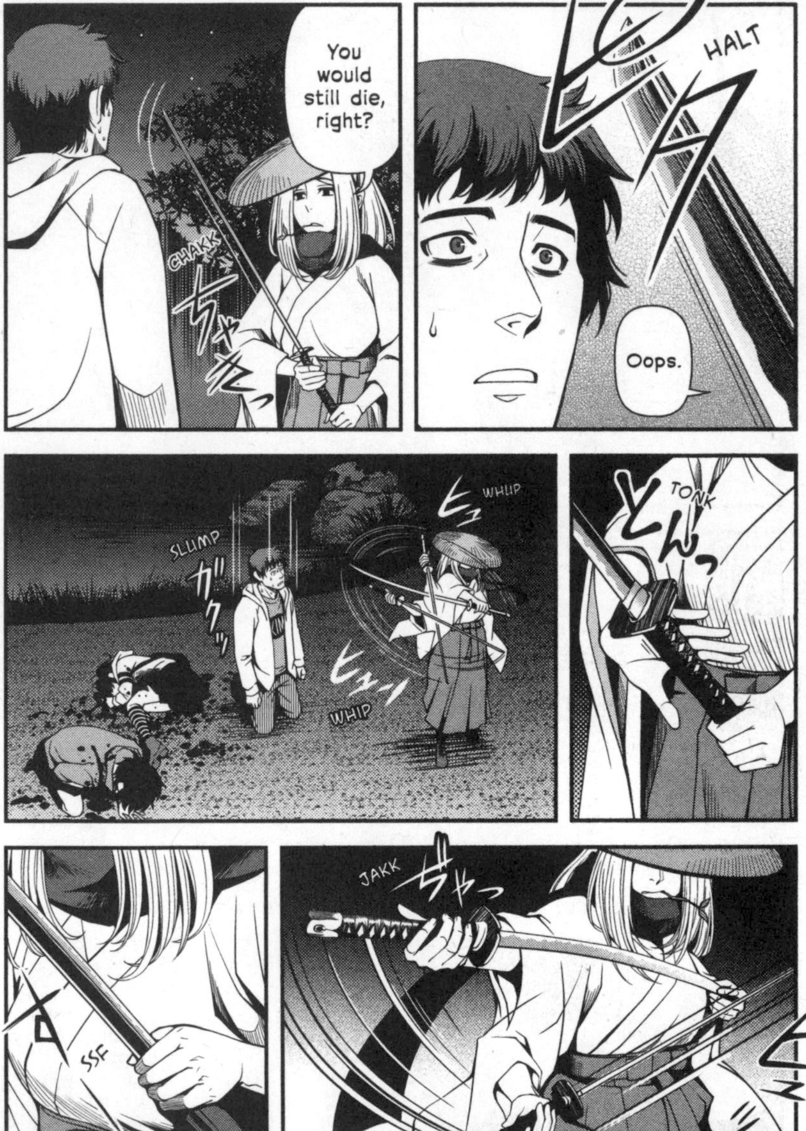
HALT
Oops.
You would still die, right?
CHAKK
ちゃきっ
TONK
とんっ
ヒュ
WHUP
SLUMP
ガクッ
ヒュー
WHIP
JAKK
SWIP
SSF

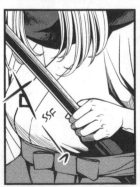

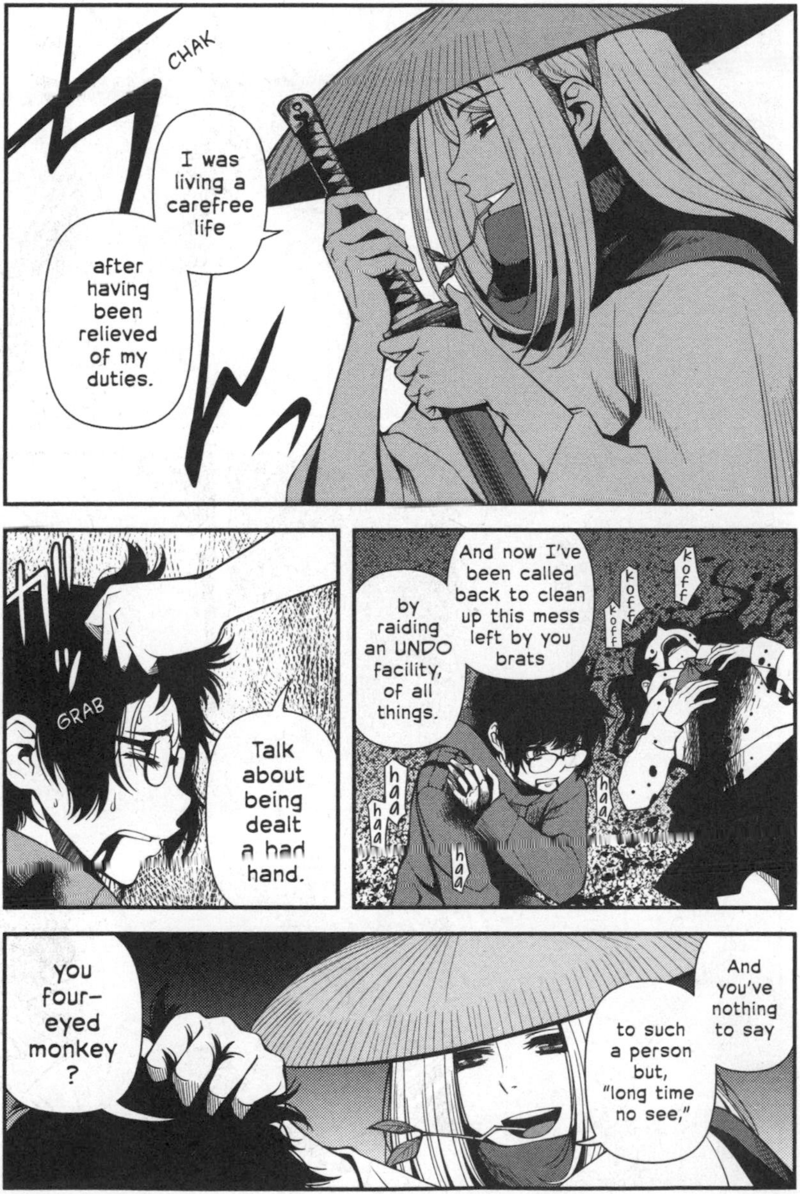
CHAK
I was living a carefree life
after having been relieved of my duties.
And now I've been called back to clean up this mess left by you brats
by raiding an UNDO facility, of all things.
koff
koff
koff
haa
haa
haa
haa
GRAB
Talk about being dealt a bad hand.
And you've nothing to say
to such a person but, "long time no see,"
you four-eyed monkey?

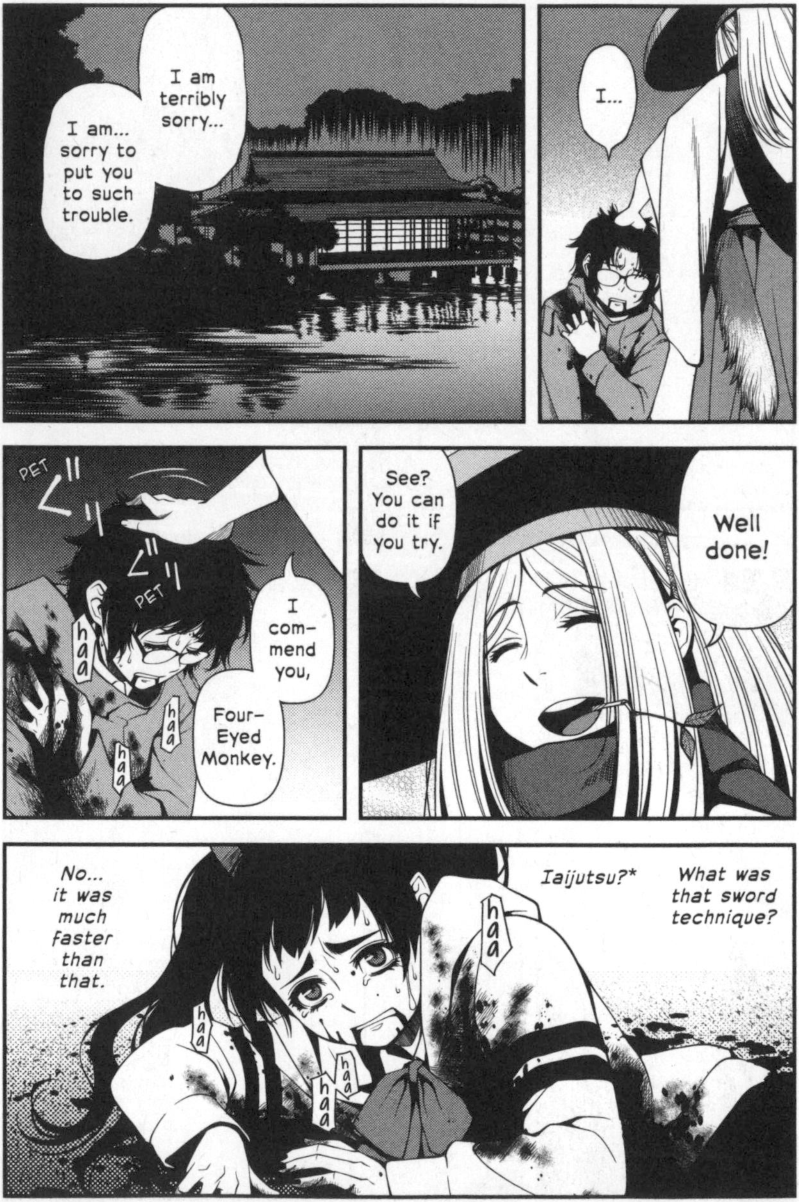
I...
I am terribly sorry...
I am... sorry to put you to such trouble.
Well done!
See? You can do it if you try.
PET
PET
I com-mend you,
Four-Eyed Monkey.
haa
haa
haa
What was that sword technique?
Iaijutsu?*
No... it was much faster than that.
haa
haa
haa
haa
haa

*quick-draw sword technique

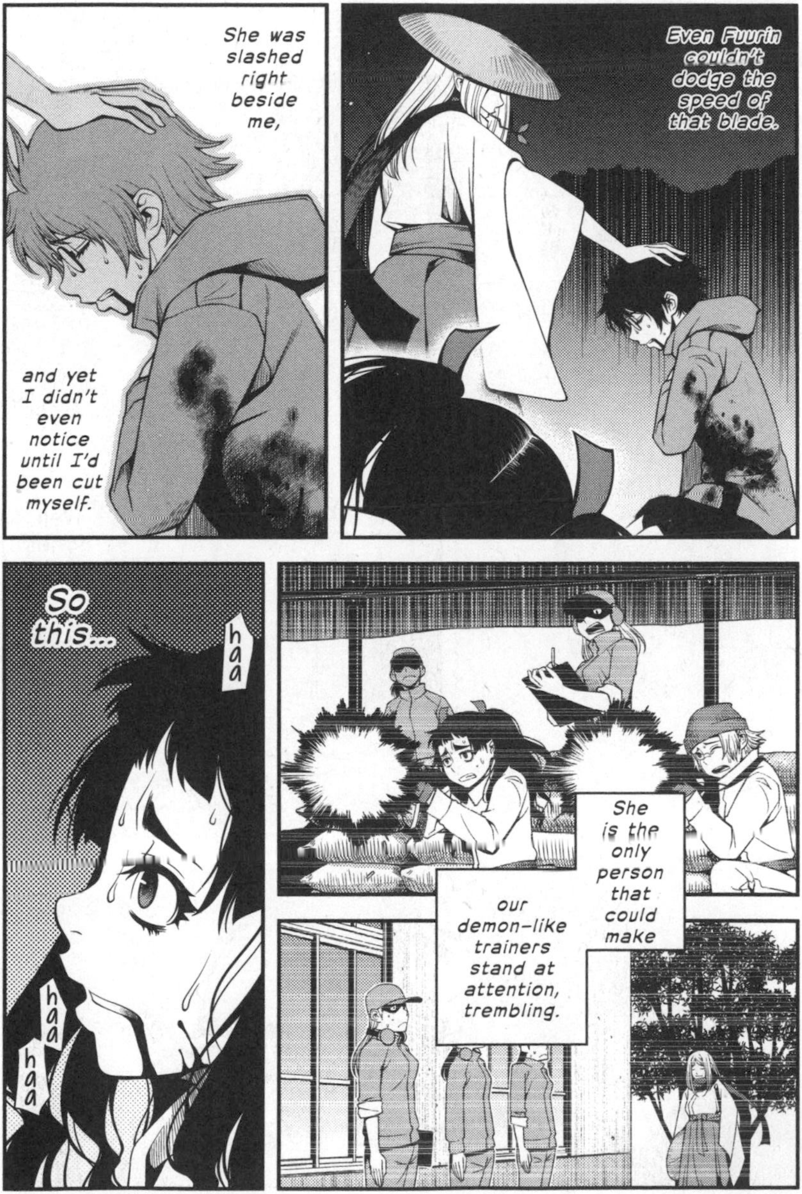
Even Fuurin couldn't dodge the speed of that blade.
She was slashed right beside me,
and yet I didn't even notice until I'd been cut myself.
She is the only person that could make
our demon-like trainers stand at attention, trembling.
So this...
haa
haa
haa

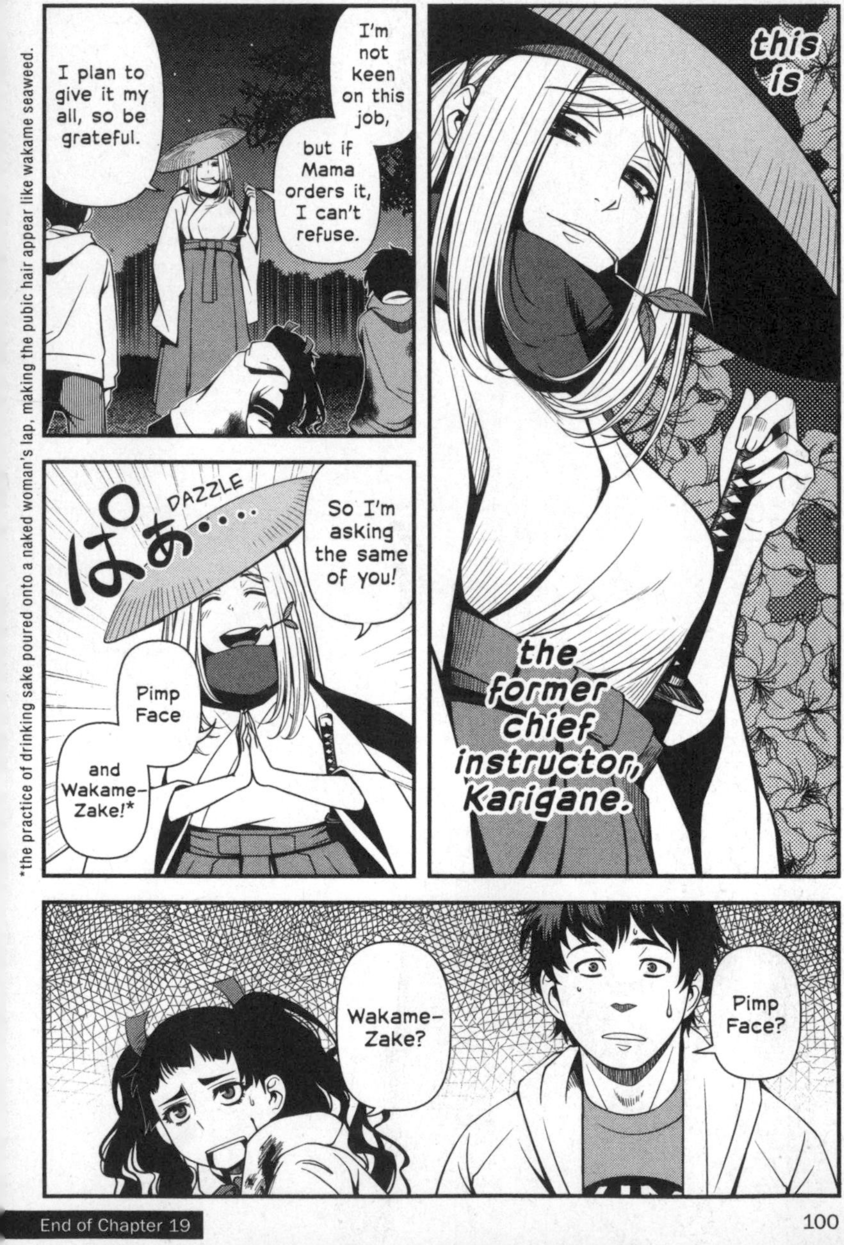
this is
the former chief instructor, Karigane.
I'm not keen on this job,
but if Mama orders it, I can't refuse.
I plan to give it my all, so be grateful.
So I'm asking the same of you!
ぱあ・・・
DAZZLE
Pimp Face
and Wakame-Zake!*
Pimp Face?
Wakame-Zake?

*the practice of drinking sake poured onto a naked woman's lap, making the pubic hair appear like wakame seaweed.

20
Karigane (Part 2)

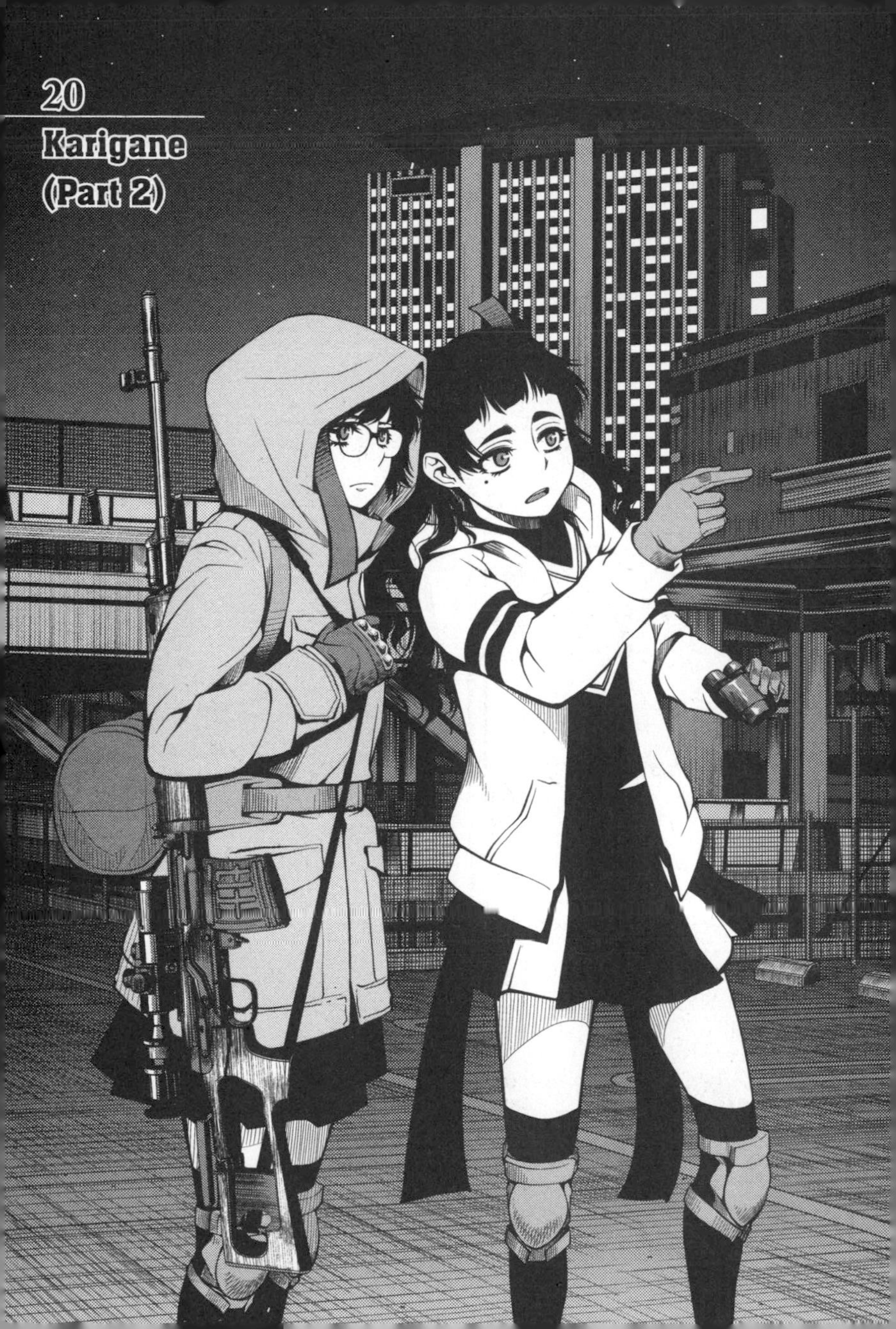

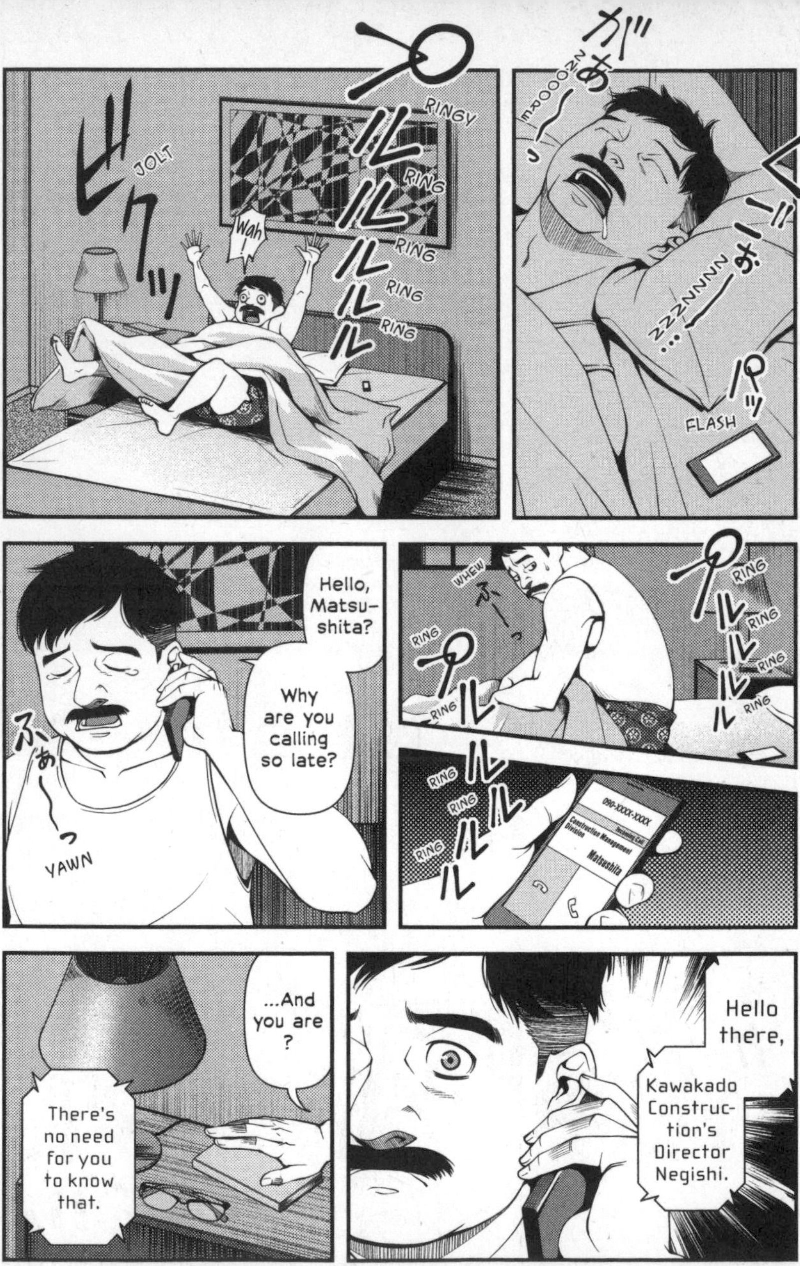
がぁ~
ZNOOOORE
ぐごーー
ZZZNNNN...
パッ
FLASH
プルルルルル
RINGY
RING
RING
RING
RING
ビクッ
JOLT
Wah!
プルルルル
RING
RING
RING
RING
プル
RING
RING
WHEW
ふーっ
ルルル
RING
RING
RING
090-XXXX-XXXX
Construction Management Division
Matsushita
Hello, Matsushita?
Why are you calling so late?
ふぁ~っ
YAWN
Hello there,
Kawakado Construction's Director Negishi.
...And you are?
There's no need for you to know that.

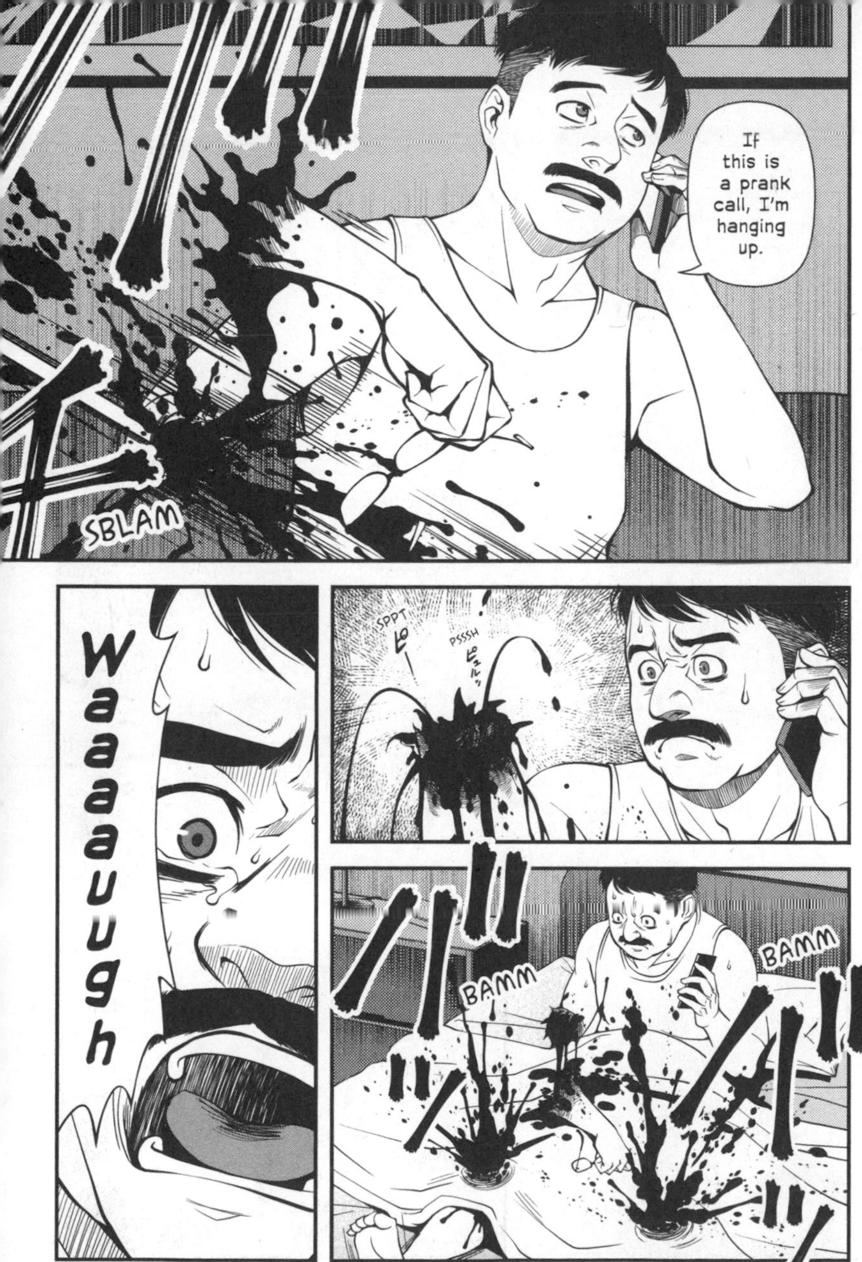
If this is a prank call, I'm hanging up.
SBLAM
SPPT
PSSSH
BAMM
BAMM
Waaaauugh

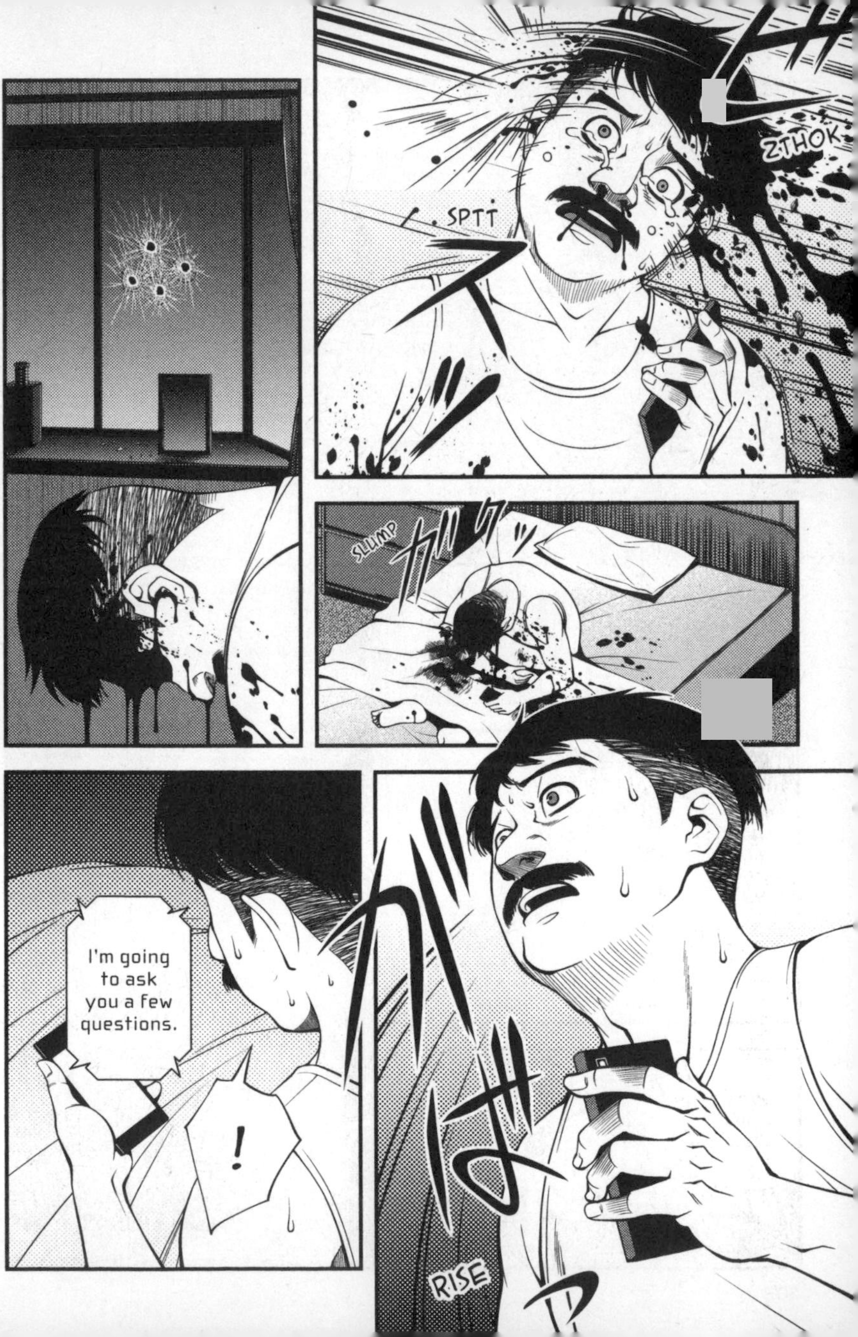
ZTHOK
SPTT
SLUMP
RISE
I'm going to ask you a few questions.
!

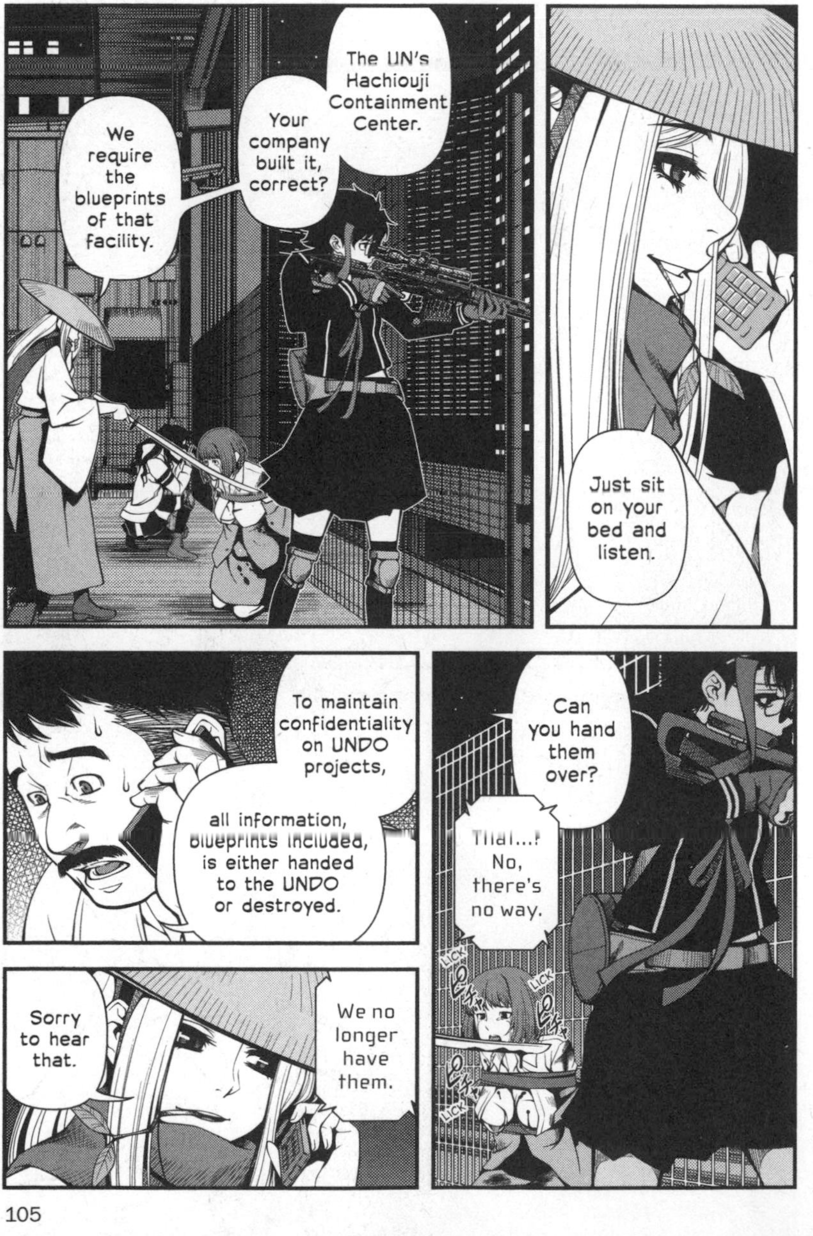
Just sit on your bed and listen.
The UN's Hachiouji Containment Center.
Your company built it, correct?
We require the blueprints of that facility.
Can you hand them over?
That...? No, there's no way.
LICK
LICK
LICK
To maintain confidentiality on UNDO projects,
all information, blueprints included, is either handed to the UNDO or destroyed.
We no longer have them.
Sorry to hear that.

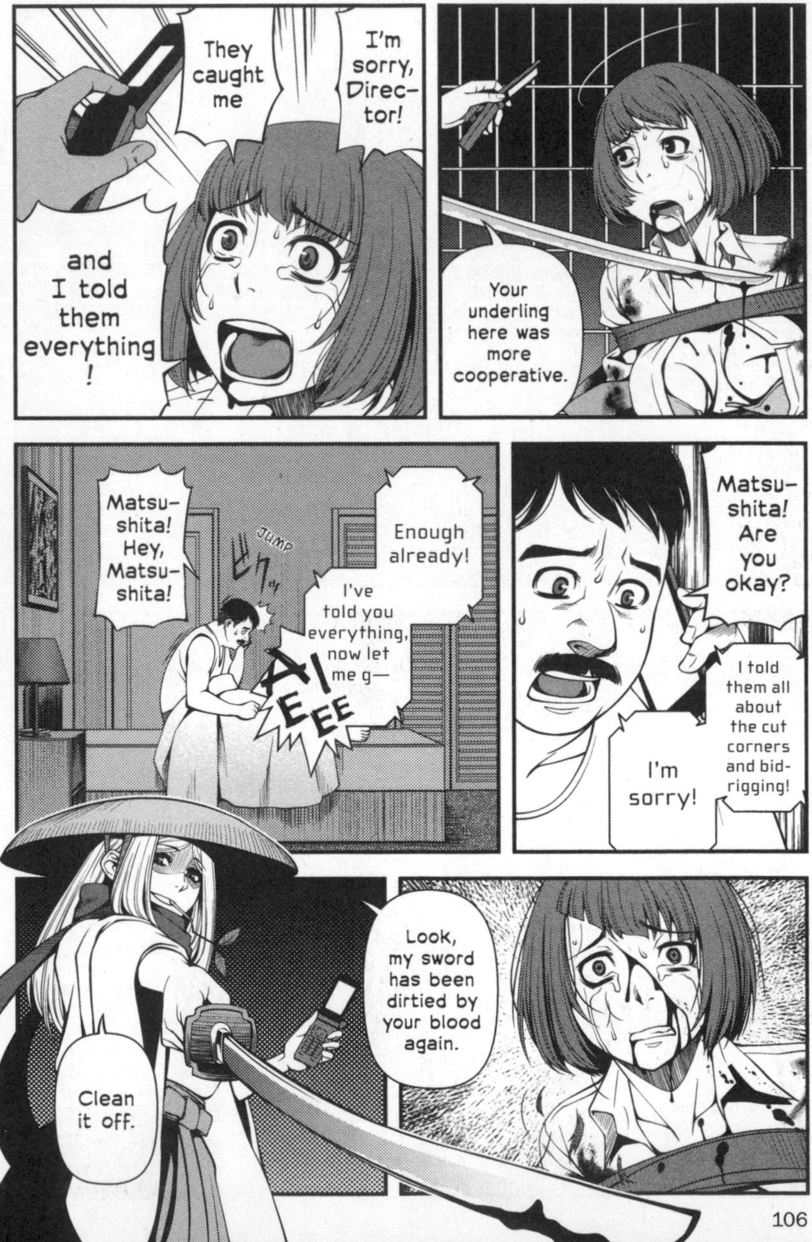

Your underling here was more cooperative.
I'm sorry, Director!
They caught me
and I told them everything!
Matsu-shita! Are you okay?
I told them all about the cut corners and bid-rigging!
I'm sorry!
Enough already!
I've told you everything, now let me g—
JUMP
Matsu-shita! Hey, Matsu-shita!
AIEEE
Look, my sword has been dirtied by your blood again.
Clean it off.

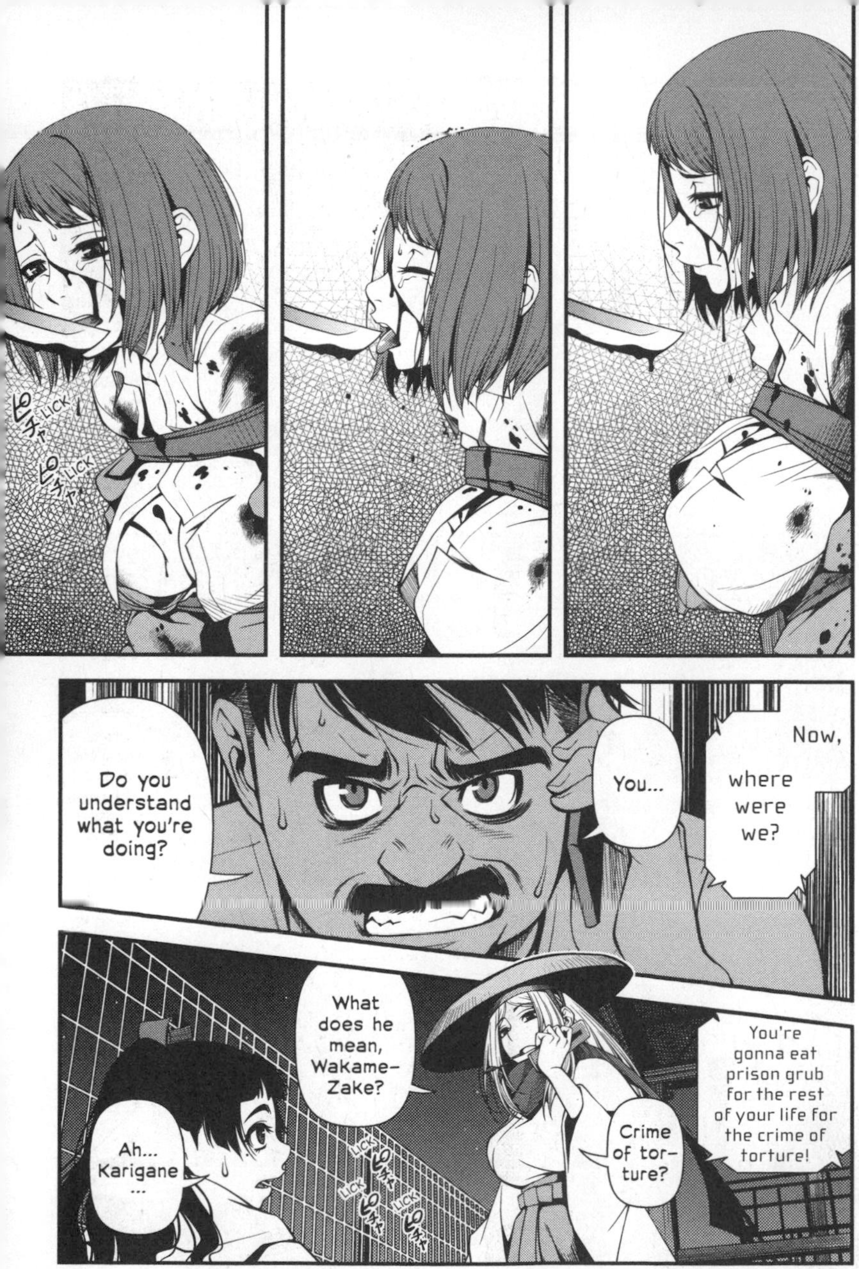
ピチャ LICK
ピチャ LICK
Now, where were we?
You...
Do you understand what you're doing?
You're gonna eat prison grub for the rest of your life for the crime of torture!
Crime of tor-ture?
What does he mean, Wakame-Zake?
Ah... Karigane ...
LICK ピチャ
LICK ピチャ
LICK ピチャ

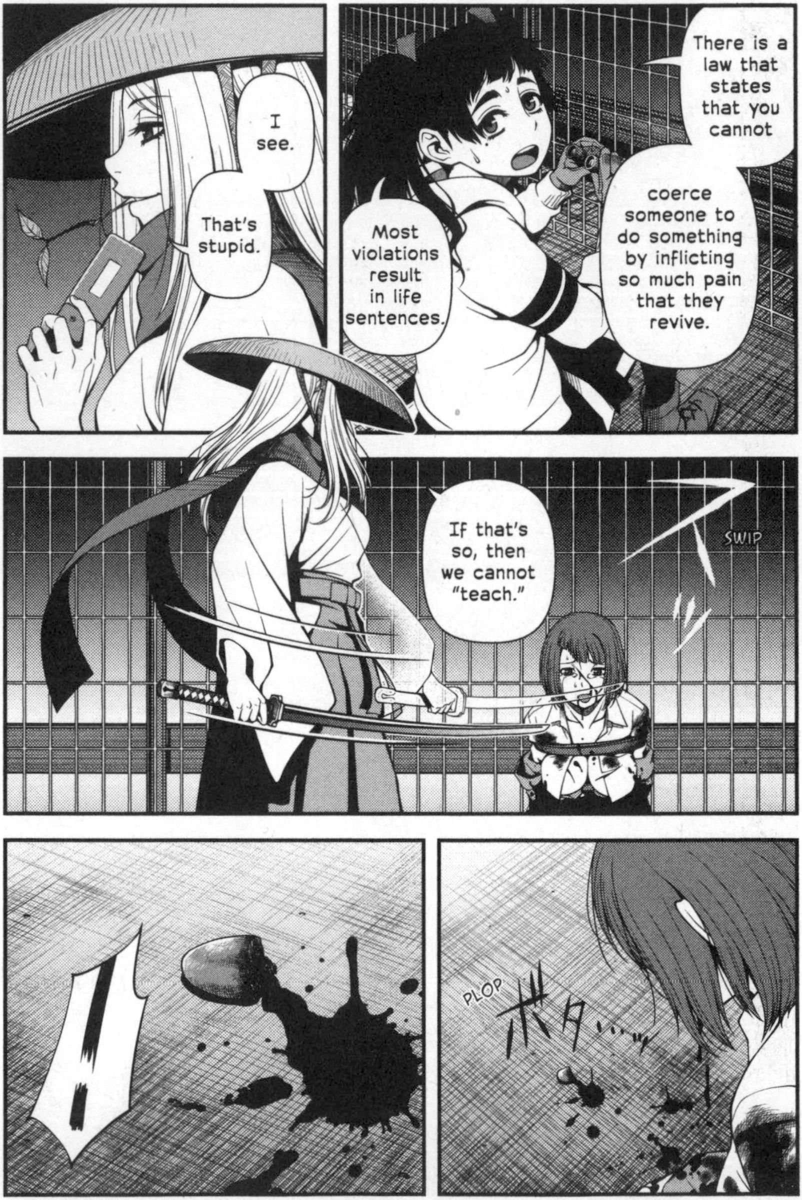
There is a law that states that you cannot
coerce someone to do something by inflicting so much pain that they revive.
Most violations result in life sentences.
I see.
That's stupid.
If that's so, then we cannot "teach."
SWIP
PLOP
ボタ…ッ

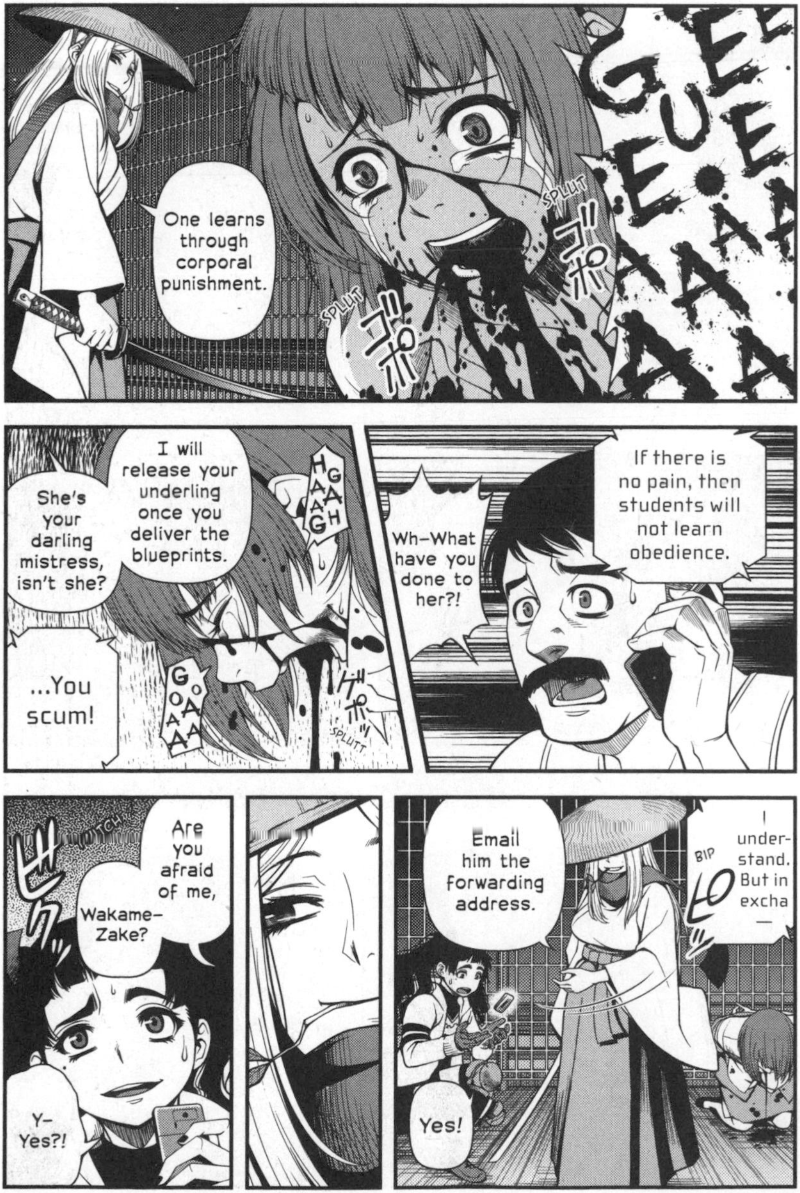
GUEEEEAAAAA
SPLUUT
One learns through corporal punishment.
SPLUUT
If there is no pain, then students will not learn obedience.
Wh-What have you done to her?!
I will release your underling once you deliver the blueprints.
HAAGH
GAAGH
She's your darling mistress, isn't she?
...You scum!
GOAAAA
SPLUTT
I under-stand. But in excha—
BIP
Email him the forwarding address.
Yes!
Are you afraid of me, Wakame-Zake?
TWITCH
Y-Yes?!

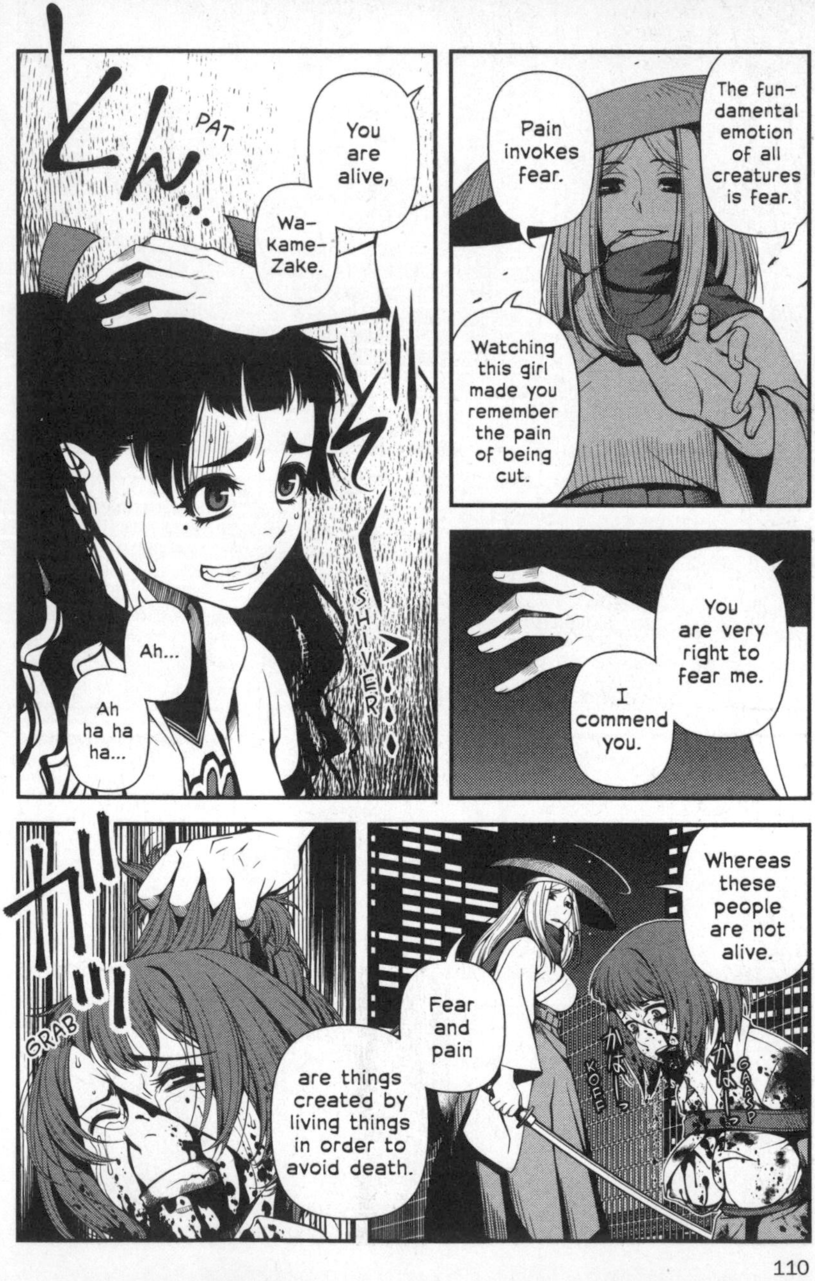
The fun-damental emotion of all creatures is fear.
Pain invokes fear.
Watching this girl made you remember the pain of being cut.
You are very right to fear me.
I commend you.
PAT
You are alive,
Wa-kame-Zake.
SHIVER
Ah...
Ah ha ha ha...
Whereas these people are not alive.
Fear and pain
are things created by living things in order to avoid death.
GAASP
KOFF
GRAB

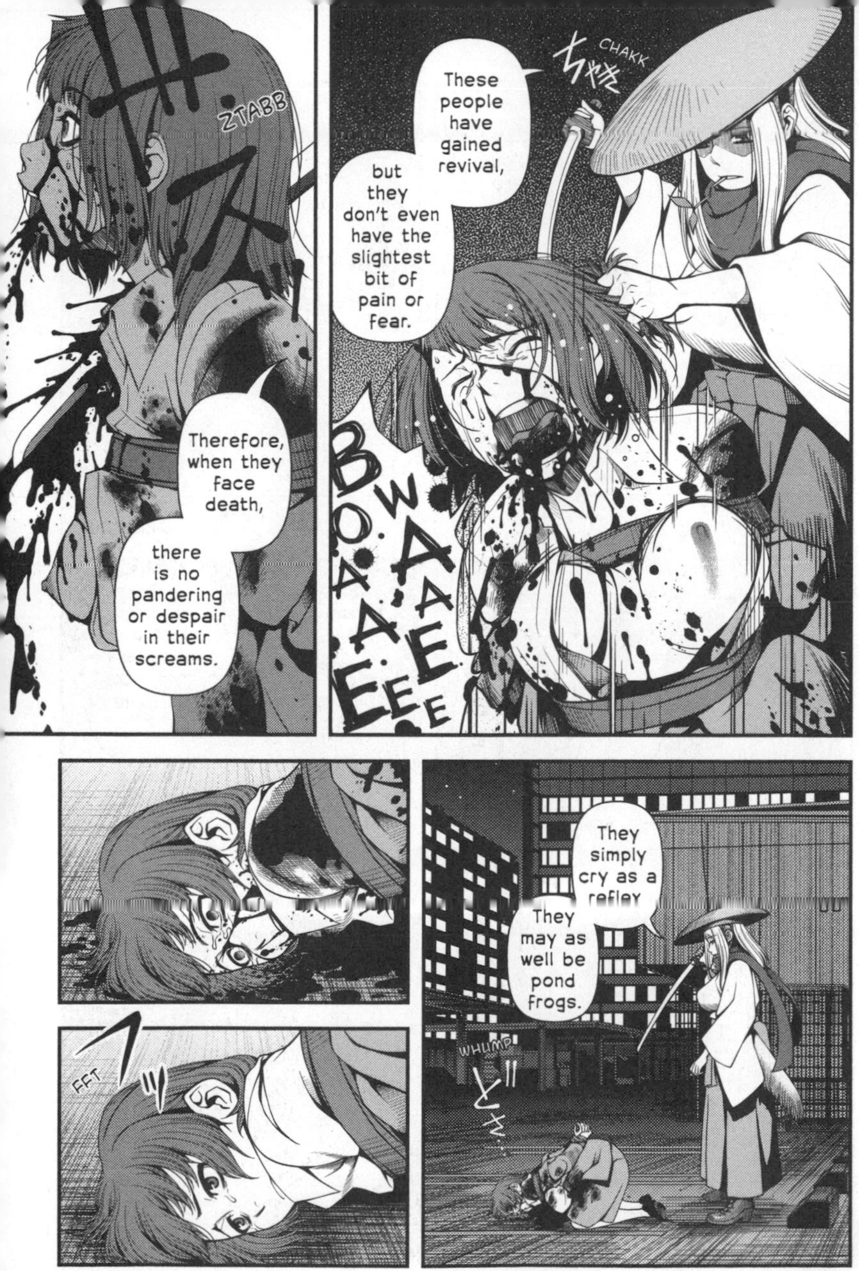

CHAKK
ちゃき
These people have gained revival,
but they don't even have the slightest bit of pain or fear.
BOWAAAEEE
ZTABB
Therefore, when they face death,
there is no pandering or despair in their screams.
They simply cry as a reflex.
They may as well be pond frogs.
WHUMP
FFT

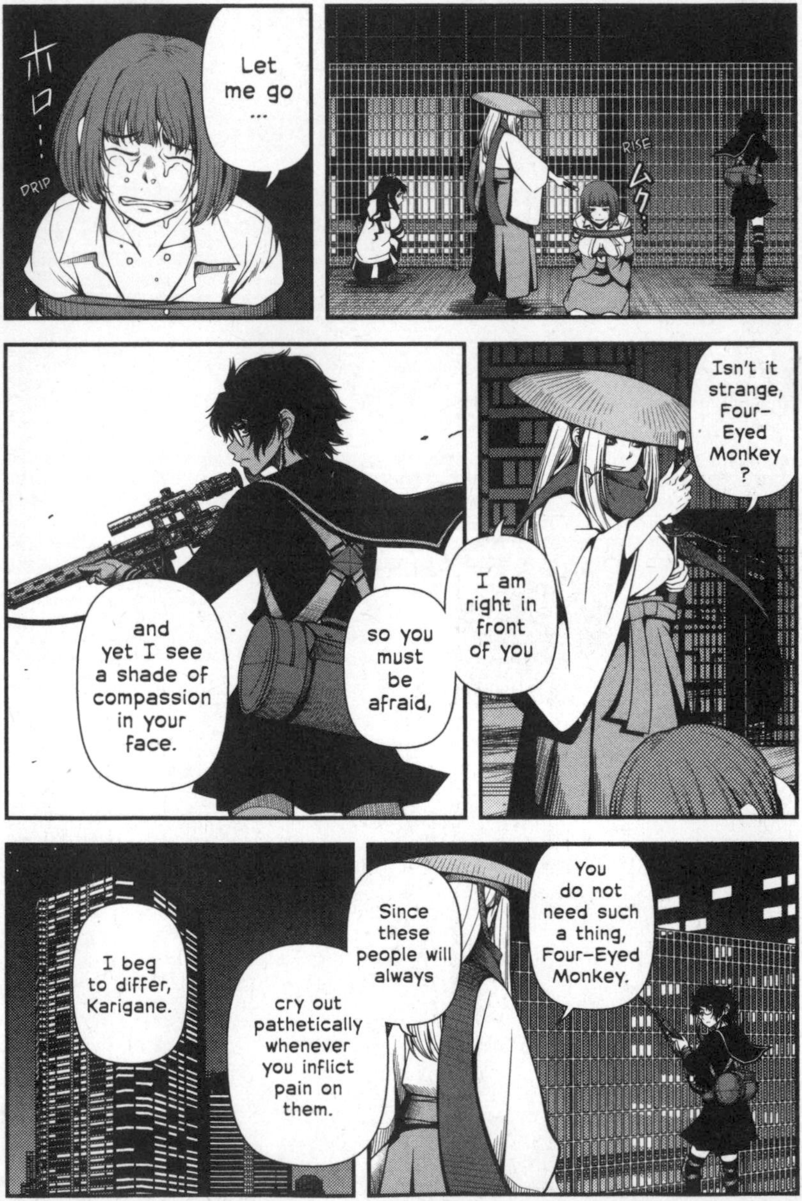
RISE
ムク
ホロ...
DRIP
Let me go ...
Isn't it strange, Four-Eyed Monkey ?
I am right in front of you
so you must be afraid,
and yet I see a shade of compassion in your face.
You do not need such a thing, Four-Eyed Monkey.
Since these people will always
cry out pathetically whenever you inflict pain on them.
I beg to differ, Karigane.

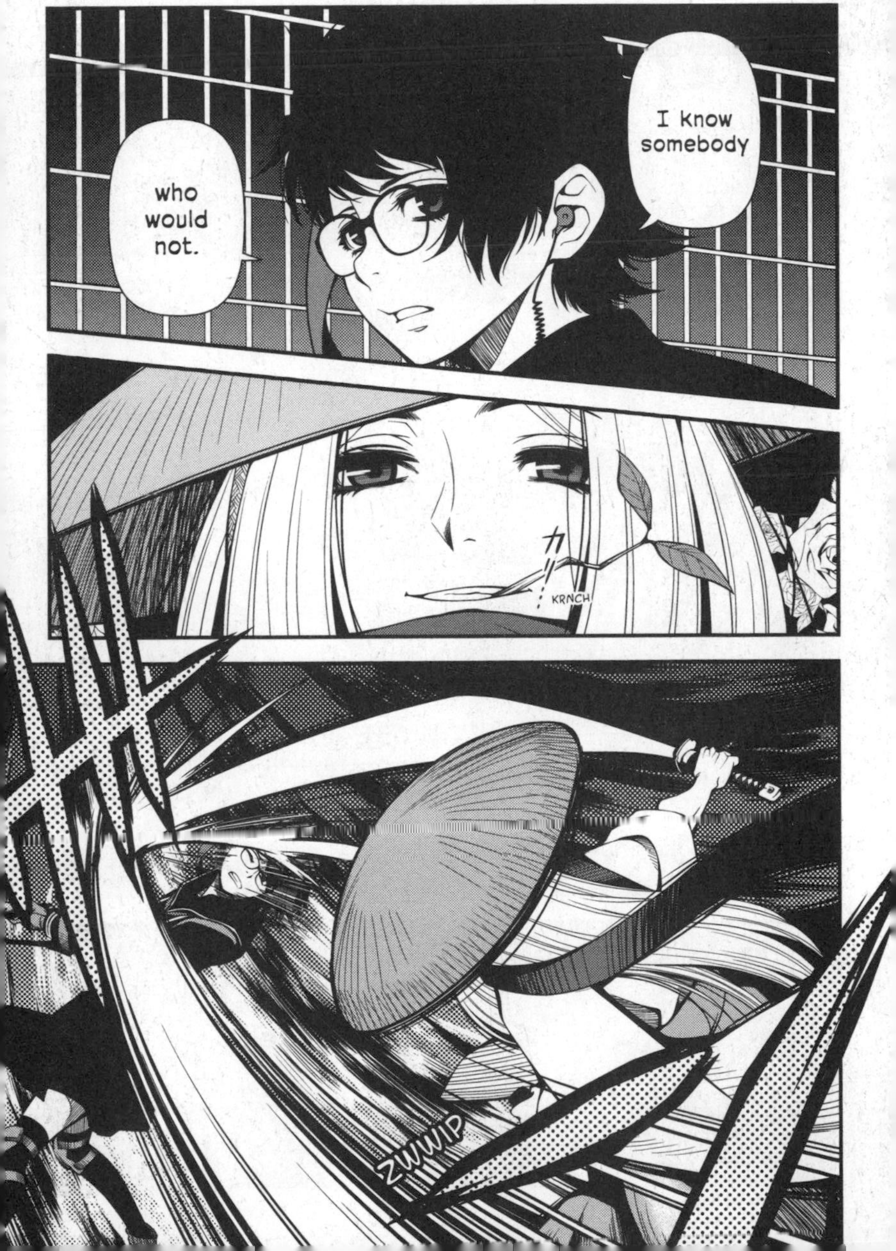
I know somebody
who would not.
KRNCH
ZWWIP

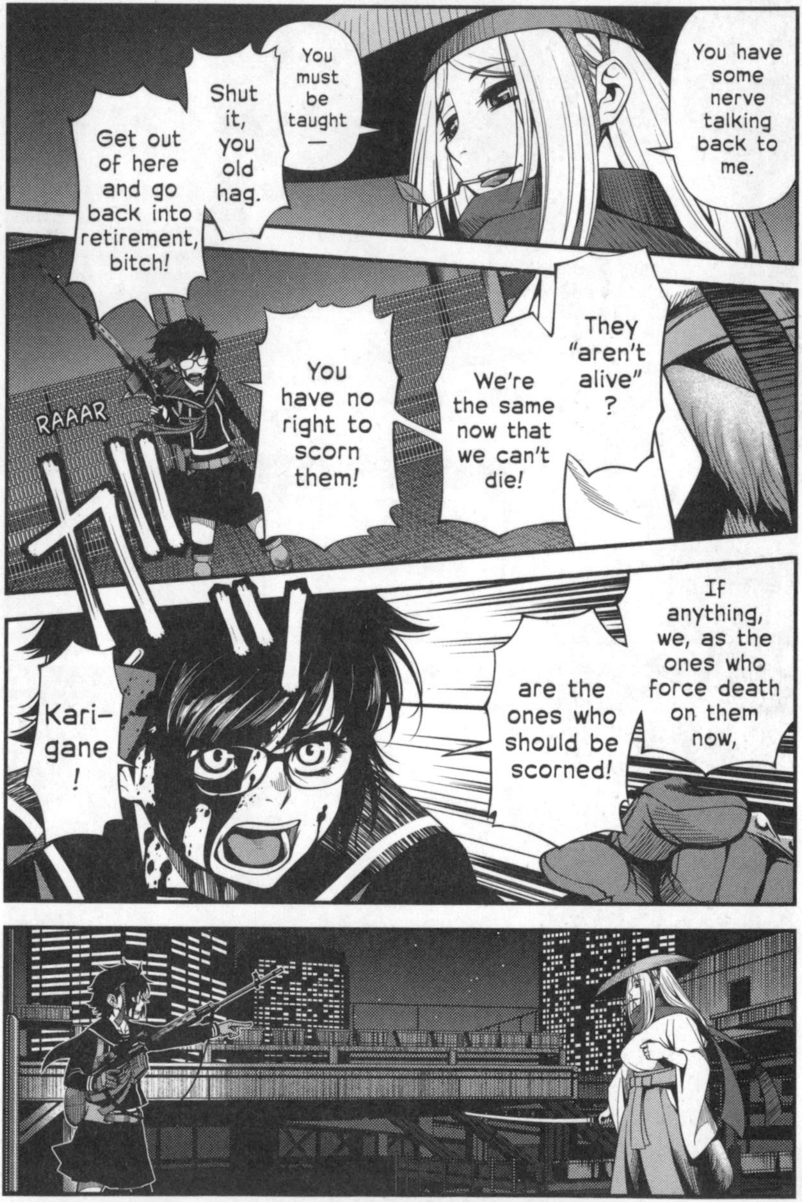
You have some nerve talking back to me.
You must be taught—
Shut it, you old hag.
Get out of here and go back into retirement, bitch!
They "aren't alive"?
We're the same now that we can't die!
You have no right to scorn them!
RAAAR
If anything, we, as the ones who force death on them now,
are the ones who should be scorned!
Kari-gane!

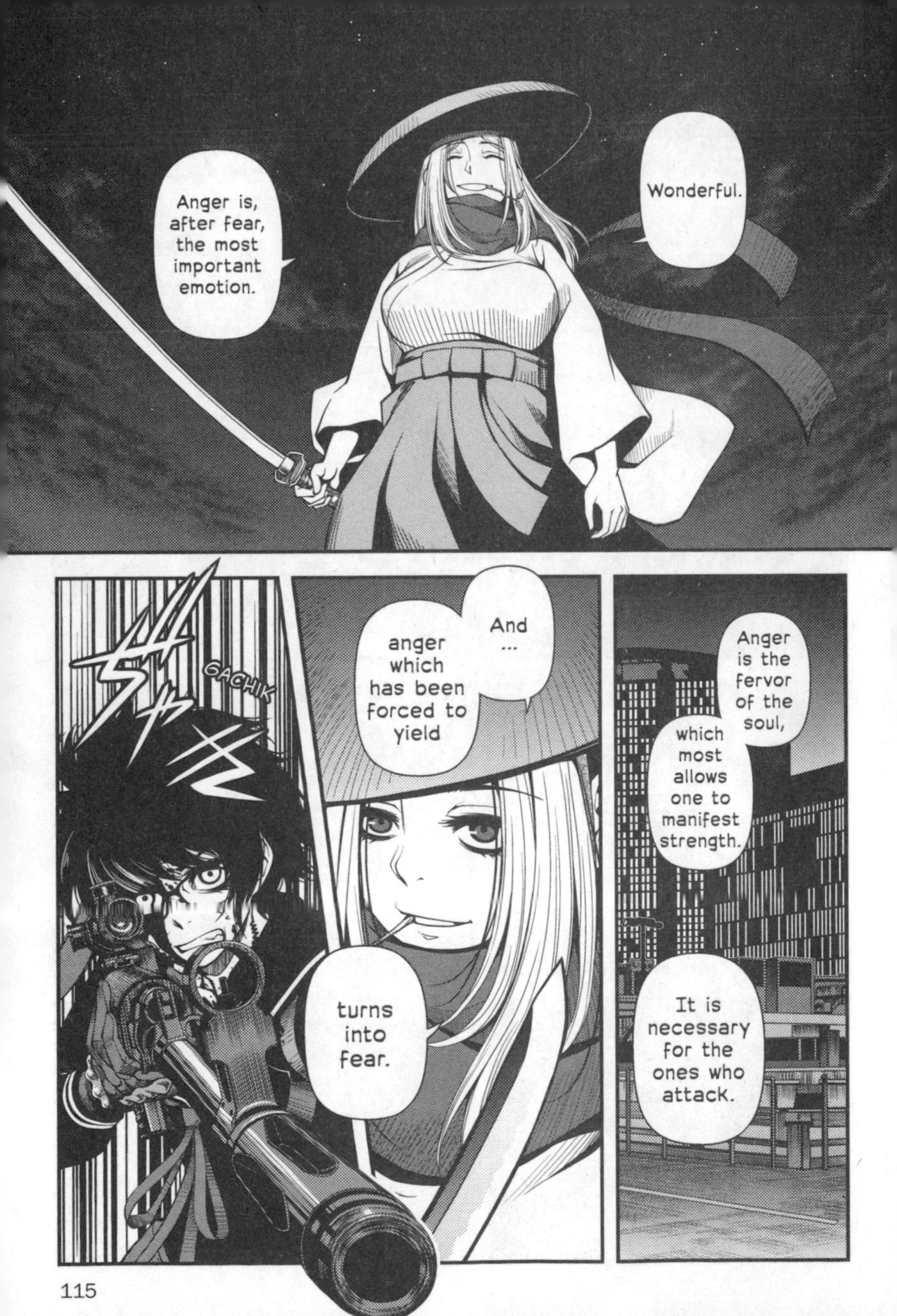
Wonderful.
Anger is, after fear, the most important emotion.
Anger is the fervor of the soul,
which most allows one to manifest strength.
It is necessary for the ones who attack.
And ...
anger which has been forced to yield
turns into fear.
GACHIK

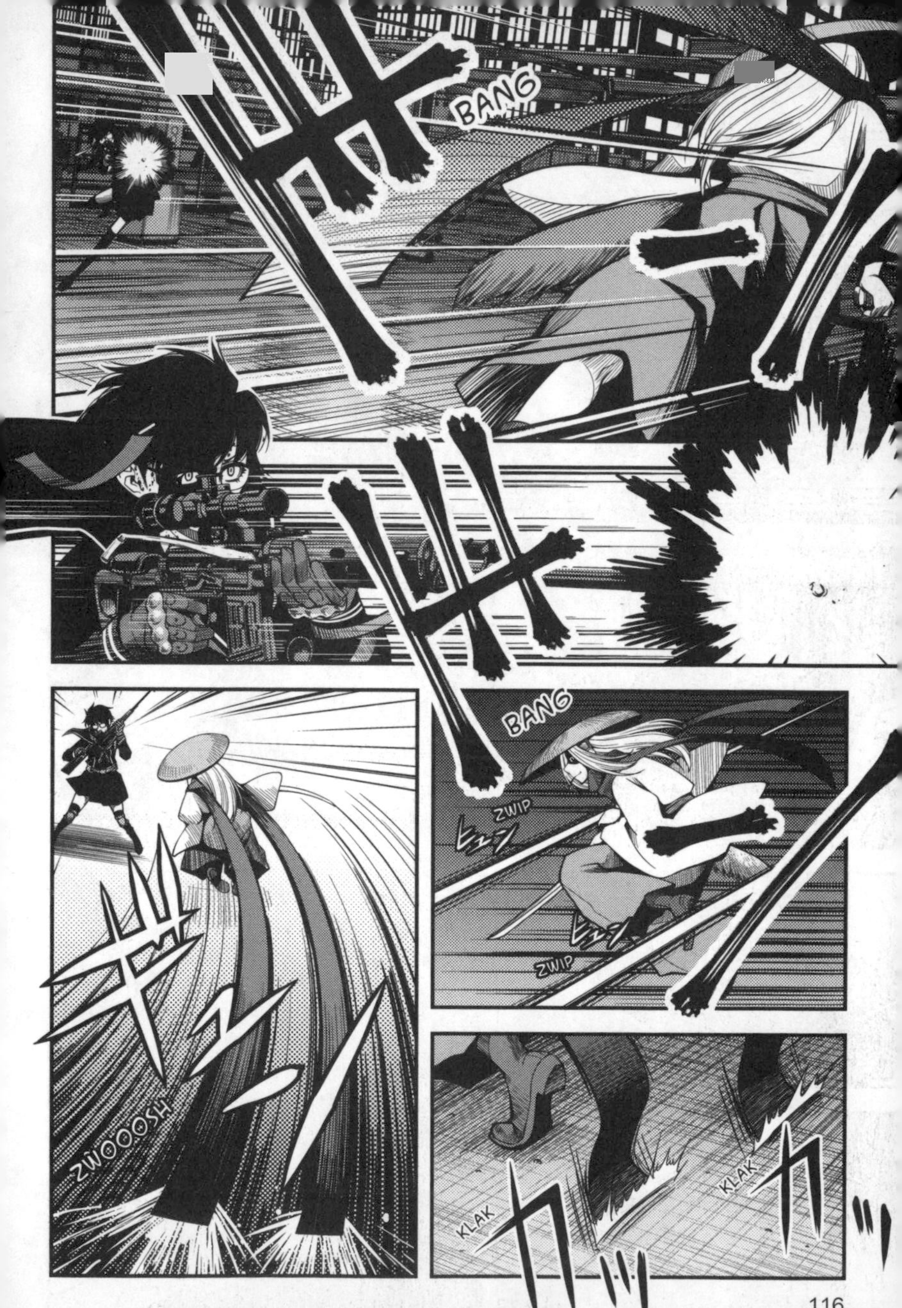
BANG
BANG
ZWIP
ZWIP
KLAK
KLAK
ZWOOOSH

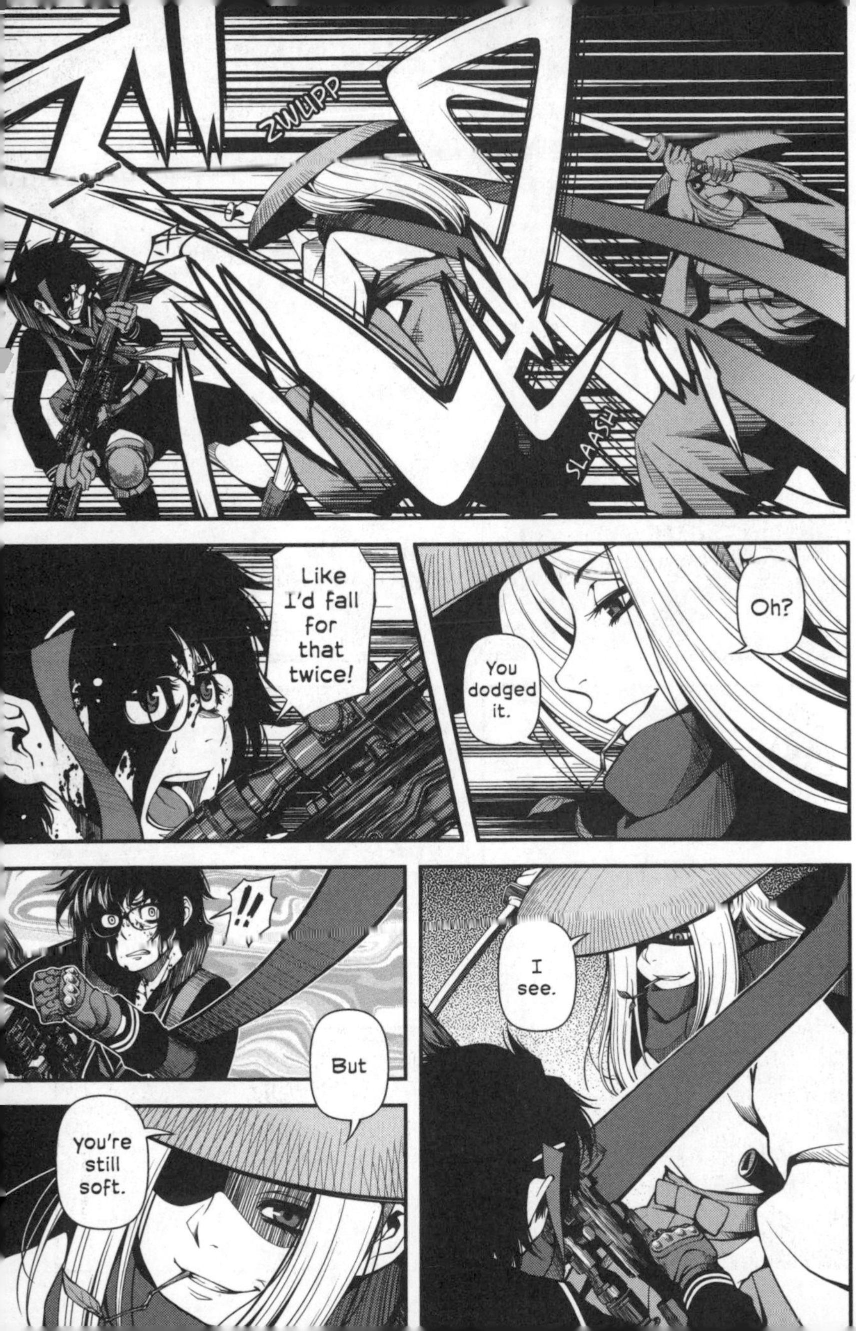
ZWUPP
SLAASH
Oh?
You dodged it.
Like I'd fall for that twice!
I see.
!!
But
you're still soft.

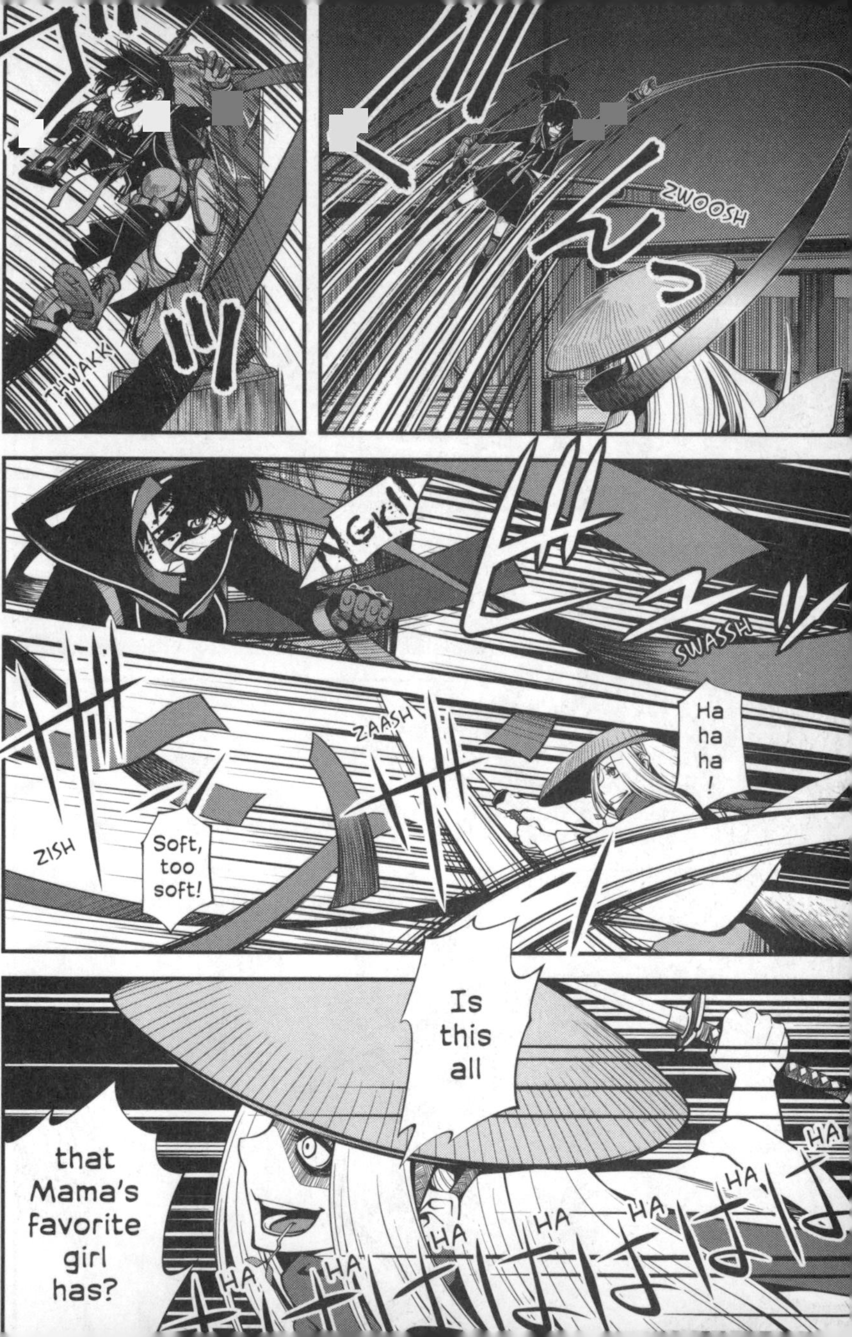
ZWOOSH
THWAKK
GK!
SWASSH
Ha ha ha!
ZAASH
Soft, too soft!
ZISH
Is this all
that Mama's favorite girl has?
HA HA HA HA HA HA HA

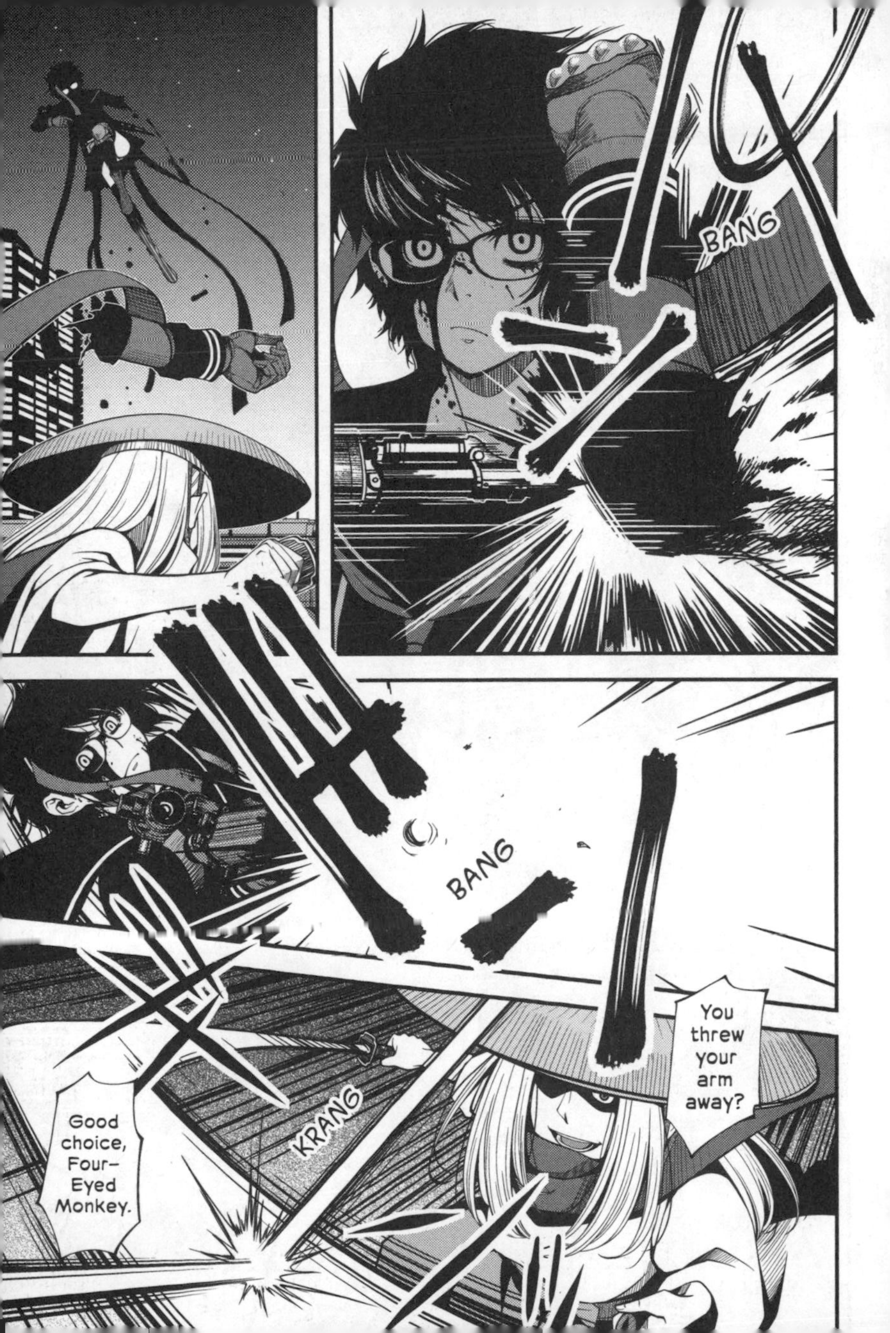
BANG
BANG
You threw your arm away?
KRANG
Good choice, Four-Eyed Monkey.

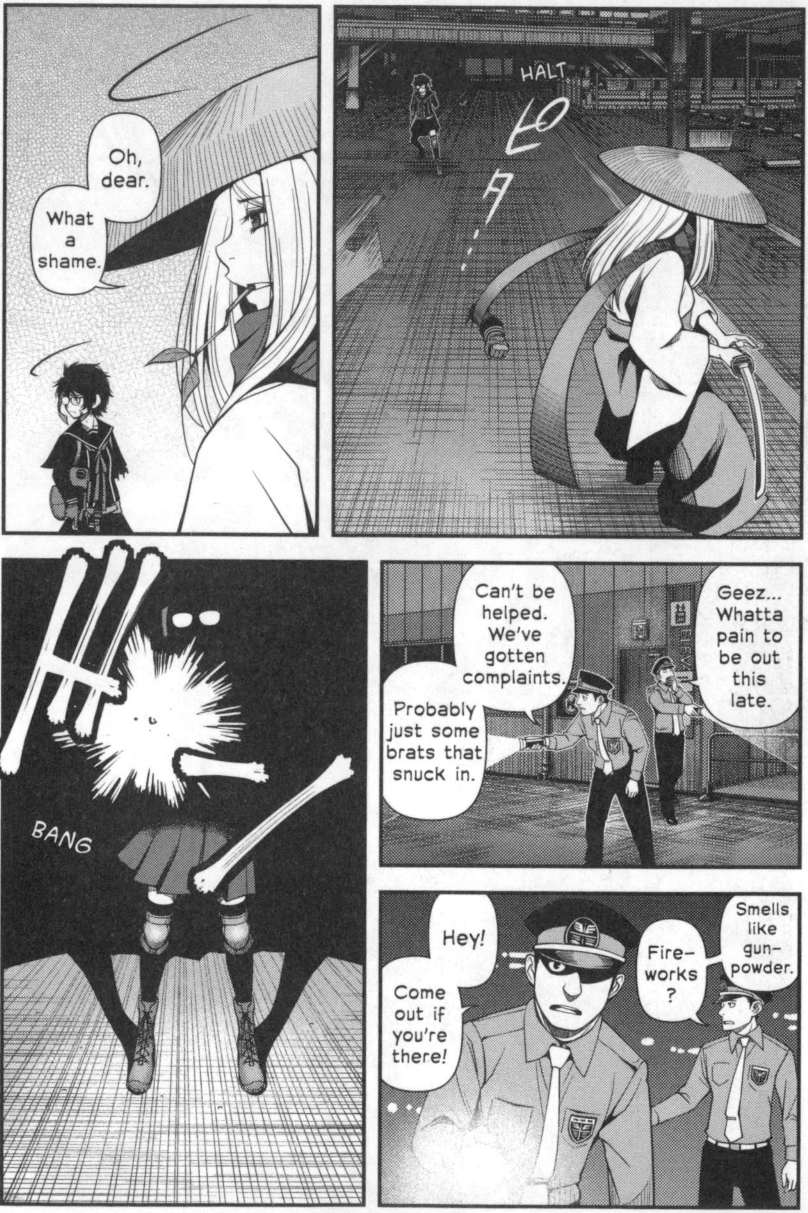
HALT
Oh, dear.
What a shame.
Geez... Whatta pain to be out this late.
Can't be helped. We've gotten complaints.
Probably just some brats that snuck in.
Smells like gun-powder.
Fire-works?
Hey!
Come out if you're there!
BANG

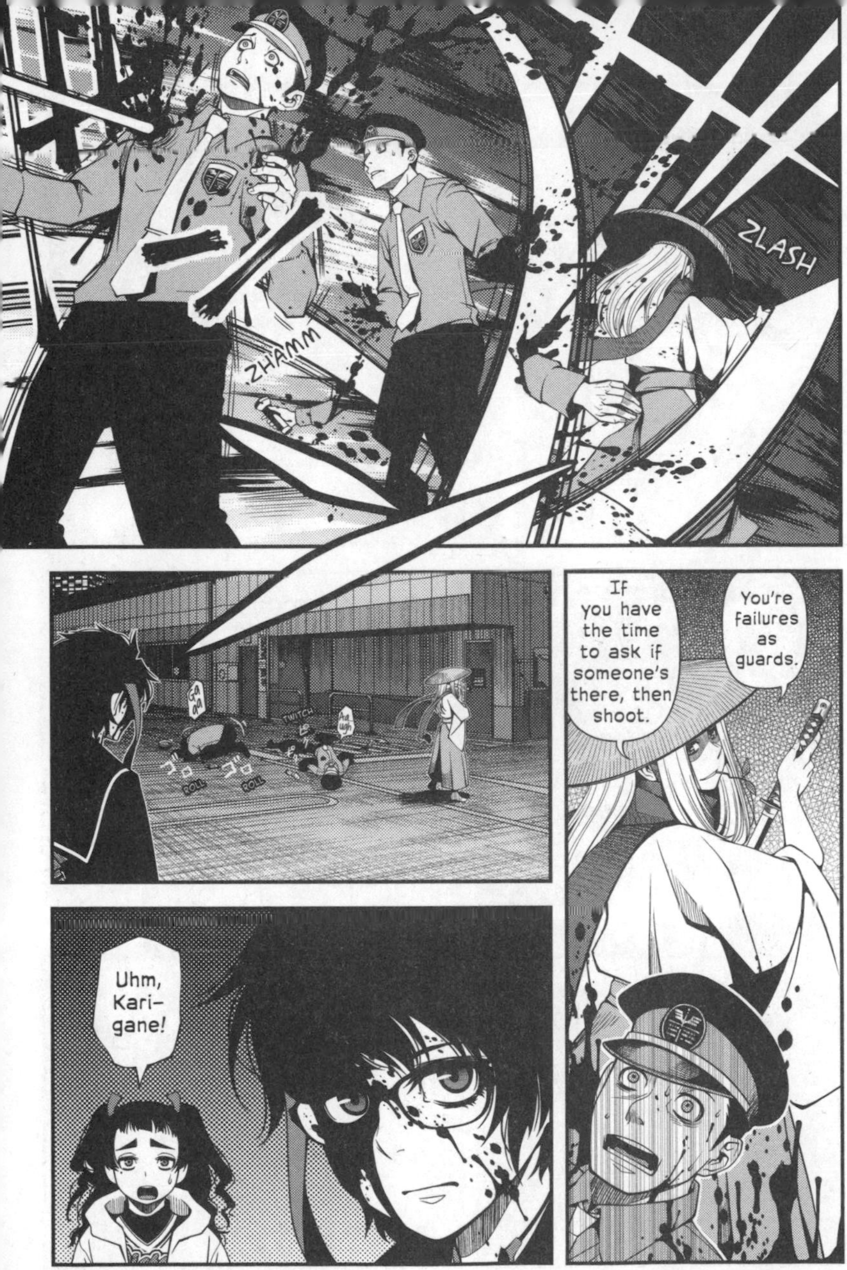
ZLASH
ZHAMM
You're failures as guards.
If you have the time to ask if someone's there, then shoot.
Aaugh
TWITCH
Gaaa
ROLL
ROLL
Uhm, Kari-gane!

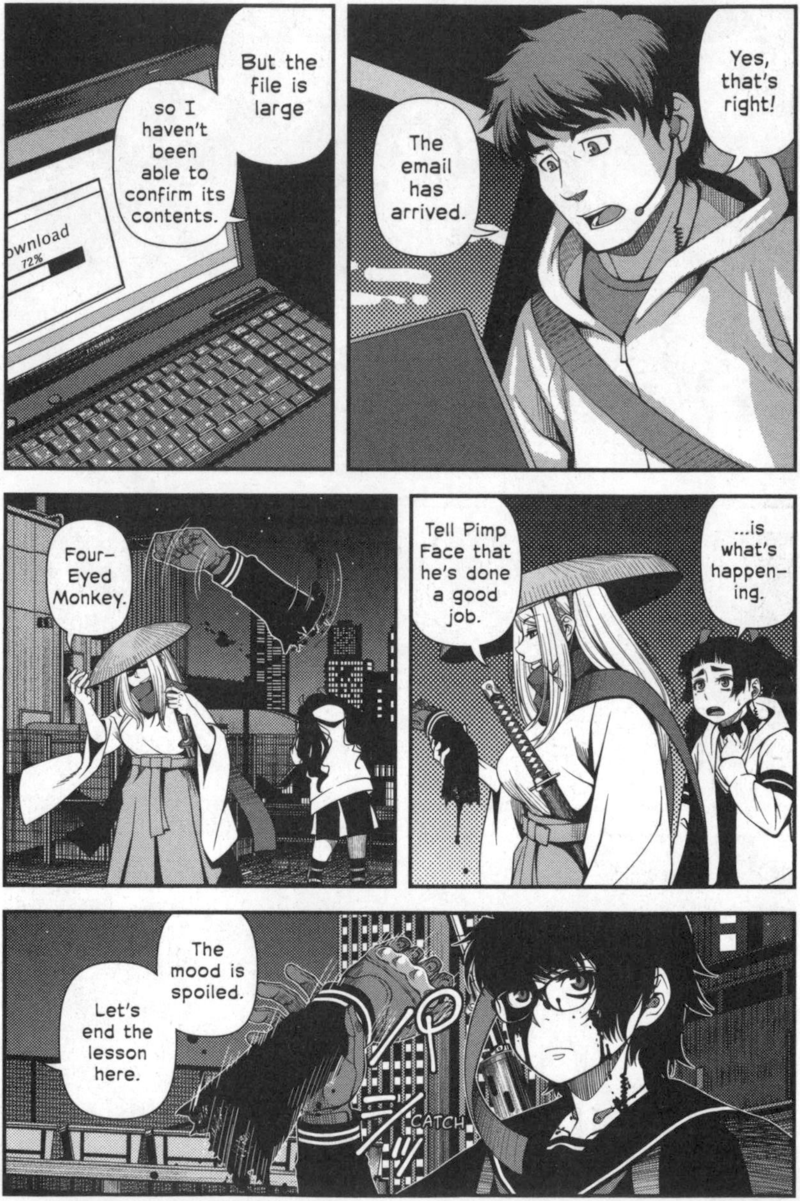
Yes, that's right!
The email has arrived.
But the file is large
so I haven't been able to confirm its contents.
...is what's happening.
Tell Pimp Face that he's done a good job.
Four-Eyed Monkey.
The mood is spoiled.
Let's end the lesson here.
CATCH

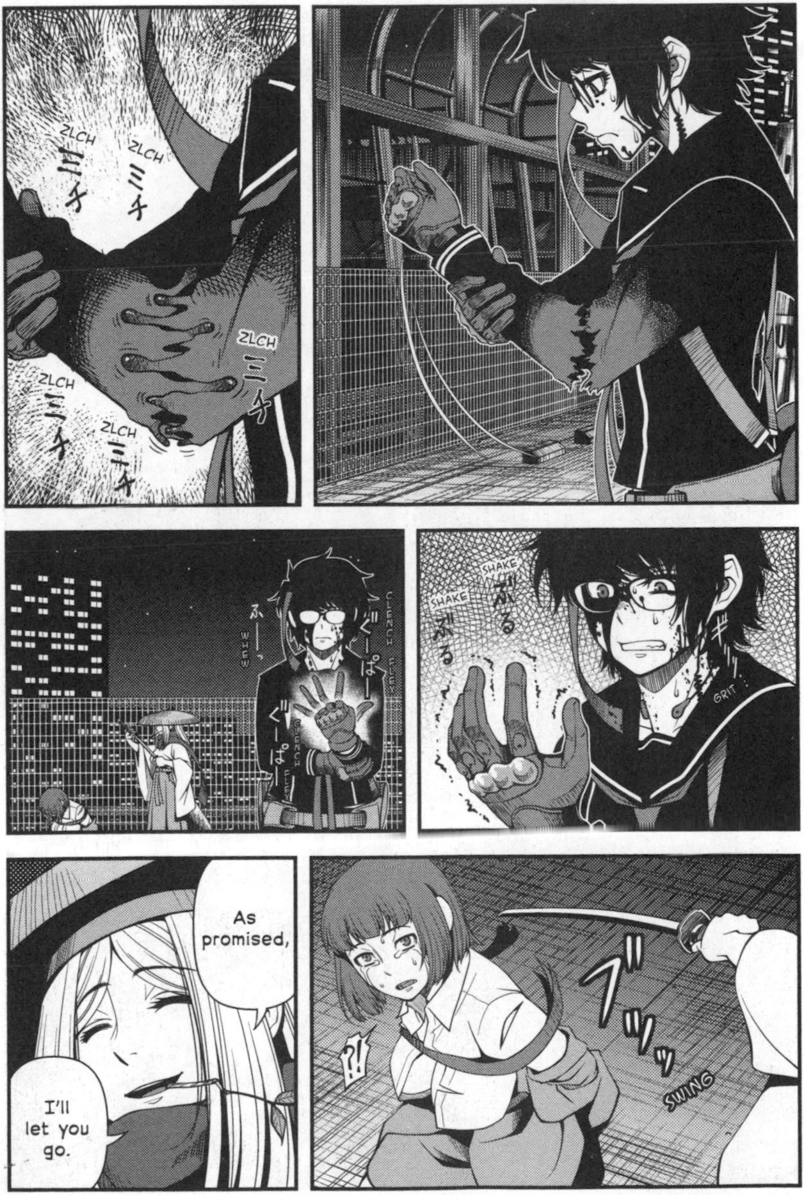
ZLCH
ZLCH
ZLCH
ZLCH
ZLCH
SHAKE ぶる
SHAKE ぶる
GRIT
CLENCH ぐーぱー
FLEX
CLENCH ぐーぱー
FLEX
WHEW ふー
SWING
?!
As promised,
I'll let you go.

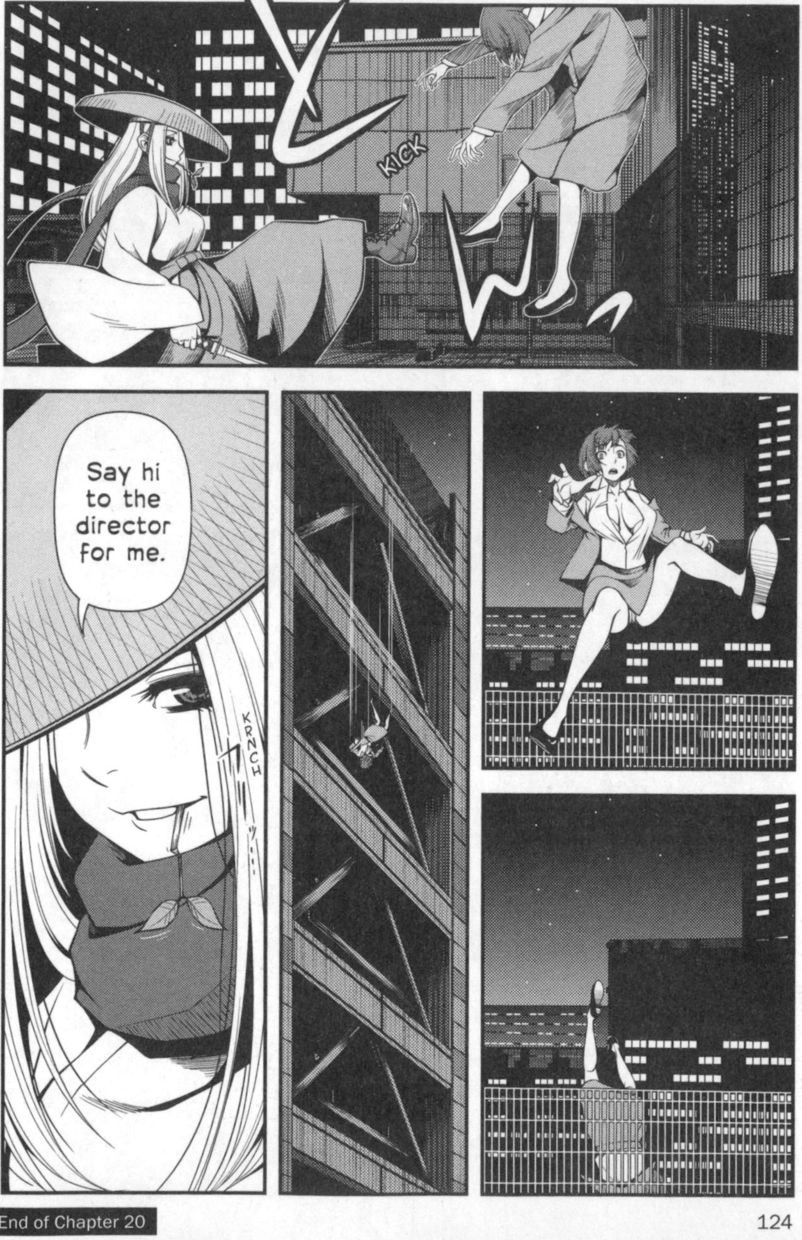
KICK
Say hi to the director for me.
KRNCH

21
Karigane (Part 3)

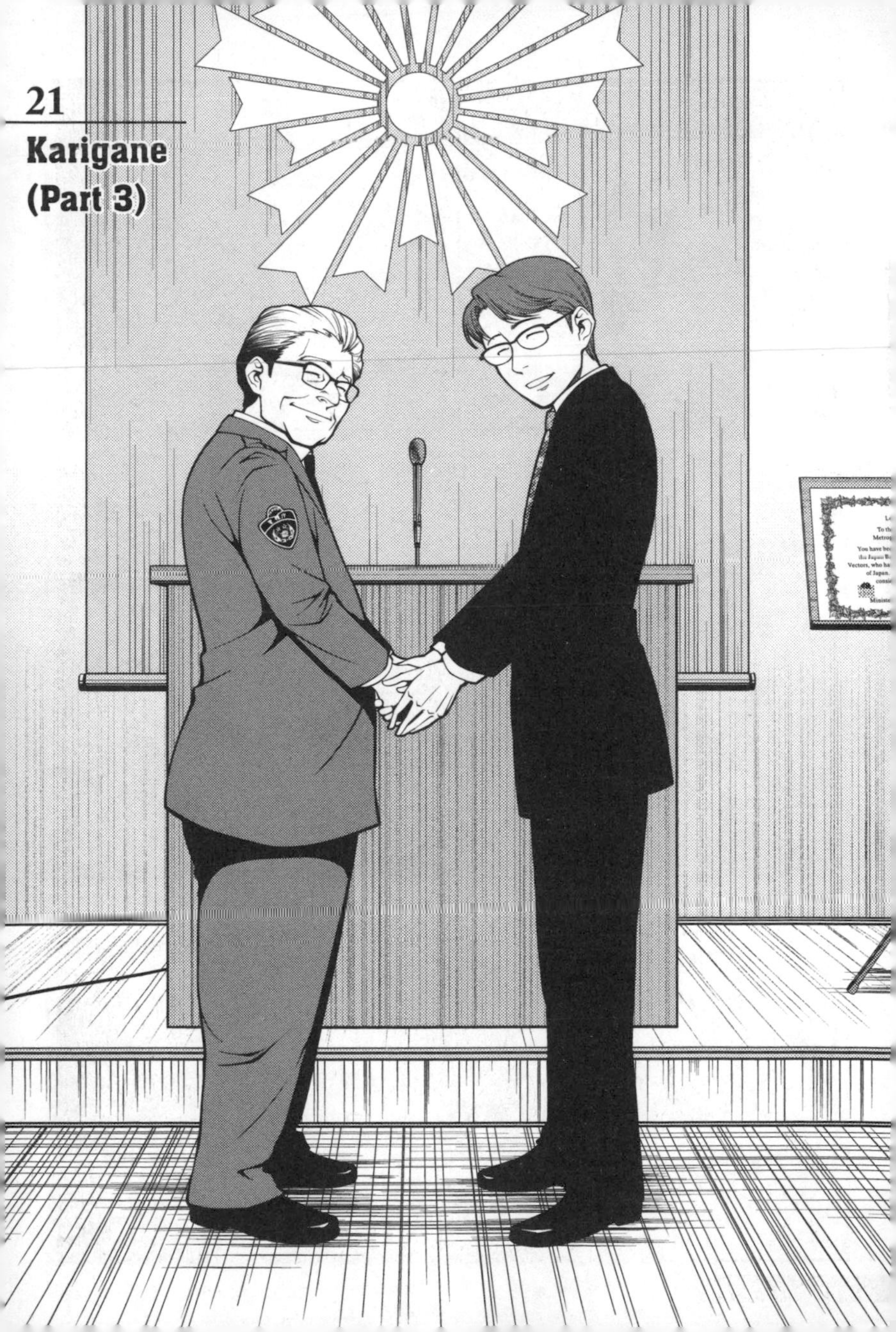

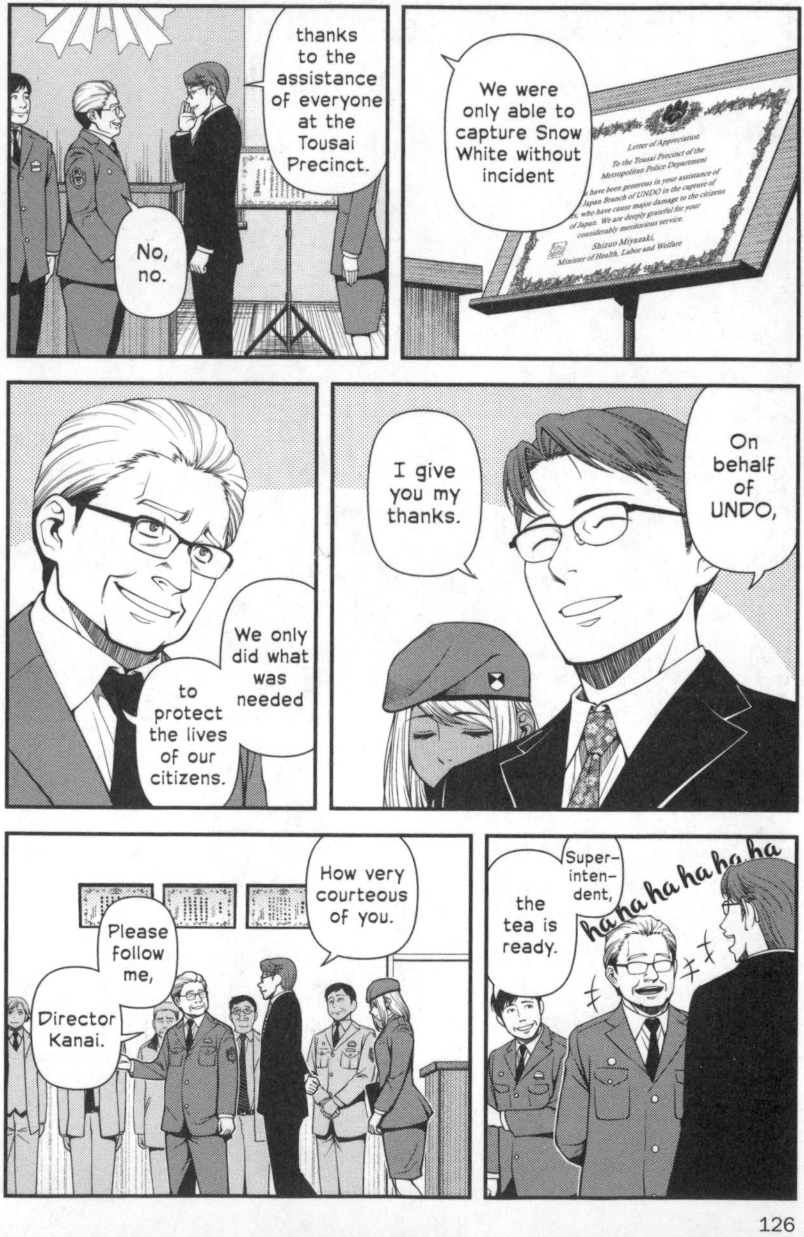
We were only able to capture Snow White without incident
Letter of Appreciation
To the Tousai Precinct of the
Metropolitan Police Department
Japan Branch of UNDO in the capture of
who have cause major damage to the citizens
of Japan. We are deeply grateful for your
considerably meritorious service.
Shizuo Miyazaki,
Minister of Health, Labor and Welfare
thanks to the assistance of everyone at the Tousai Precinct.
No, no.
On behalf of UNDO,
I give you my thanks.
We only did what was needed
to protect the lives of our citizens.
Superintendent,
the tea is ready.
hahahahahaha
How very courteous of you.
Please follow me,
Director Kanai.

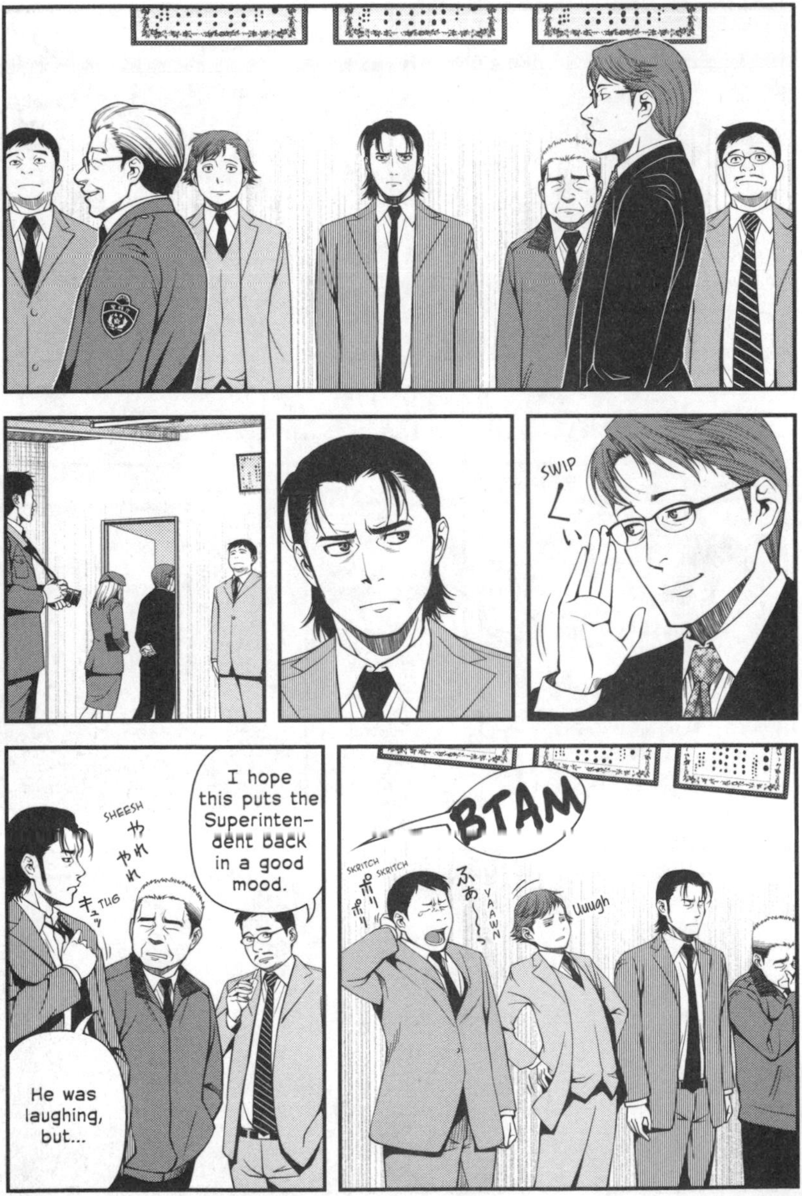
SWIP
くい
BTAM
SKRITCH SKRITCH
ポリポリ
ふあ~っ
YAAWN
Uuugh
I hope this puts the Superinten-dent back in a good mood.
SHEESH
やれやれ
キュッ
TUG
He was laughing, but...

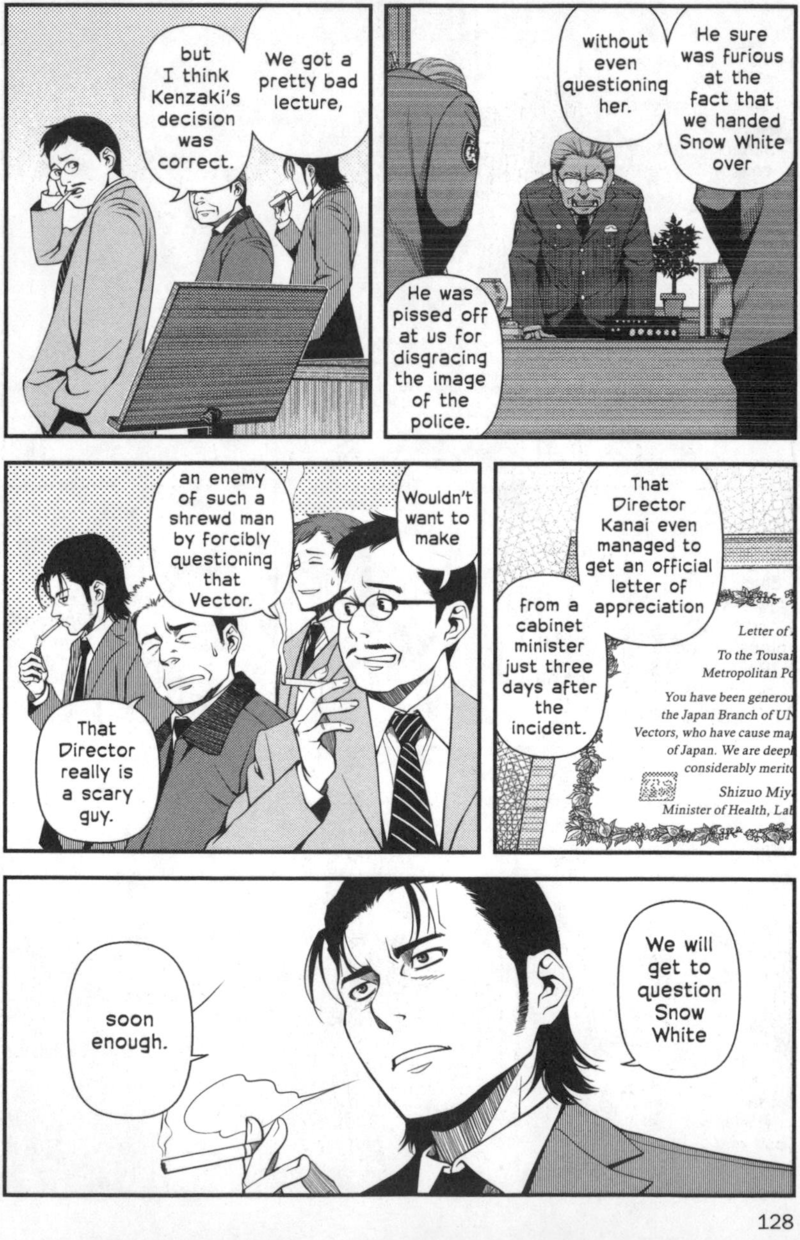
He sure was furious at the fact that we handed Snow White over
without even questioning her.
He was pissed off at us for disgracing the image of the police.
We got a pretty bad lecture,
but I think Kenzaki's decision was correct.
That Director Kanai even managed to get an official letter of appreciation
from a cabinet minister just three days after the incident.
Wouldn't want to make
an enemy of such a shrewd man by forcibly questioning that Vector.
That Director really is a scary guy.
We will get to question Snow White
soon enough.

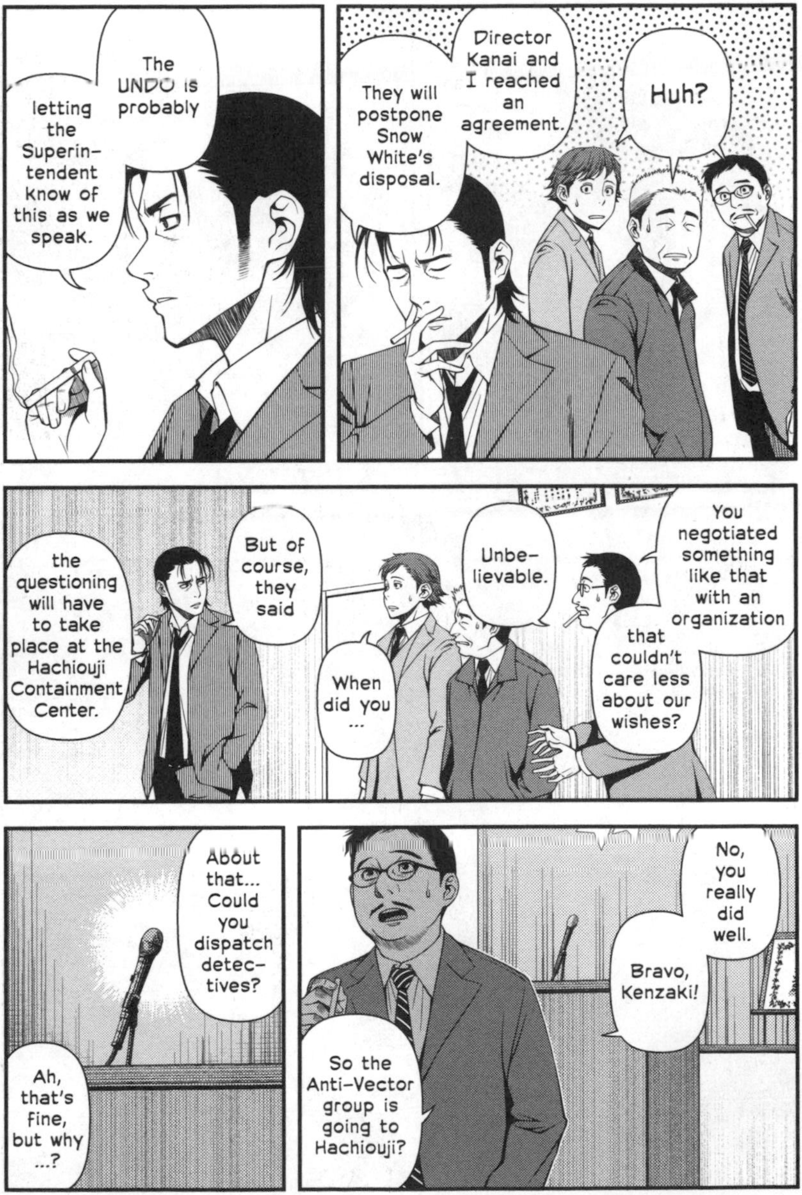
Huh?
Director Kanai and I reached an agreement.
They will postpone Snow White's disposal.
The UNDO is probably
letting the Superintendent know of this as we speak.
You negotiated something like that with an organization
that couldn't care less about our wishes?
Unbelievable.
When did you ...
But of course, they said
the questioning will have to take place at the Hachiouji Containment Center.
No, you really did well.
Bravo, Kenzaki!
So the Anti-Vector group is going to Hachiouji?
About that... Could you dispatch detectives?
Ah, that's fine, but why ...?

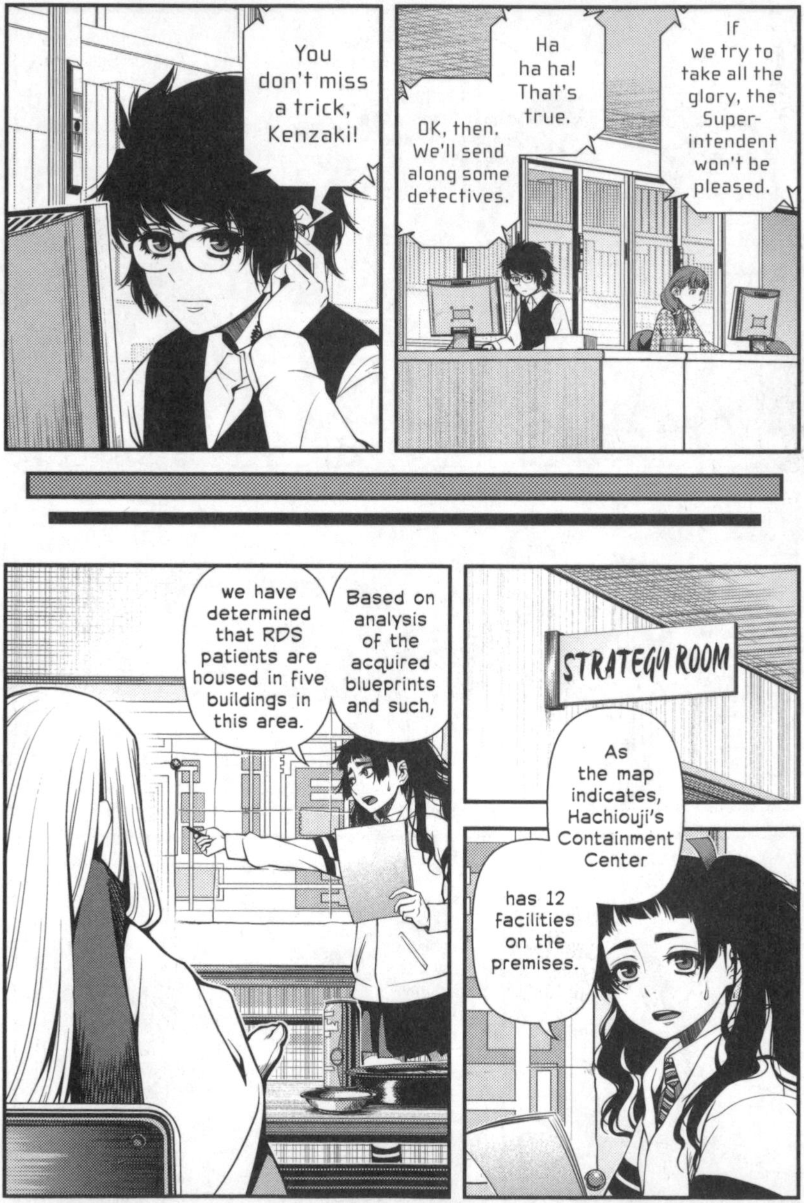
If we try to take all the glory, the Super-intendent won't be pleased.
Ha ha ha! That's true.
OK, then. We'll send along some detectives.
You don't miss a trick, Kenzaki!
STRATEGY ROOM
As the map indicates, Hachiouji's Containment Center
has 12 facilities on the premises.
Based on analysis of the acquired blueprints and such,
we have determined that RDS patients are housed in five buildings in this area.

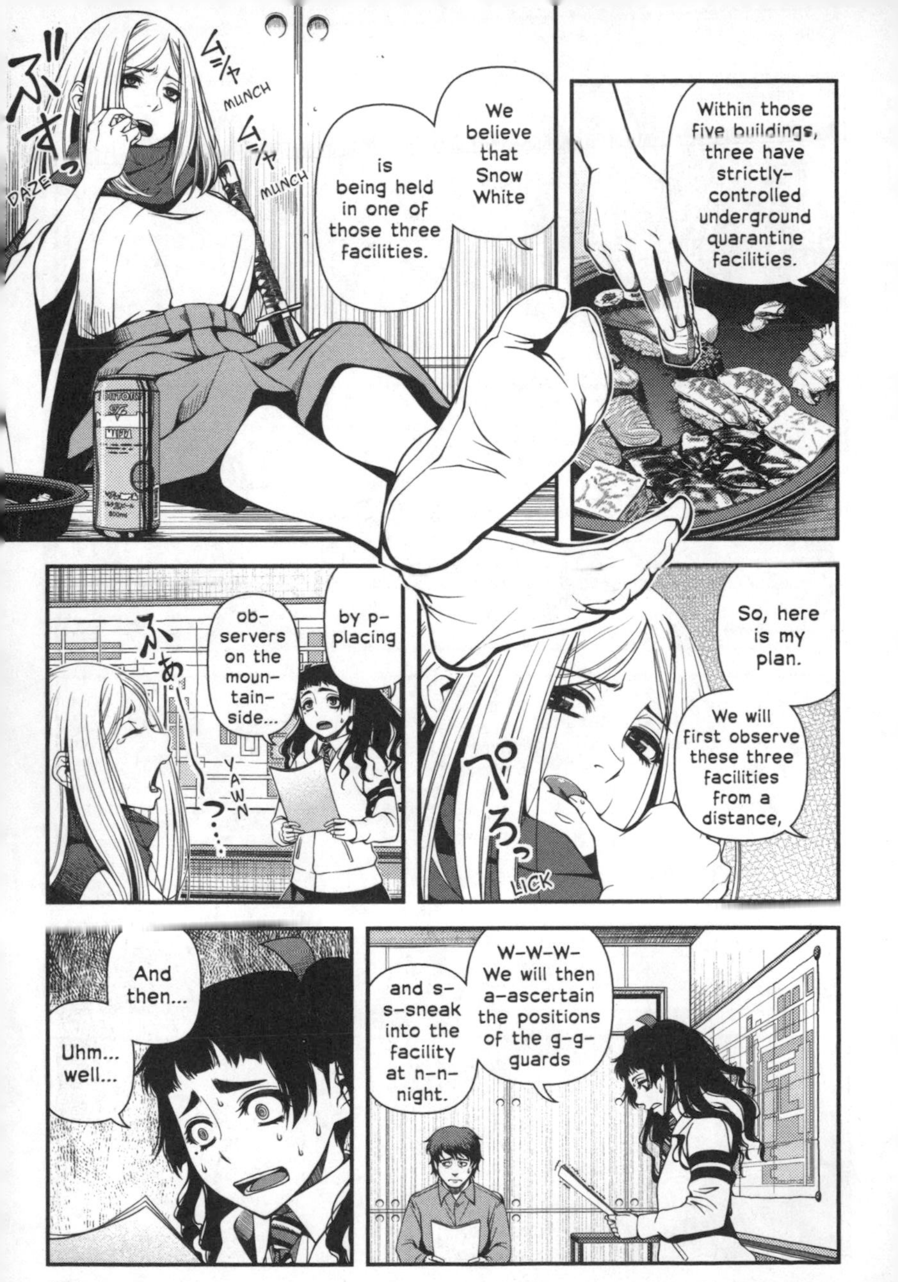

Within those five buildings, three have strictly-controlled underground quarantine facilities.
We believe that Snow White
is being held in one of those three facilities.
ムシャ
MUNCH
ムシャ
MUNCH
ぶすっ
DAZE
So, here is my plan.
We will first observe these three facilities from a distance,
ぺろっ
LICK
by p-placing
ob-servers on the moun-tain-side...
ふぁ
YAWN
W-W-W-We will then a-ascertain the positions of the g-g-guards
and s-s-sneak into the facility at n-n-night.
And then...
Uhm... well...

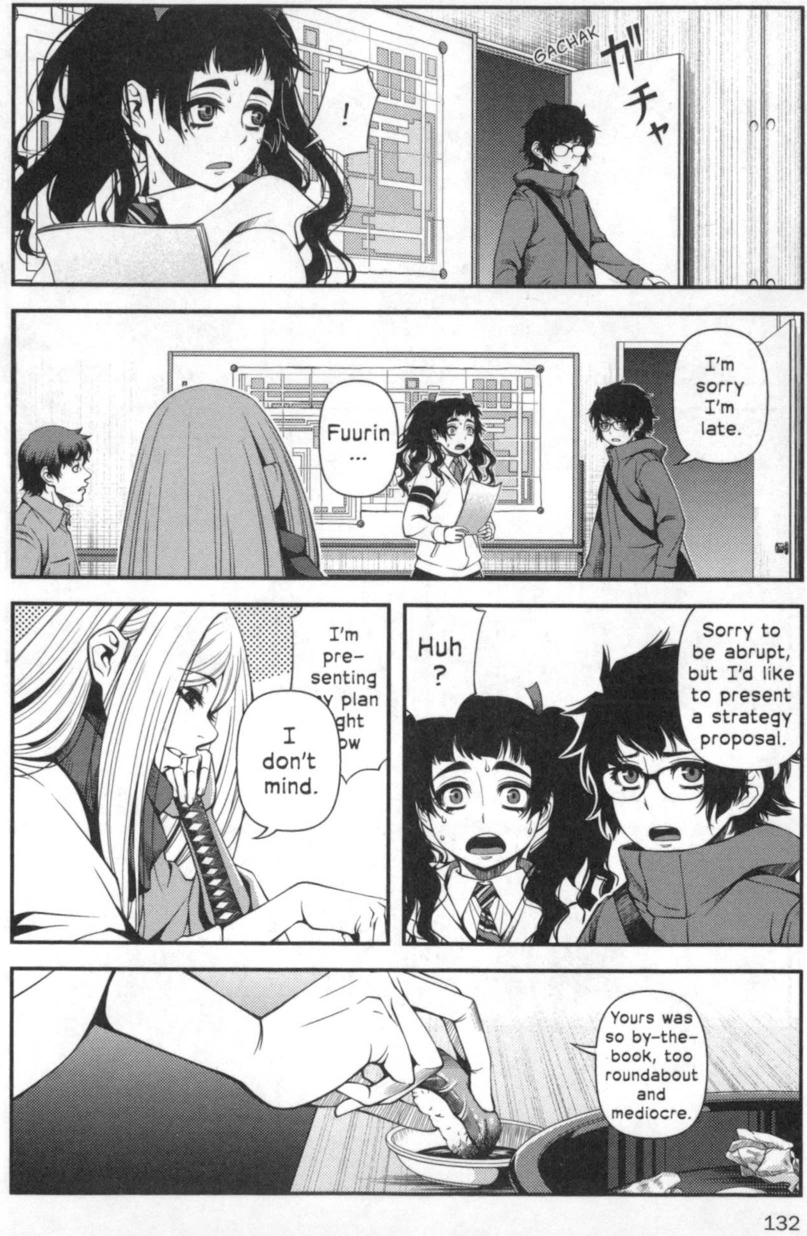
ガチャ
GACHAK
!
I'm sorry I'm late.
Fuurin ...
Sorry to be abrupt, but I'd like to present a strategy proposal.
Huh ?
I'm presenting
I don't mind.
Yours was so by-the-book, too roundabout and mediocre.

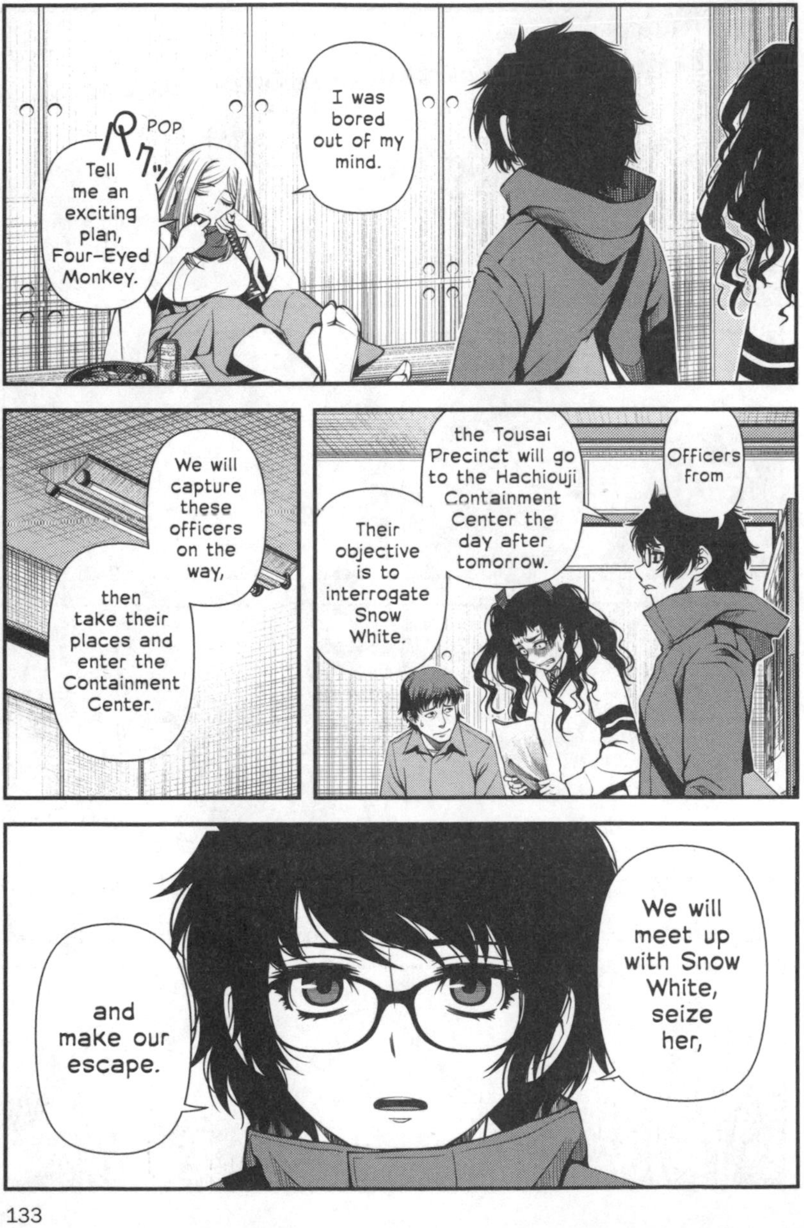

I was bored out of my mind.
パクッ
POP
Tell me an exciting plan, Four-Eyed Monkey.
Officers from
the Tousai Precinct will go to the Hachiouji Containment Center the day after tomorrow.
Their objective is to interrogate Snow White.
We will capture these officers on the way,
then take their places and enter the Containment Center.
We will meet up with Snow White, seize her,
and make our escape.

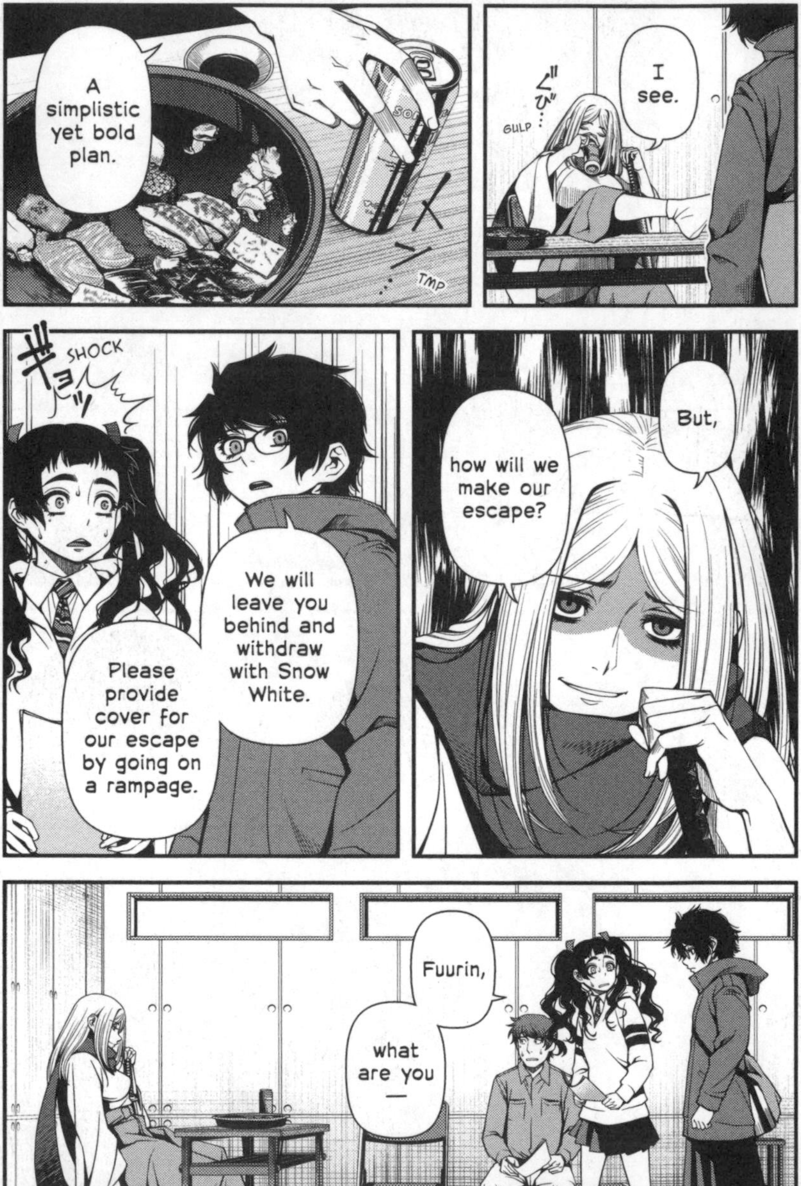
I see.
GULP
A simplistic yet bold plan.
TMP
But,
how will we make our escape?
SHOCK
We will leave you behind and withdraw with Snow White.
Please provide cover for our escape by going on a rampage.
Fuurin,
what are you —

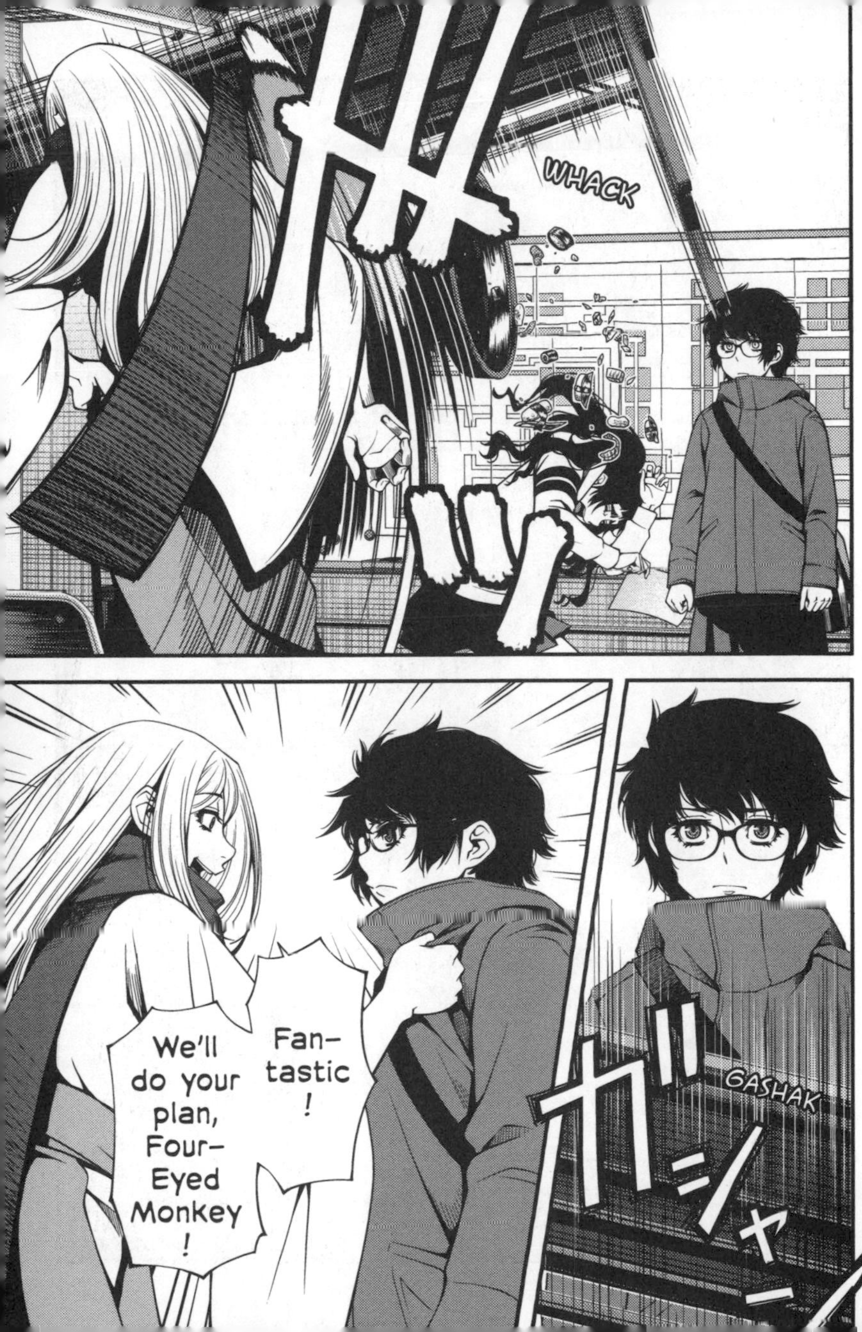
WHACK
GASHAK
Fan-tastic!
We'll do your plan, Four-Eyed Monkey!

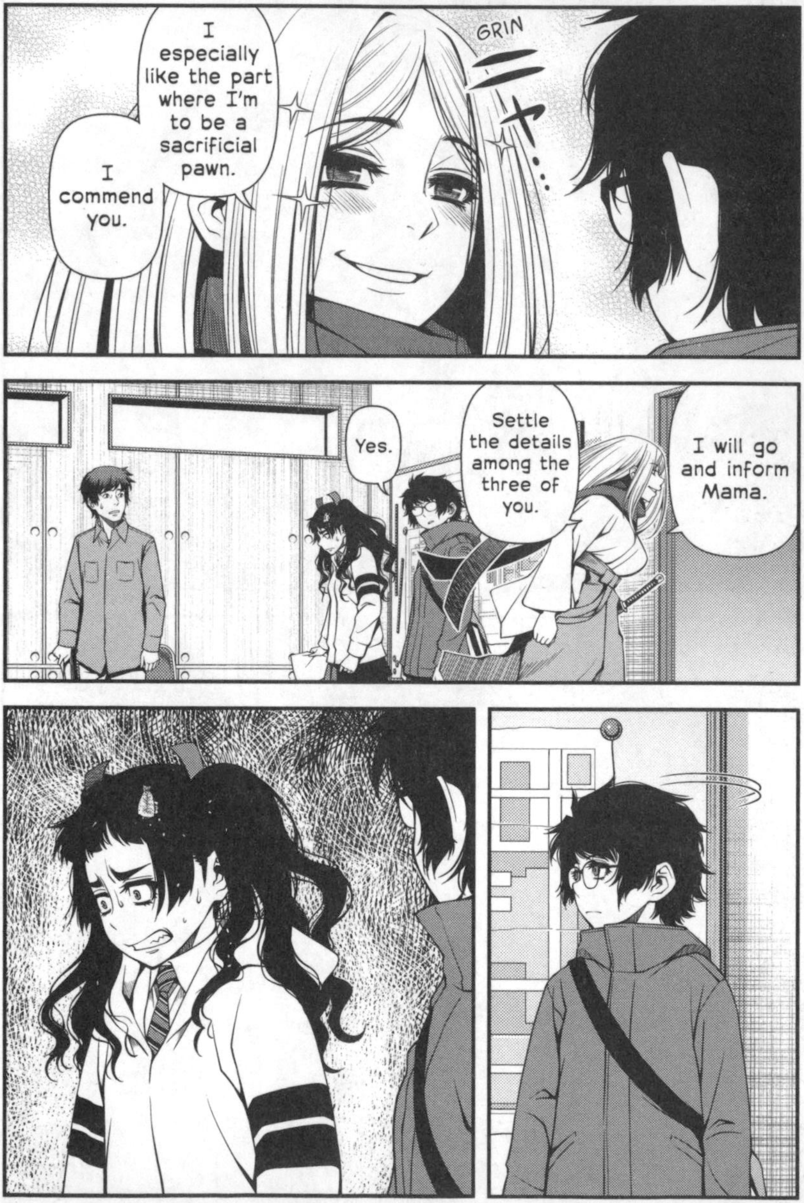
GRIN
I especially like the part where I'm to be a sacrificial pawn.
I commend you.
I will go and inform Mama.
Settle the details among the three of you.
Yes.

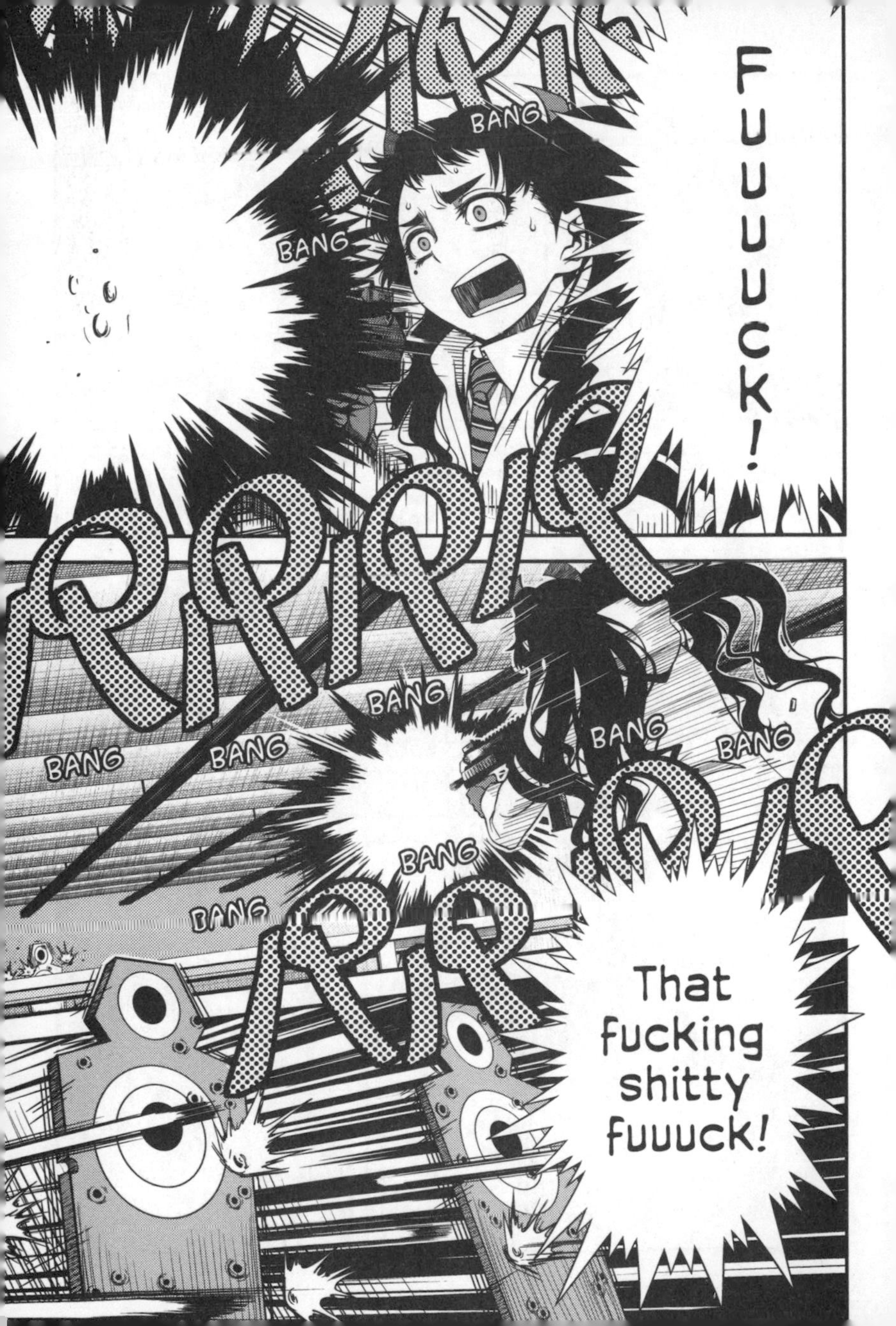
FUUUUCK!
BANG
BANG
BANG
BANG
BANG
BANG
BANG
BANG
That fucking shitty fuuuck!

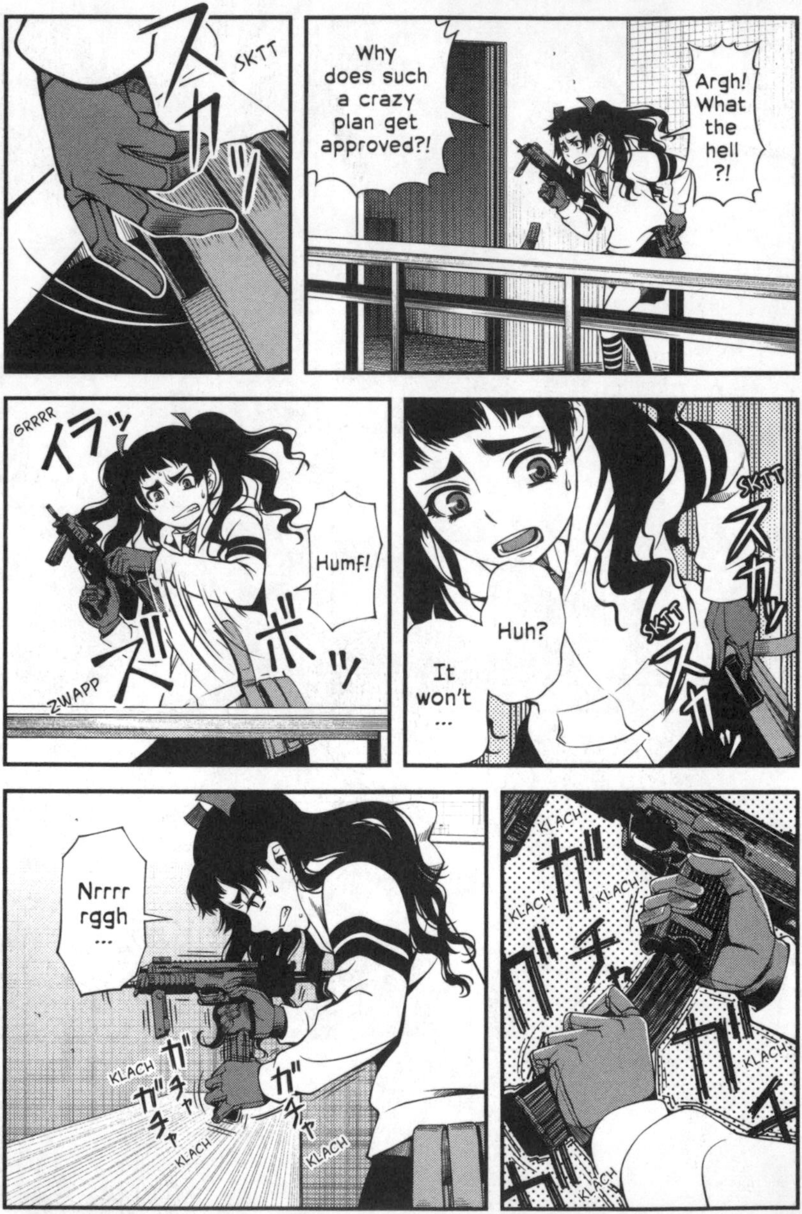
Argh! What the hell ?!
Why does such a crazy plan get approved?!
SKTT
SKTT
Huh?
It won't ...
SKTT
GRRRR
Humf!
ZWAPP
KLACH
KLACH
KLACH
KLACH
KLACH
Nrrrr rggh ...
KLACH
KLACH
KLACH

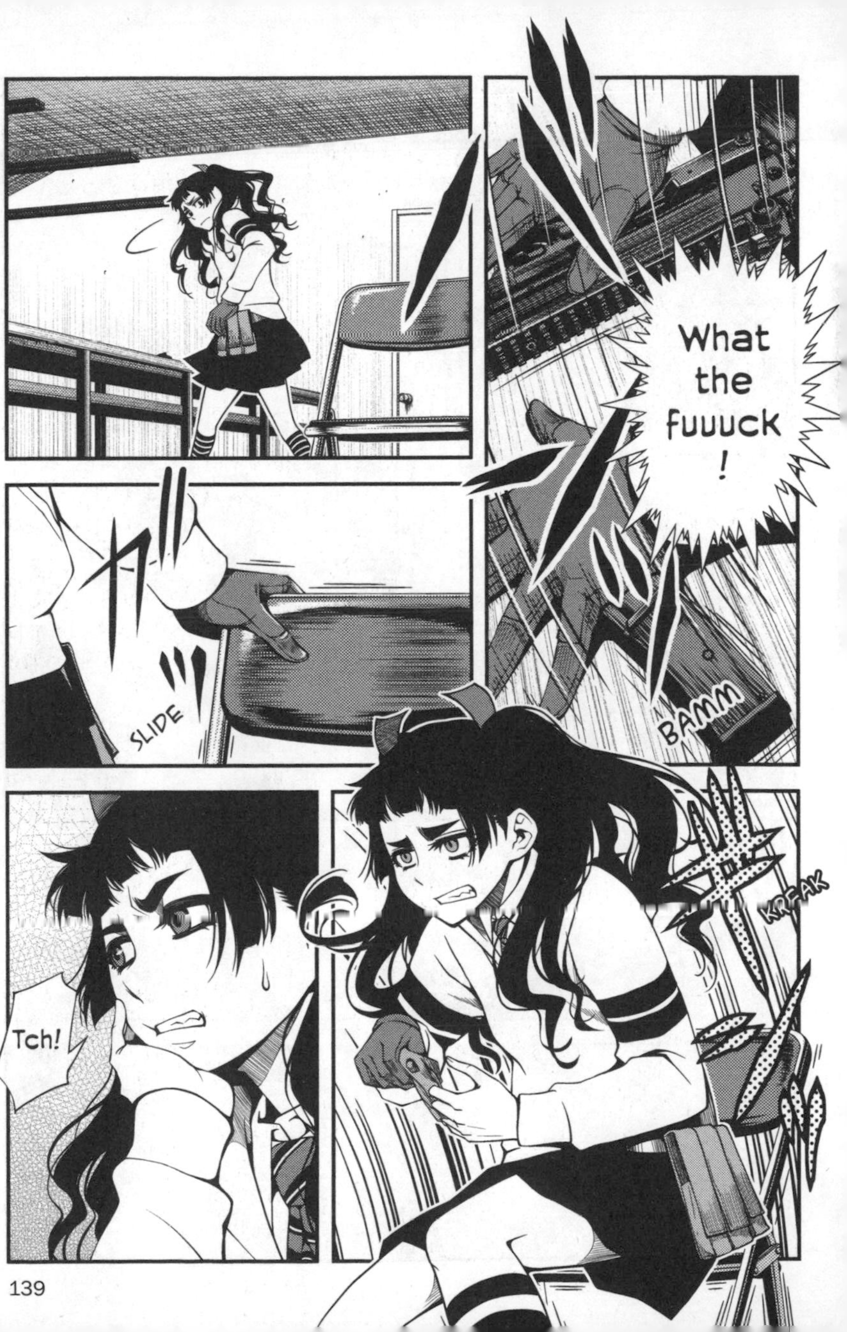

What the fuuuck!
BAMM
SLIDE
KRAK
Tch!

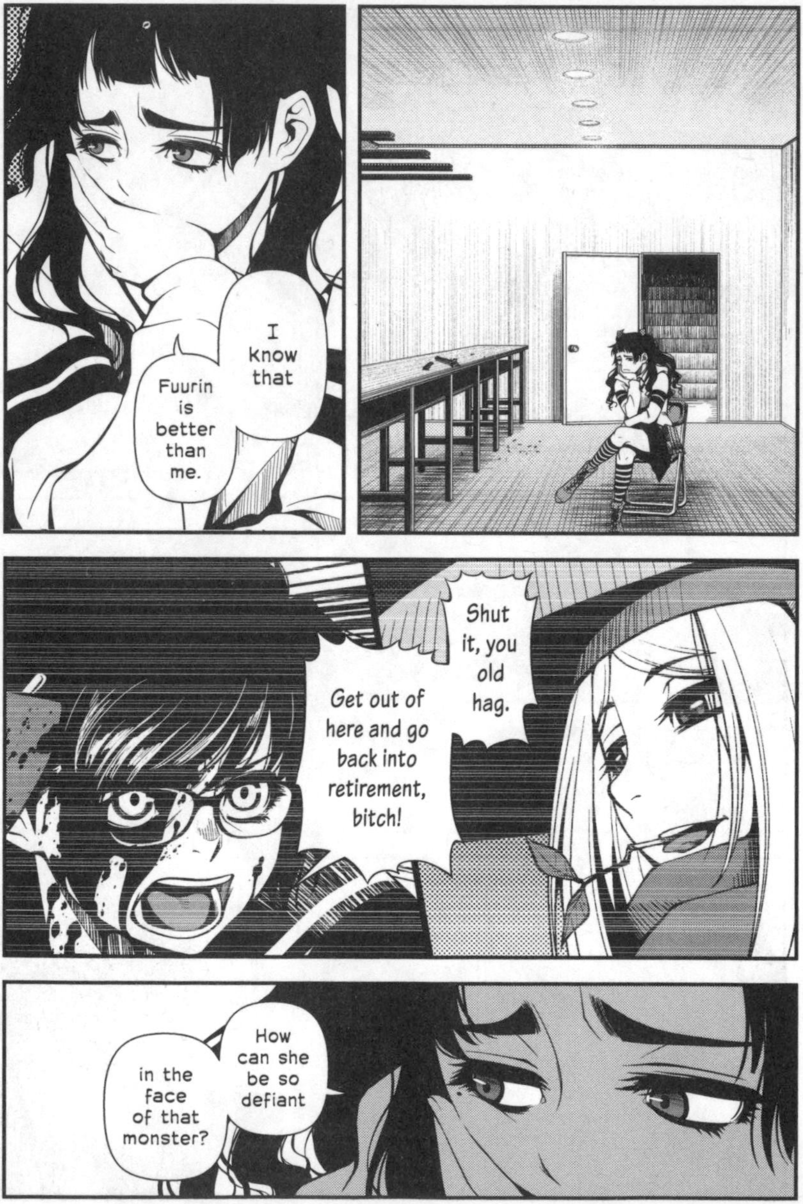

I know that
Fuurin is better than me.
Shut it, you old hag.
Get out of here and go back into retirement, bitch!
How can she be so defiant
in the face of that monster?

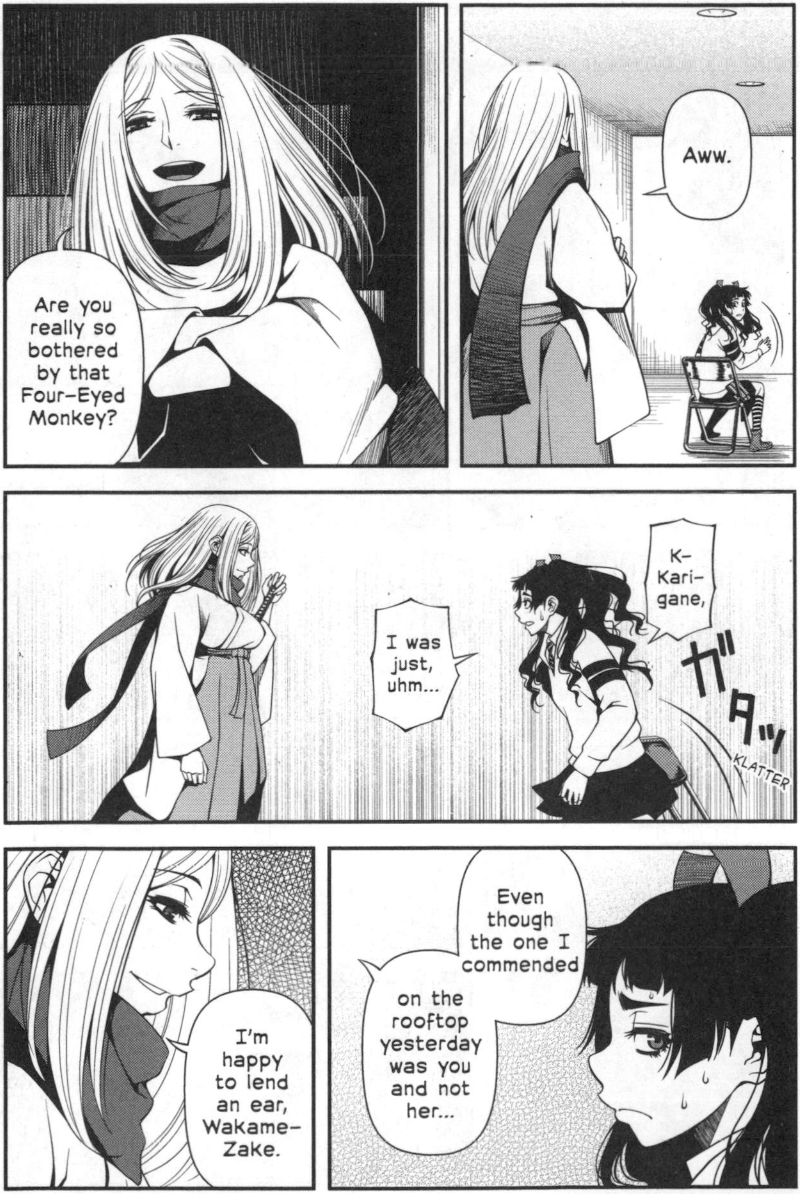
Aww.
Are you really so bothered by that Four-Eyed Monkey?
K-Kari-gane,
ガタッ
KLATTER
I was just, uhm...
Even though the one I commended
on the rooftop yesterday was you and not her...
I'm happy to lend an ear, Wakame-Zake.

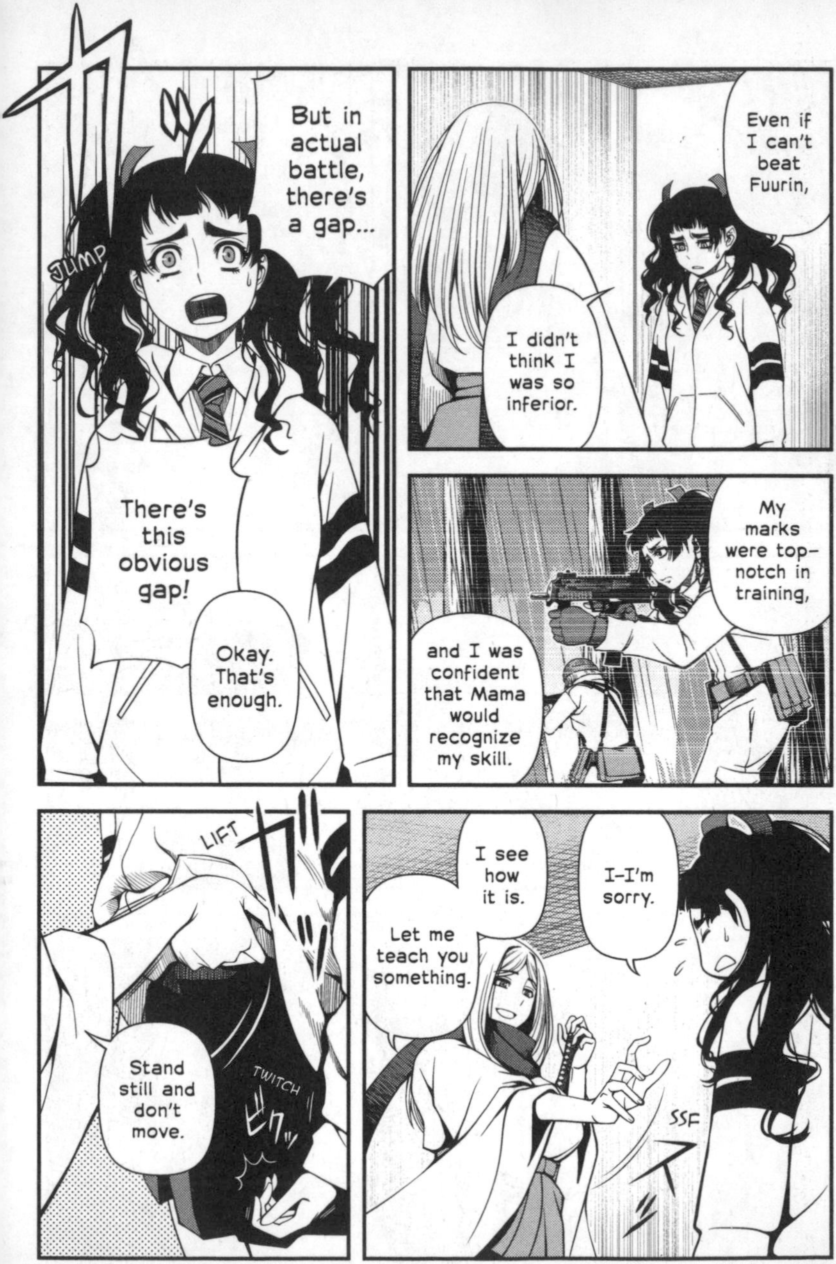
Even if I can't beat Fuurin,
I didn't think I was so inferior.
My marks were top-notch in training,
and I was confident that Mama would recognize my skill.
JUMP
But in actual battle, there's a gap...
There's this obvious gap!
Okay. That's enough.
I-I'm sorry.
I see how it is.
Let me teach you something.
SSF
LIFT
Stand still and don't move.
TWITCH

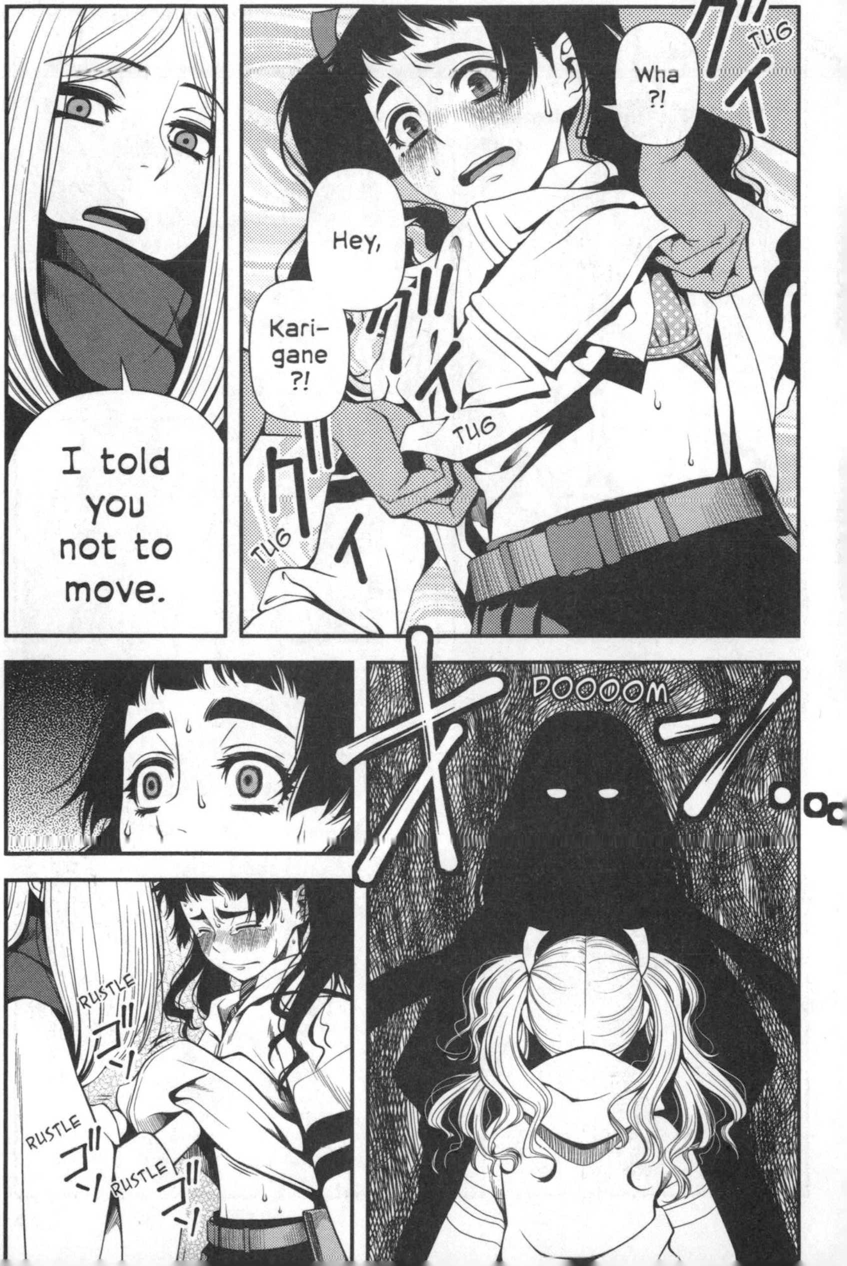
Wha ?!
TUG
Hey,
Kari- gane ?!
TUG
TUG
I told you not to move.
DOOOOM
RUSTLE
RUSTLE
RUSTLE

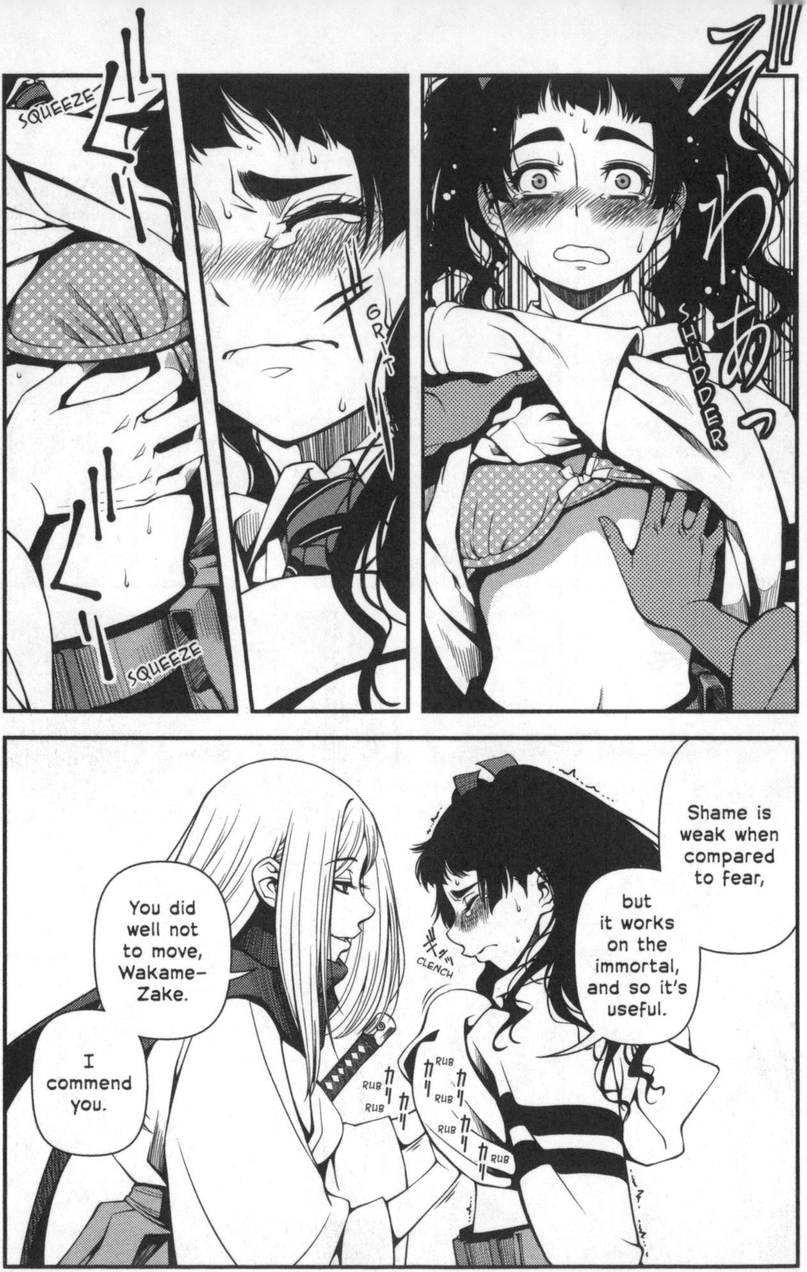
SHUDDER
GRIT
SQUEEZE
SQUEEZE
Shame is weak when compared to fear,
but it works on the immortal, and so it's useful.
CLENCH
You did well not to move, Wakame-Zake.
I commend you.
RUB
RUB
RUB
RUB
RUB
RUB

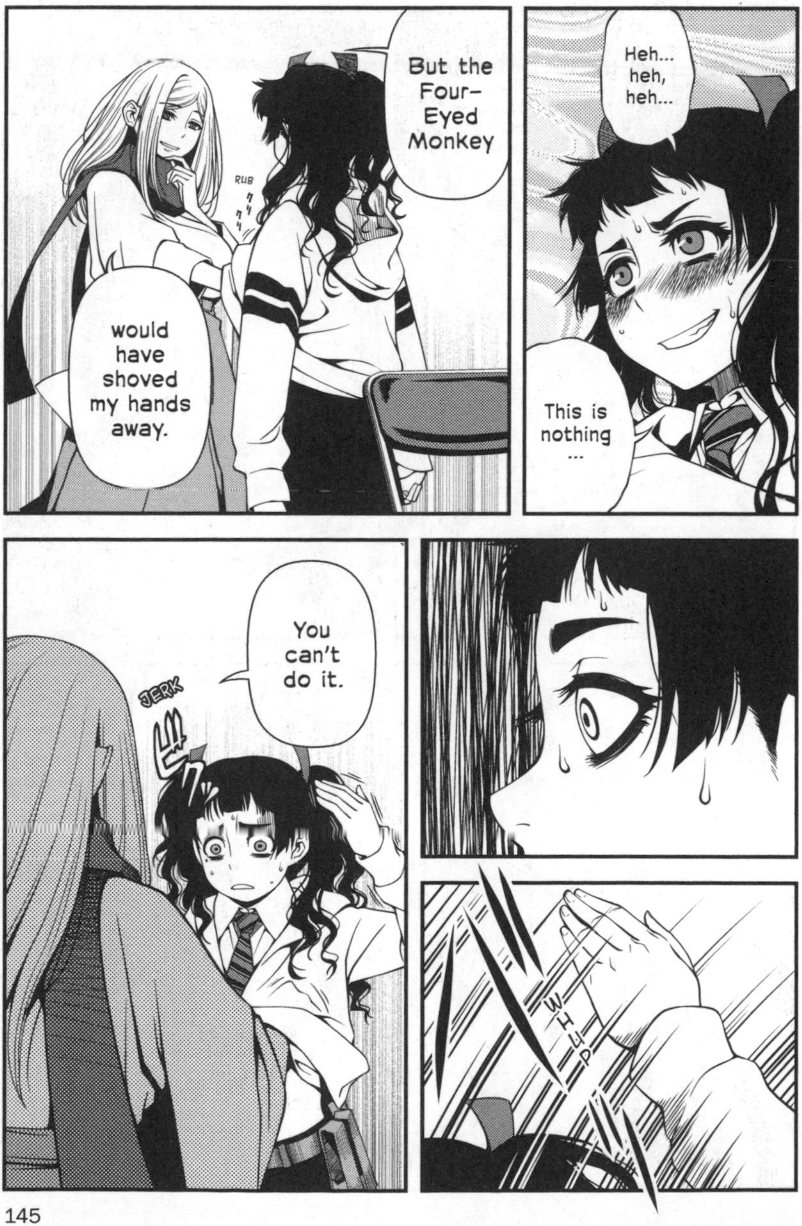
Heh... heh, heh...
This is nothing ...
But the Four-Eyed Monkey
RUB
would have shoved my hands away.
WHUP
JERK
You can't do it.

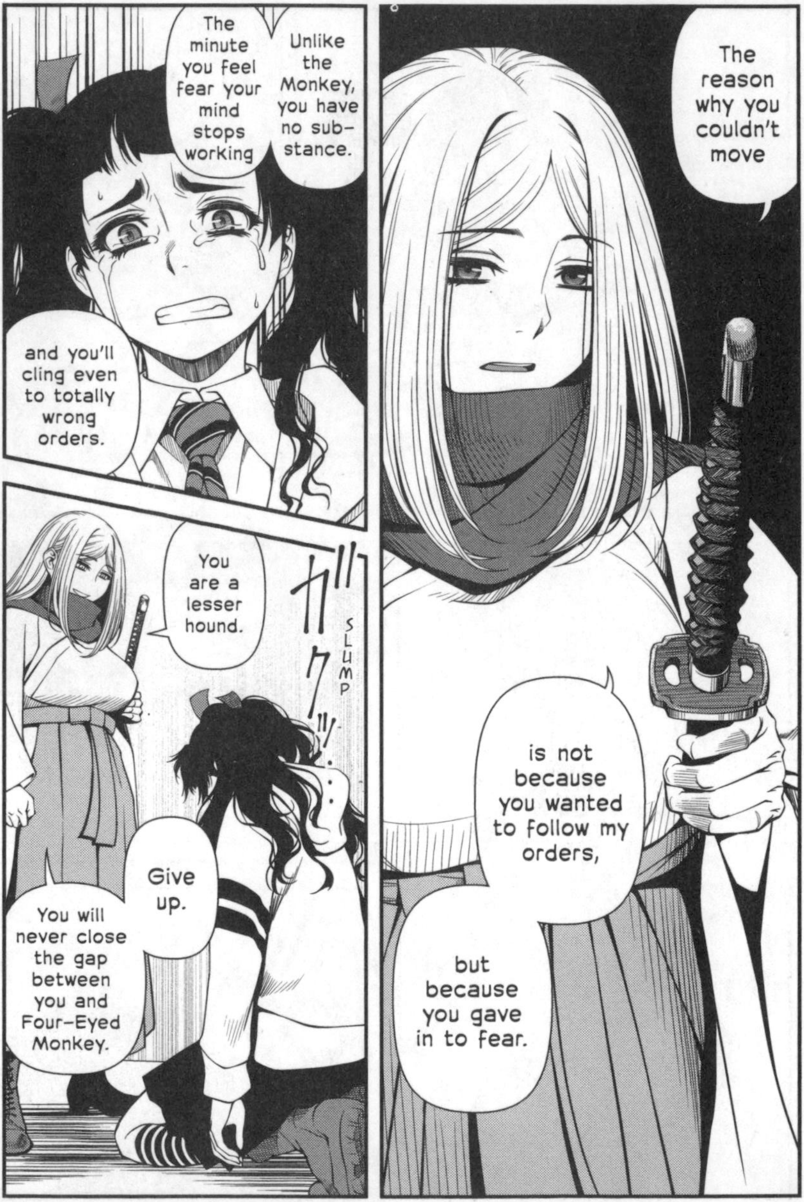
The reason why you couldn't move
is not because you wanted to follow my orders,
but because you gave in to fear.
Unlike the Monkey, you have no sub-stance.
The minute you feel fear your mind stops working
and you'll cling even to totally wrong orders.
SLUMP
You are a lesser hound.
Give up.
You will never close the gap between you and Four-Eyed Monkey.

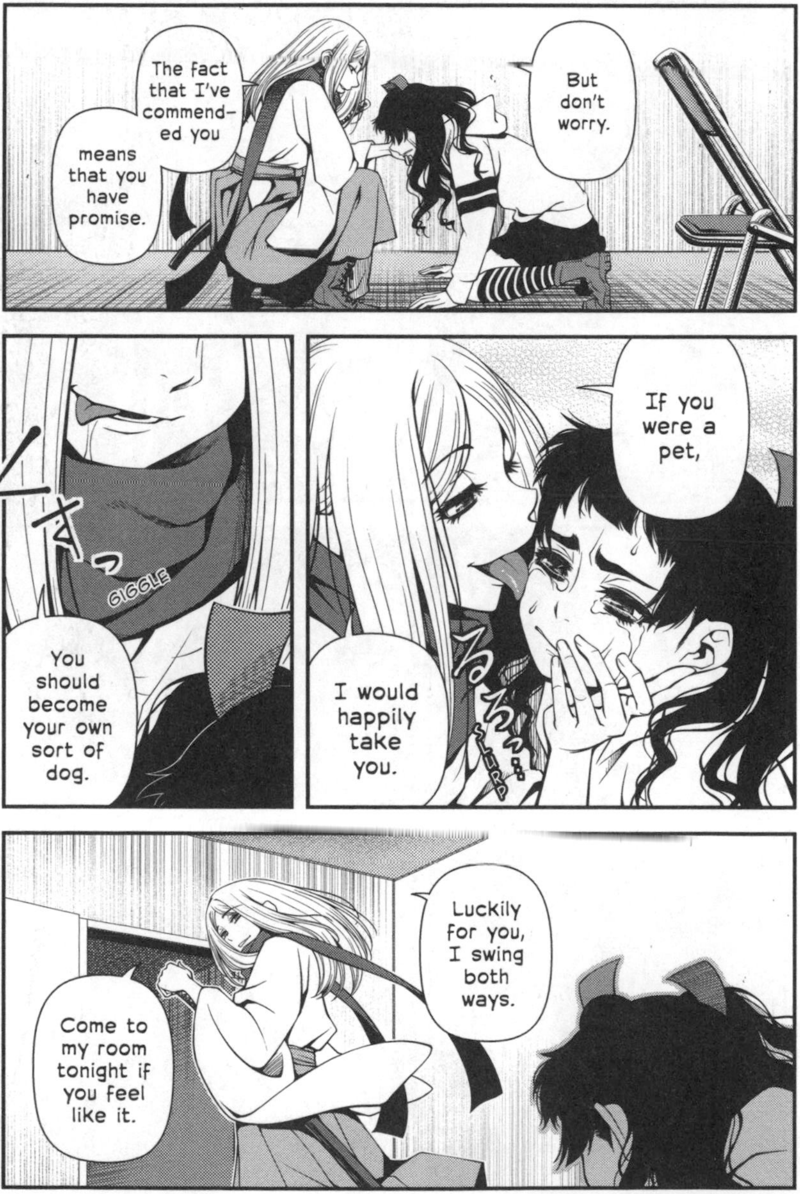
But don't worry.
The fact that I've commend-ed you
means that you have promise.
If you were a pet,
I would happily take you.
SLURP
GIGGLE
You should become your own sort of dog.
Luckily for you, I swing both ways.
Come to my room tonight if you feel like it.

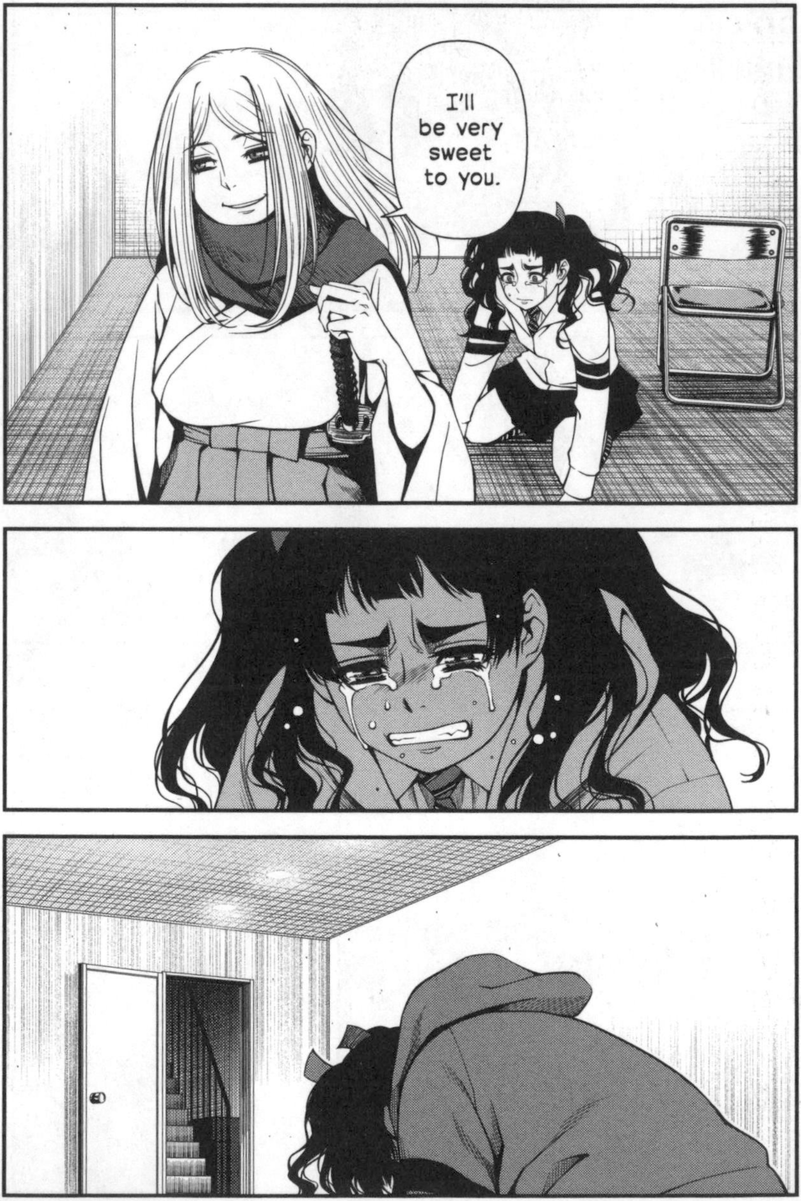
I'll be very sweet to you.

Bonus
Sandwich

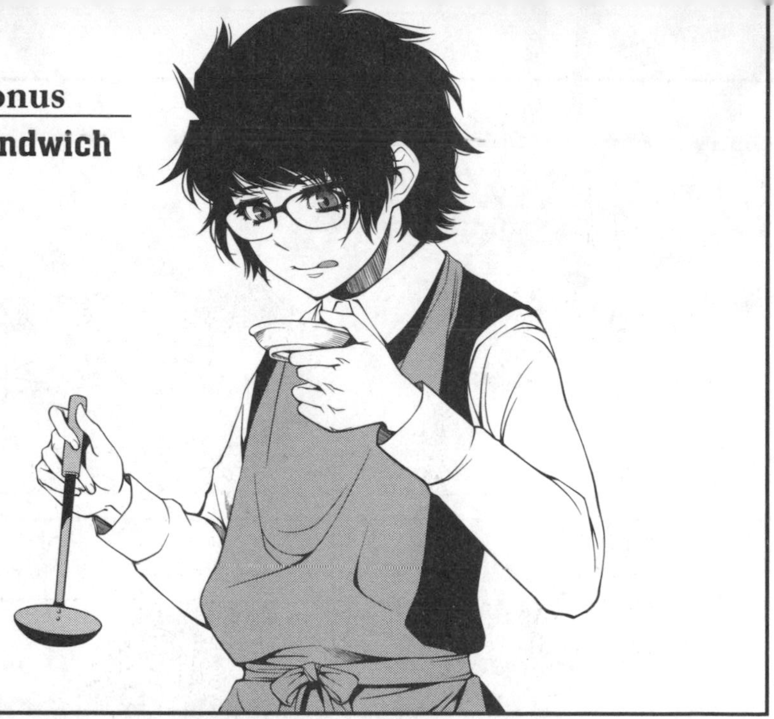

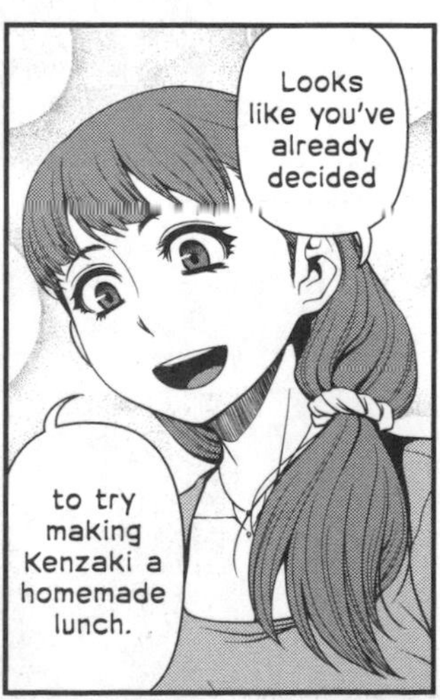
Looks like you've already decided
to try making Kenzaki a homemade lunch.

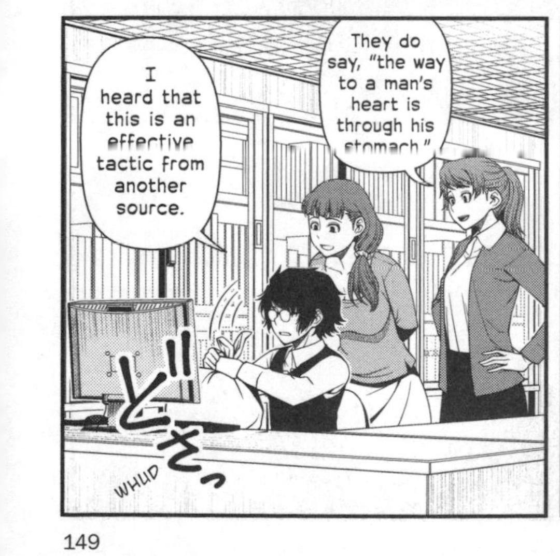
They do say, "the way to a man's heart is through his stomach."
I heard that this is an effective tactic from another source.
どさっ
WHUD

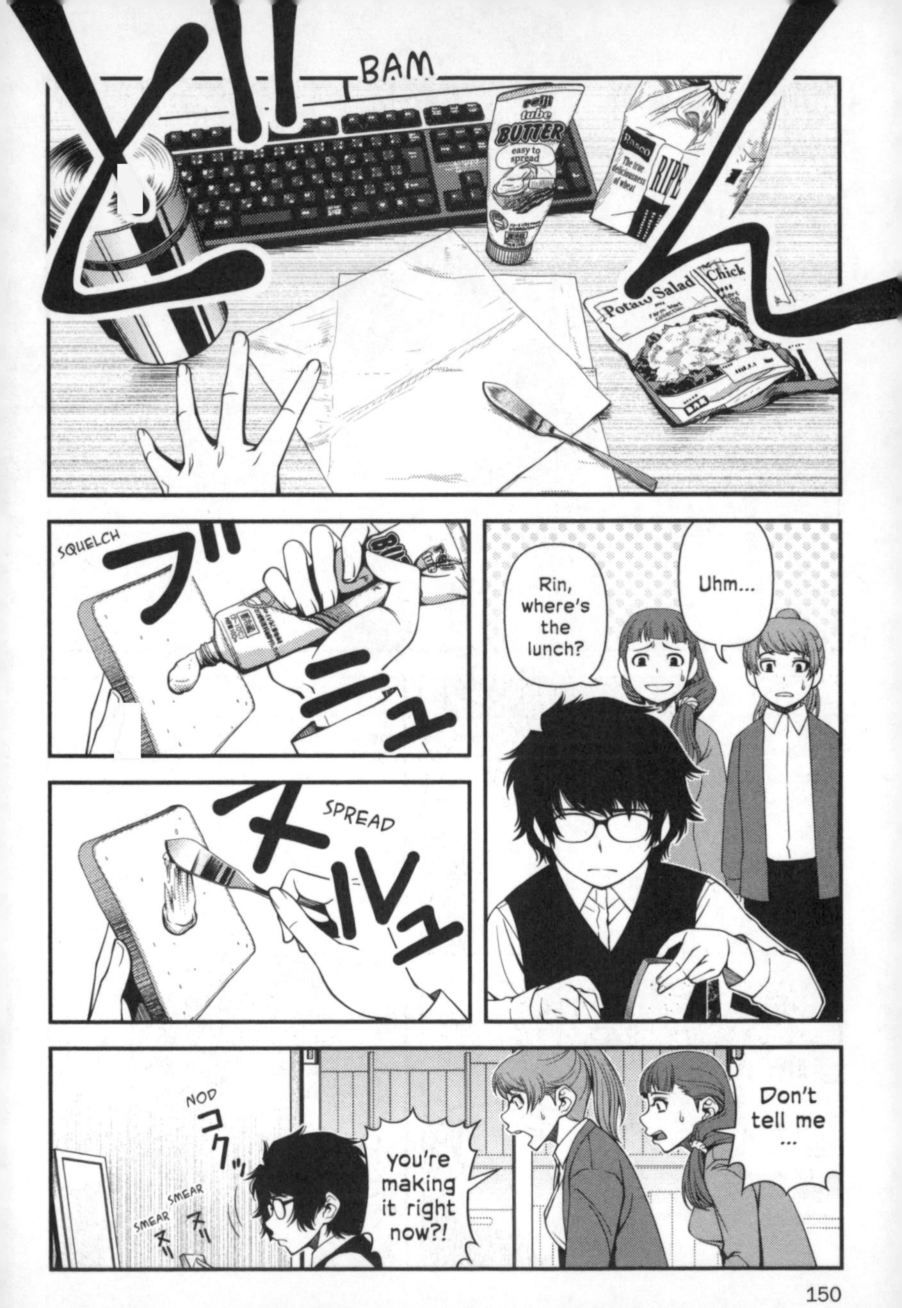
BAM
BUTTER
easy to spread
Pasco
The true deliciousness of wheat
RIPE
Potato Salad
Chick
Uhm...
Rin, where's the lunch?
SQUELCH
SPREAD
Don't tell me ...
you're making it right now?!
NOD
コクッ
SMEAR
SMEAR
ズリ
ズリ

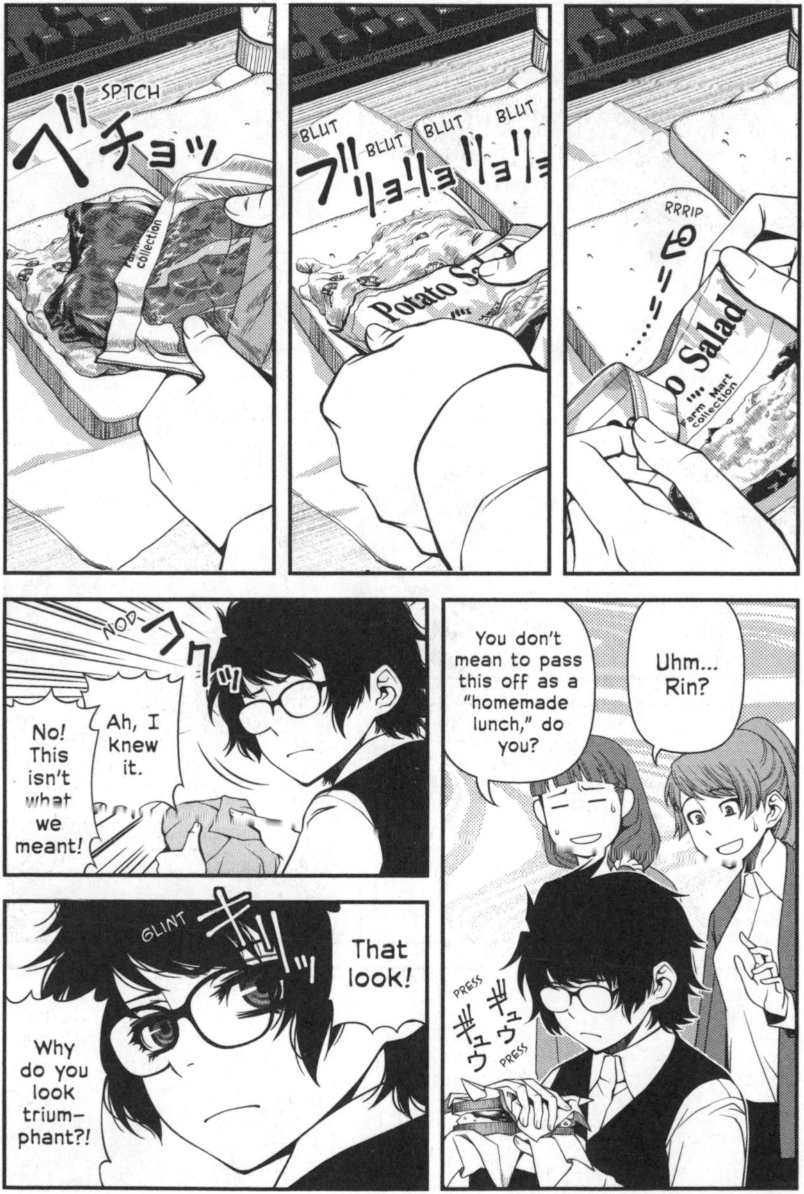
RRRIP
o Salad
Farm Mart collection
BLUT BLUT BLUT BLUT
Potato S
SPTCH
collection
Uhm... Rin?
You don't mean to pass this off as a "homemade lunch," do you?
PRESS PRESS
NOD
Ah, I knew it.
No! This isn't what we meant!
GLINT
That look!
Why do you look trium-phant?!

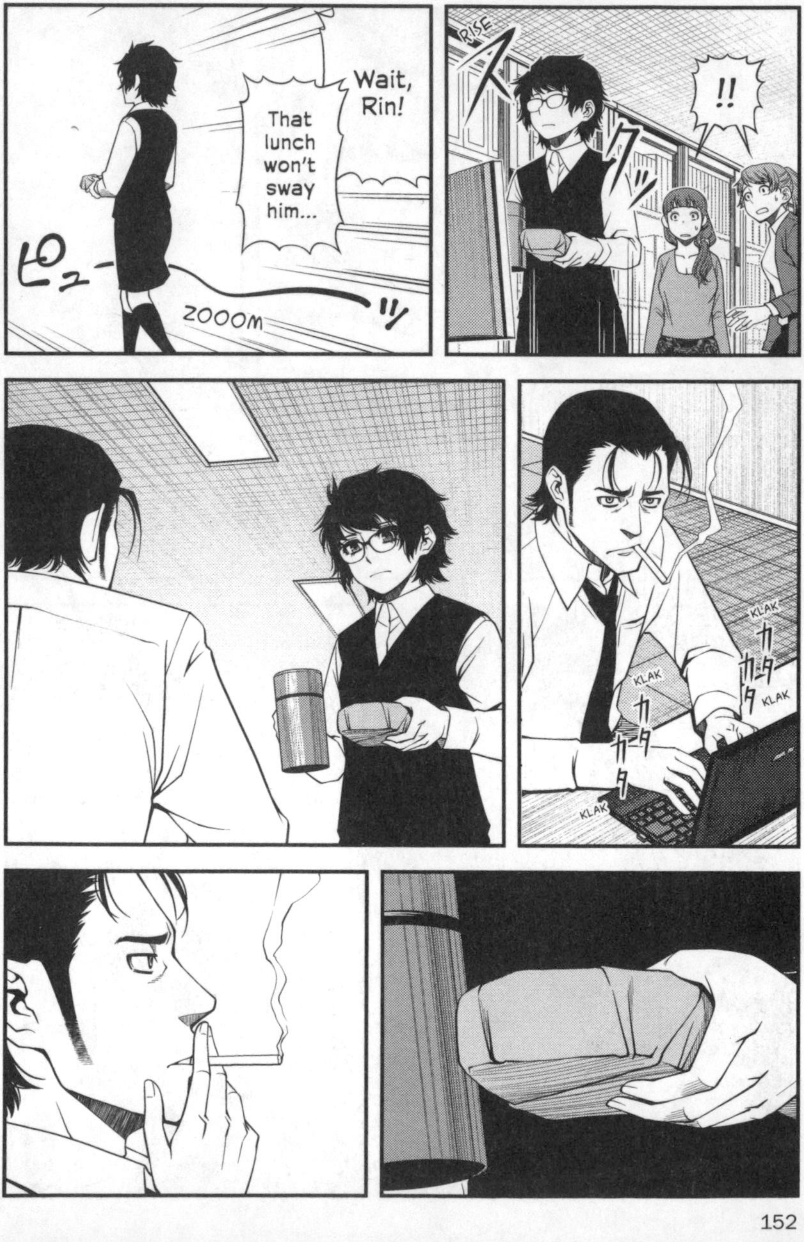
RISE
スクッ
!!
Wait, Rin!
That lunch won't sway him...
ピュー
ッ
ZOOOM
KLAK
カタ
カタ
KLAK
KLAK
カタ
カタ
KLAK

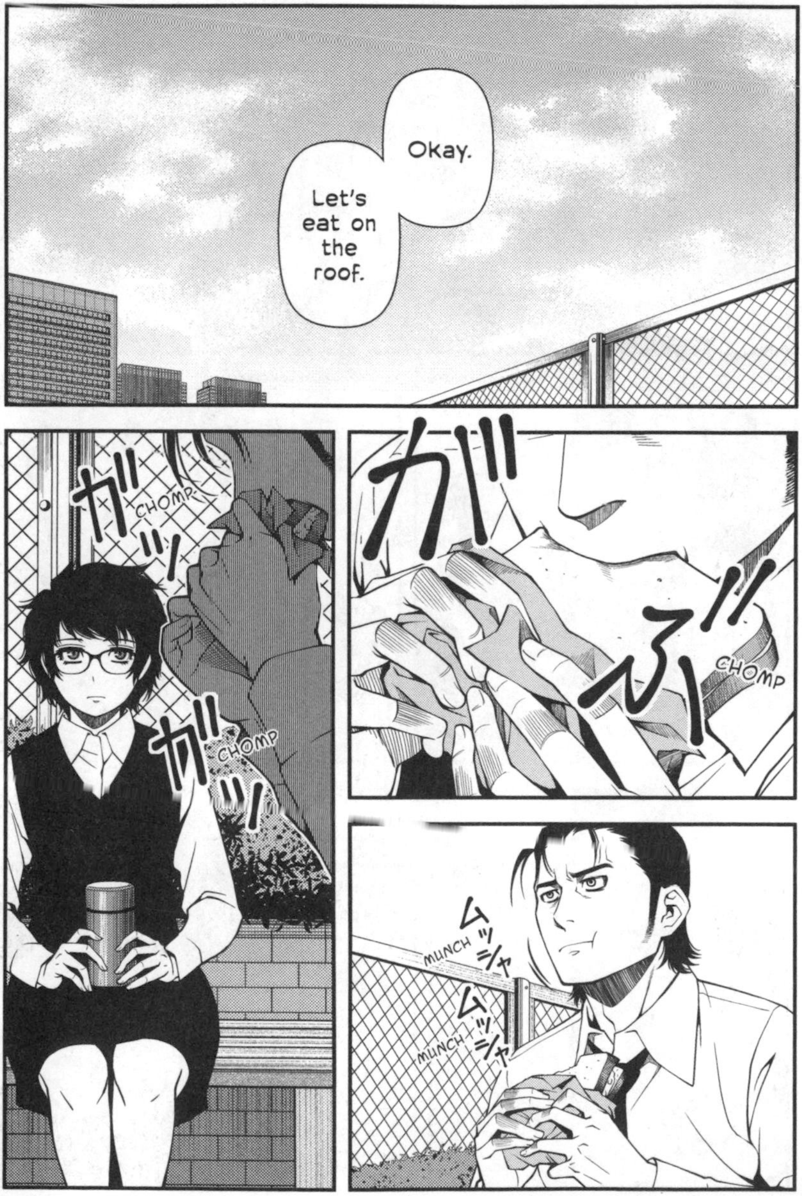

Okay.
Let's eat on the roof.
がぶッ
CHOMP
ムッシャ
MUNCH
ムッシャ
MUNCH
ガッ
CHOMP
ガッ
CHOMP

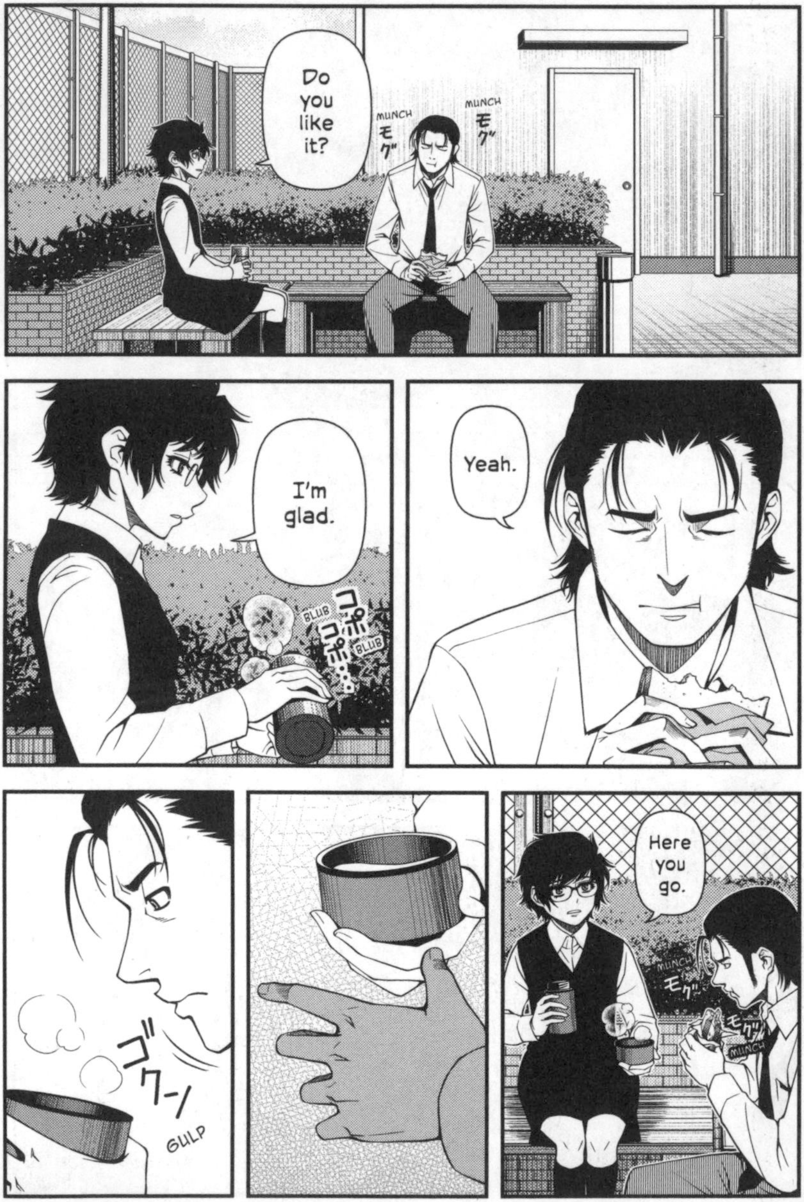
Do you like it?
MUNCH
モグ
MUNCH
モグ
Yeah.
I'm glad.
コポコポ…
BLUB
BLUB
Here you go.
MUNCH
モグ
モグ
MUNCH
ゴクーン
GULP

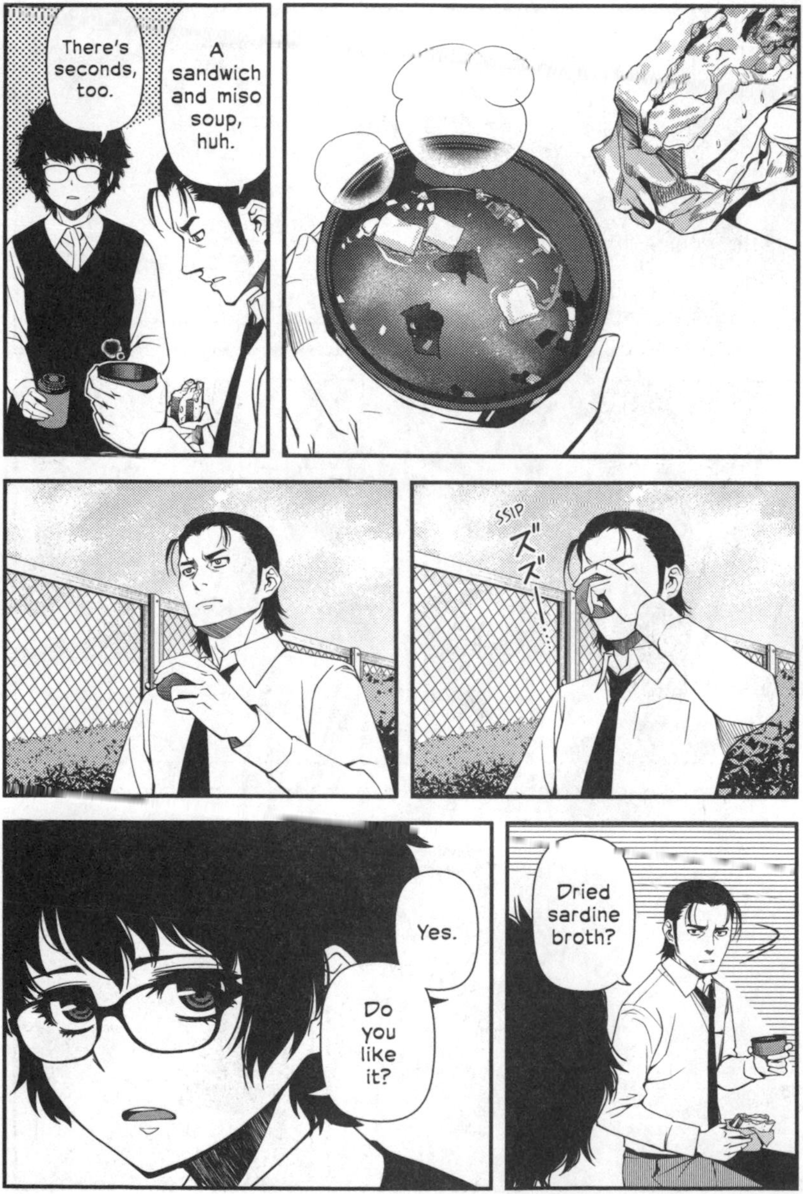
A sandwich and miso soup, huh.
There's seconds, too.
SSIP
ズズー…
Dried sardine broth?
Yes.
Do you like it?

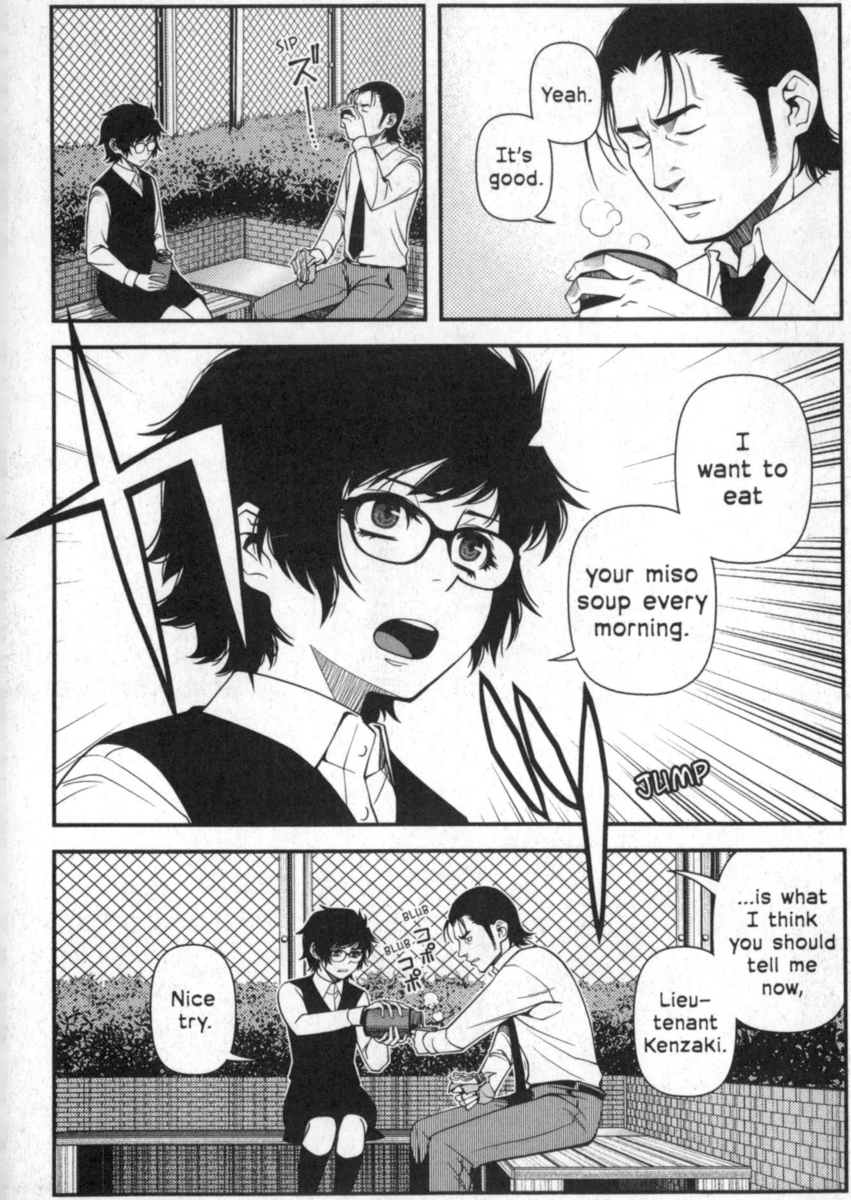
Yeah.
It's good.
SIP
ズー……
I want to eat
your miso soup every morning.
JUMP
...is what I think you should tell me now,
Lieu-tenant Kenzaki.
BLUB
BLUB
コポコポ
Nice try.

[Bonus] Secondary Character Introduction

[Members of the Tousai Precinct]

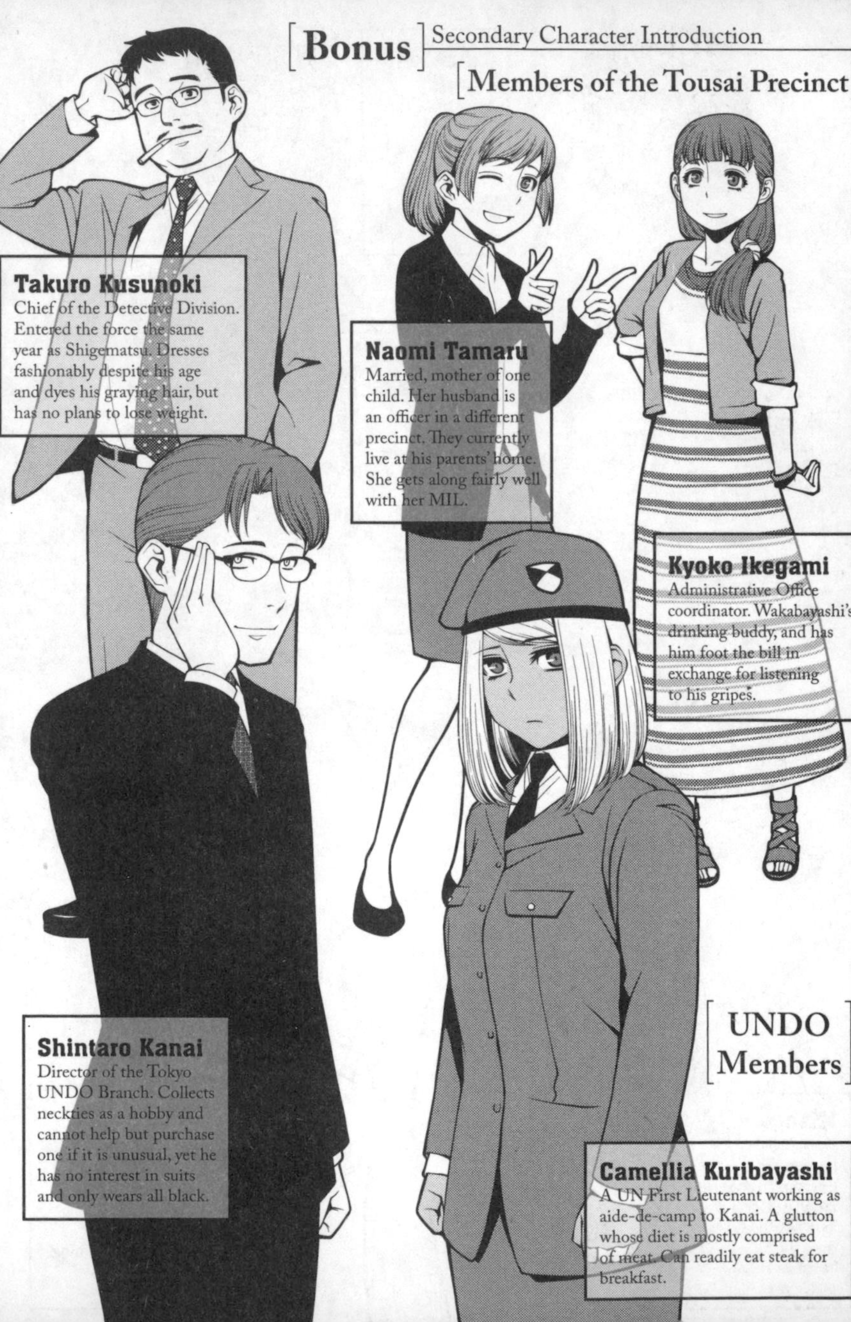

Takuro Kusunoki
Chief of the Detective Division. Entered the force the same year as Shigematsu. Dresses fashionably despite his age and dyes his graying hair, but has no plans to lose weight.

Naomi Tamaru
Married, mother of one child. Her husband is an officer in a different precinct. They currently live at his parents' home. She gets along fairly well with her MIL.

Kyoko Ikegami
Administrative Office coordinator. Wakabayashi's drinking buddy, and has him foot the bill in exchange for listening to his gripes.

[UNDO Members]

Shintaro Kanai
Director of the Tokyo UNDO Branch. Collects neckties as a hobby and cannot help but purchase one if it is unusual, yet he has no interest in suits and only wears all black.

Camellia Kuribayashi
A UN First Lieutenant working as aide-de-camp to Kanai. A glutton whose diet is mostly comprised of meat. Can readily eat steak for breakfast.

Escape Artists

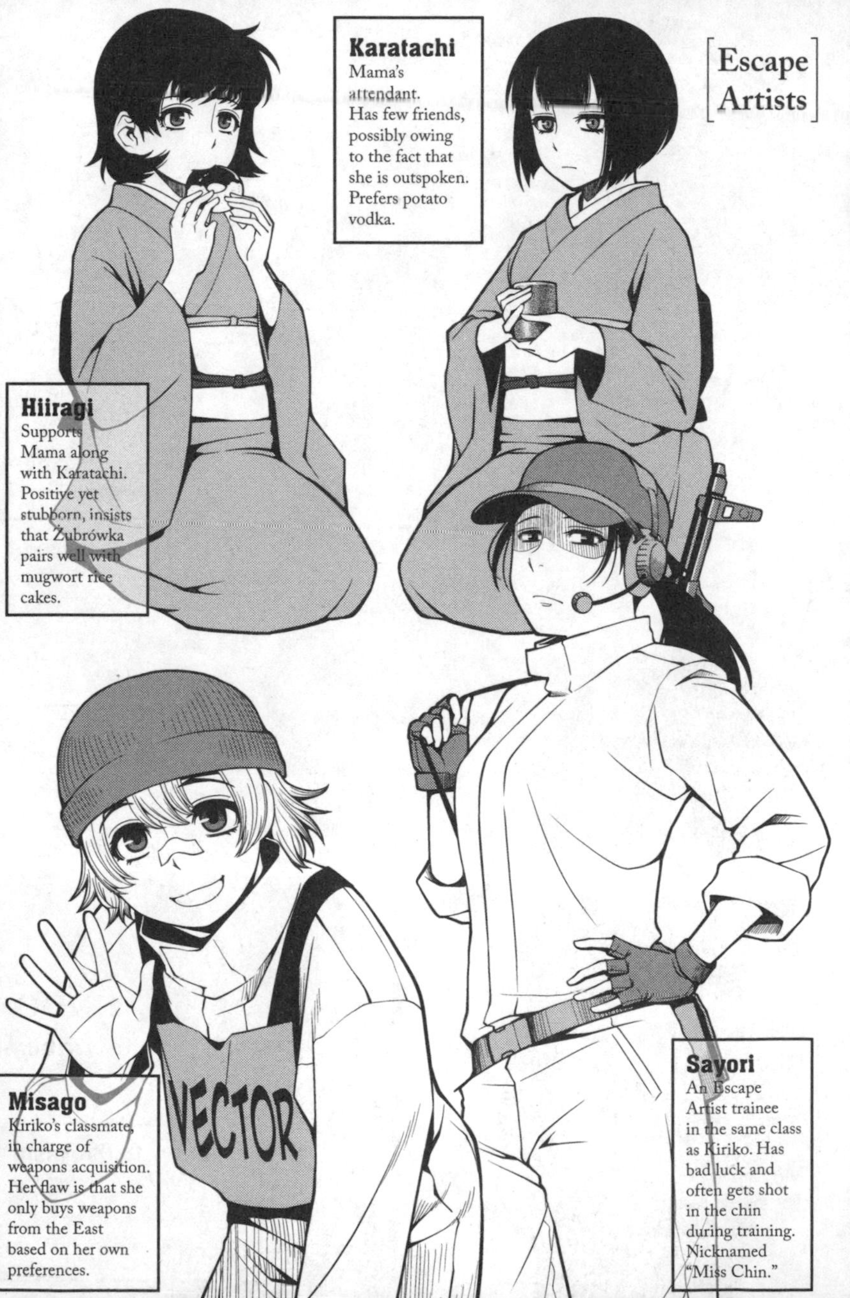

Karatachi
Mama's attendant. Has few friends, possibly owing to the fact that she is outspoken. Prefers potato vodka.

Hiiragi
Supports Mama along with Karatachi. Positive yet stubborn, insists that Żubrówka pairs well with mugwort rice cakes.

Sayori
An Escape Artist trainee in the same class as Kiriko. Has bad luck and often gets shot in the chin during training. Nicknamed "Miss Chin."

Misago
Kiriko's classmate, in charge of weapons acquisition. Her flaw is that she only buys weapons from the East based on her own preferences.

Immortal Hounds 3

A Vertical Comics Edition

Translation: Yota Okutani
Production: Grace Lu
         Anthony Quintessenza

© 2015 Ryo Yasohachi
First published in Japan in 2015 by KADOKAWA CORPORATION ENTERBRAIN.
English translation rights arranged with KADOKAWA CORPORATION ENTERBRAIN
through TUTTLE-MORI AGENCY, INC., Tokyo.

Translation provided by Vertical Comics, 2017
Published by Vertical Comics, an imprint of Vertical, Inc., New York

Originally published in Japanese as *Shinazu no Ryouken 3* by Kadokawa Corporation, 2015
Shinazu no Ryouken first serialized in *Harta*, Kadokawa Corporation, 2013-

This is a work of fiction.

ISBN: 978-1-942993-61-2

Manufactured in Canada

First Edition

Vertical, Inc.
451 Park Avenue South
7th Floor
New York, NY 10016
www.vertical-comics.com

Vertical books are distributed through Penguin-Random House Publisher Services.